TRANSFORMATIONAL
PARENTING

THE LIFE-CHANGING
MAGIC
OF PARENTING
AS PERSONAL GROWTH

DR. JENNIFER JOHNSTON-JONES, PHD

Published by Roots & Wings Institute Publishing
www.RootsnWings.org

First paperback edition 2019

ISBN 978-1-7328201-0-4
Photographs by Gabby Sage Smith and various family members for other family photos
Cover design by Emir Orucevic
Illustrations/Shutterstock

DEDICATION

This book is dedicated with all my heart and soul to my sun and my moon, my ocean and my stars: my children Océane and Orion.

Thank you for the gift of being my children.

And also to my Lionheart husband, Mike, who is my universe.

CONTENTS

PART THREE : ESSENTIALS FOR RAISING REMARKABLE HUMANS ★ 259

FOREWORD

Sarah Ferguson, Duchess of York

It is not often that you read a book that resonates so strongly with your own beliefs. *Transformational Parenting* is a rich source of practical ideas for any parent who needs help along the way.

"You will learn to rely more on yourself as you become your own guru. You will begin to notice and deprogram all the leftover 'beliefs' that were created during your childhood. You will decipher the unconscious patterns that have been passed down from generation to generation and decide what works and what can be left behind. You will also learn to heal your past, release emotions that are locked and no longer serving you, and unravel your story for a wonderfully cleansing and freeing emotional detox. And best of all, you will be exposed to ideas that will make being a parent the most joyful experience of your life."

This book is packed with sensible, workable ideas that will appeal to and inspire parents throughout the world. Behaviour can change and this is a route map complete with helpful exercises to changing the behaviour of you as a parent and that of your child. To paraphrase Jennifer, parenting is a developmental relationship, not just a verb. It goes two ways and is an opportunity for personal transformation as well as providing our children with the framework for their own future.

I thoroughly endorse this book and hope you enjoy reading it, find it inspiring and also get a sense of hope — I feel that the age 0-5 is so important in a child's development for a healthy future and this book and Dr. Jennifer Johnston-Jones confirms this. A wonderful book and I feel so relieved I followed this advice without realizing I was following good mothering as confirmed here. My two beautiful girls are a testament to this now.

With my Bestest wishes
Sarah
The Duchess of York.
2018.

The Duchess' Daughters,
Princesses of York

PART ONE

YOU

INTRODUCTION

Dear Parents,

The work of parenting is more exhausting than it needs to be! We are thinking of parenting all wrong. It can be joyful and energy-fueling if we shift the lens inward. Through my professional work with hundreds of parents, my research into happiness, personal growth and authentic success, as well as my own personal development, it has become clear that what we really need to do to raise exceptional children is to work on ourselves.

Personal development is different for parents. First, we are on a firm deadline! With only 18 years (realistically 12 or 13) to get our act together until we lose our direct influence on our children, we are a motivated bunch! Also, it is during the first five years of life that the neurological foundation for a human is developed. This should not be a guessing game; we need to be prepared. Second, because our children are our mirror and are constantly reflecting our emotional state, we have a direct feedback loop available for advanced personal growth. Third, the relationship we create with our children now will be the foundation for our relationship with them as adults. We have no time to dilly-dally around with that which distracts from the heart of the matter.

What's more, when we move the lens inward, we not only raise our children to their potential, we transform ourselves and transform the world along the way. This is why it is called *Transformational Parenting*: it has the potential to change the world while it transforms us. The evidence behind *Transformational Parenting* is powerful. It's a gathering of the most meaningful parenting science and personal growth science together in one place. You don't have to question the relevance of this book or read 50 other books; I've done all that for you. In fact, it may just be the only parenting book you will need. *Transformational Parenting* moves us beyond trends and into the substance of what is needed to grow children, ourselves, and our world into one of kindness and compassion, even a world of joy. A world where every human can meet their potential without hurting another along the way. It's time for a paradigm shift.

When I first became a mother I was clueless. Although I had been teaching parenting for years before I had children (not ideal), my parenting was "by the book" – literally. I had read almost every parenting book I could get my hands on and was well-versed in the latest neuroscience, child development, and psychology, but in no way was I prepared for the inner work that was required of me. In times of stress such as middle of the night feedings where I was so exhausted I wanted to cry, I would refer to my internal catalog of parenting research looking for the most appropriate response or an answer to "What would Dr. Siegel do?" "What new neuroscience research do we know about infant sleep?" As you can see, I was coming from an intellectual rather than relational mindset. And, no surprise, more often than not there were no answers.

Sometimes, when my daughter broke down in a temper tantrum, I became so upset myself that I would distract her to try to get her to stop crying. At the time, I wasn't aware that this distraction tactic didn't allow her to feel or express what was inside of her and also a sign that I was having trouble with handling such behavior. While I had the psychological understanding that tantrums are an important way of releasing negative emotions, seeing my baby sad was almost intolerable to me because I hadn't completed healing my own internal wounds.

For each age that she passed, I would have a slight subconscious awareness of my own feelings at that age. As she yearned for me to hold her, I recognized my own preverbal memories as a baby yearning to be held, so I held her deeply. I began to realize that her cries triggered an awareness in my own subconscious wounds that were asking to be healed. I didn't always have specific memories, but I had feelings that came up. This is common as before we learn to speak, our memories are less related to words, and more related to feelings. And of course, I also was aware of memories that I could recall clearly that still brought up feelings. I didn't want to pass onto my children any unhelpful patterns or ways of thinking I had learned in my own childhood, whether I was aware of them or not. I wanted to raise both of my children to their highest potential.

That is when I became aware of the need to go *raise myself* and started my examination of the true meaning of parenting as a relationship, rather than as a verb. I realized that parenting is a developmental relationship process rather than something we "do" to our children. I came to realize the power of raising children as a deeply powerful transformational opportunity to heal our wounds and grow into our truest potential, our best selves.

So I give you my life's work. I hope you use it as a gateway to deeper exploration of your true self, and allow yourself to manifest into who you are meant to be. It is an honor to be on this journey with you. Your courage in this process will provide your children with freedom to live their lives on their own terms, will allow you to break free from generational wounds, to deeply love yourself while teaching your children to love themselves, and help create a future that is more joyful and peaceful.

A COMPILATION OF VOICES

This book is a summary of a multi-faceted approach drawn from the fields of psychology, neurology, human development, spirituality, and sociology. As if Jung, Freud, the Dalai Lama, Marshall Rosenberg, Martin Seligman, Magda Gerber, Dan Siegel, and Jane Nelson all came into one room and compiled their teachings with a scientific twist. While I am the author, these ideas are not unique to me. I have been inspired by many teachers before me and have incorporated teachings from them. *Transformational Parenting* is a compilation of my twenty years of professional critical thinking as well as a byproduct of many critical thinkers who have come before me. I share many ideas and concepts in this book that were introduced to me through my studies as a psychologist. I want to share them with you because I believe that one shouldn't have to get a PhD in Clinical Psychology to have the tools that are necessary to manifest personal growth or to raise joyful humans.

Transformational Parenting is therefore, in my opinion, the best of what psychology and parenting have to offer for personal growth. It proposes that we view people through a lens of strengths versus pathology (Martin Seligman and Positive Psychology), that our human experience is deeper than we are conscious of and extremely interconnected (Carl Jung and Sigmund Freud), and that we must look within for answers (Dan Siegel, Thomas and Eileen Paris, L.R. Knost, and Shefali Tsabary). *Transformational Parenting* is also informed by a point of view that questions authority and asks people to reconsider the status quo (Alfie Kohn, Carol Dweck, Alice Miller, Robin Grille, and Mary Pipher). *Transformational Parenting* also understands that science alone can be limited and that life is kind of magic (Esther Hicks and Napoleon Hill). Also, that there is wisdom in the ancient (Dalai Lama, Thich Nhat Hanh, and Jean Liedloff) and wisdom in the new. So if you have studied these thinkers, you will likely see some of their ideas shared here because *Transformational Parenting* is a compilation of voices who have been encouraging and doing their part for humans to become their best in this life and to create a more peaceful future as much as we, together, can imagine.

HOW TO READ THIS BOOK

This book is not meant to be read as a typical book, where you read it once and put it away. Use this book as a coach, come back to it often, teach what you have learned to someone else. It is also recommended that you read this book from the beginning to end instead of skipping around. *Transformational Parenting* is written as a process and each chapter builds upon the next. In doing so, you'll be provided with a new opportunity for healing and personal growth which doesn't rely exclusively on psychology or psychiatry, but on the building of conscious relationships. After all, there is no more intimate and profound relationship than the relationship we have with our children. Share this book with your loved ones and create a life where personal growth becomes just as ingrained as brushing your teeth.

Can you imagine what the world would be like if we took personal growth as seriously as we take exercising or dieting? But that is exactly the problem, we prioritize our external appearance while neglecting what's going on inside. We think that a special kind of diet or new exercise will be the ticket to a healthy body, but because we have been neglecting our internal needs, inevitably, the suppressed emotions re-emerge, we become triggered and behave unhealthily. We must give our internal needs as much importance as we place on the external.

It's no coincidence that we don't prioritize personal growth. Because of the way we were parented, we learned that the most important thing a child can do is to please his or her parents in order to cope in a stressful home. Therefore, the majority of humans alive today learned strategies for appearing a certain way on the outside while neglecting what they were feeling on the inside.

Here's another motivation: relationships with our children are the most important relationships we will have in our lives. When asked what regrets they had on their deathbed, most people regret having worked too hard and not having more time with their children.[1] We mustn't leave this for a time that is convenient. The journey begins now. This book will transform you if you simply open your mind to the concepts presented and take the recommended action. I can personally guarantee that if you develop a *Transformational Parenting* approach, not only will your relationship with your children improve, as they become more connected and better behaved, but more importantly, both you and your children will begin the process to grow to your highest potential together. What an opportunity!

How do I know? In my work as a psychologist teaching parenting, I have worked with hundreds of parents from all over the world, from all types of cultures and economic levels; from parents living in the slums of the city to parents in the 1% of wealth structure; from parents who are recent immigrants, to parents whose families have lived in their home country for hundreds of years. I've worked with celebrity parents, homeless parents, parents with six children, foster parents, blended fam-

---

1 Ware, B. (2012) *The top five regrets of the dying: A life transformed by the dearly departing.* Carlsbad, Calif.: Hay House.

ilies, and parents of children with special needs and many more. From my extensive work, I know that we all share the same desire: to become the best we can be and to give our children the best we can give them. And, not surprisingly, we all share the same solution: to develop the character traits that we most wish for our children to acquire by digging into our own personal growth.

Just as by not making a decision, the decision gets made for us; by not raising our children in an intentional, transformative manner, we are increasing the chances of them re-experiencing the pain we experienced in our childhoods. Raising children provides the opportunity to reprocess your childhood, and either heal or continue the pattern.

To begin *Transformational Parenting*, I've broken the process into three parts. The first is focused on you, the second on your child, and the last on resources and tools for both you and your child to grow to your highest potential.

In the first part of the book, "You," you'll learn to rely more on yourself as you become your own guru. You'll begin to notice and deprogram all the leftover "beliefs" that were created during your childhood. You will decipher the unconscious patterns that have been passed down from generation to generation and decide what works and what can be left behind. You'll also learn to heal your past, release emotions that are locked and no longer serving you, and unravel your story for a wonderfully cleansing and freeing emotional detox. And, best of all, you'll be exposed to ideas that will make being a parent the most joyful experience of your life.

In the second part of the book, "Your Child," you'll learn what it means to parent consciously and the benefits of prioritizing the relationship with your child. In the chapter, "Why Children Misbehave and What to Do About It," you'll learn specific tools for specific situations and the reasons behind unwanted behavior. You'll learn tools to deepen your connection with your child so that good behavior is simply the result of your relationship rather than the result of a bribe or punishment.

In the third part of the book, "Essentials for Raising Remarkable Humans," you'll learn about "Transformational Communication," a powerful evidence-based tool that you can apply to every relationship in your life, including your spouse or partner, business associates, other adult relationships, as well as your child. You'll also learn life tools you can use to manifest and build toward achieving the life you desire. You'll learn what brings you joy, how to take full advantage of your mindset, and how to release roles and relationships that no longer serve you.

Throughout this book, you will find a lot of writing exercises. You may be tempted to skip through them, but I encourage you to do the exercises as you read them. Take out a pen and write your authentic experiences. This is not for anyone else but you. There can be great benefits to writing down our stories. In a study[2] of the advantages of writing about emotions, people who wrote about their lives for just a few days in a row, for just 15–20 minutes a day, experienced these benefits, among others:

- fewer stress-related visits to the doctor
- improved immune system functioning
- reduced blood pressure
- improved mood / affect
- feeling of greater psychological well-being
- reduced depressive symptoms before examinations
- reduced absenteeism from work
- quicker re-employment after job loss
- improved working memory
- improved sporting performance
- higher grade point average for students.

Should you do these writing exercises and apply the lessons you read in this book to your life, you will not only be on your way to transforming yourself into the person you are meant to be, you'll provide the space for your child to do the same and transform the world along the way.

Finally, please note that in order to protect the confidentiality of the clients whose stories I have used in this book, I have changed their

2   Baikie, K.A. and Wilhelm, K. (2005) Emotional and physical health benefits of expressive writing. *Advances in Psychiatric Treatment*, 11 (5): 338–346; DOI: 10.1192/apt.11.5.338

names and any identifying information. Their stories are often composites of several clients so that they will not be recognized.

I'm thrilled you're here with me. You're brave enough to move away from the dominant paradigm that has us pointing fingers at our children and unconsciously perpetuating fear and violence. You're compassionate enough to be willing to make a change for your child. And you're smart enough to know that evidence-based psychology is the way to go. Welcome!

We're in this together,
Dr. Jennifer Johnston-Jones

CHAPTER 1

FREE YOURSELF
FROM "PARENTING"

*"Don't let yourself become so concerned with raising
a good kid that you forget you already have one."*
— Glennon Melton

I feel my belly tighten and pulse. My hands are sweaty and I'm hot all over. I'm full of excitement and anticipation of what's to come. I'm also incredibly scared. I take a breath to relax but the tightening quickens and compresses, becoming so intense that I need to lay down. I've heard the words "pain," "pressure," and "excruciating" many times when birth was described and I'm trying hard not to have that programming infect my mind. I'm trying not to be afraid. I've elected to have a home birth because I'm more afraid of hospitals than of birth, but now that it's happening, I have no "out" for what's to come. The tightening increases and I feel everything. I'm overwhelmed.

I use a tool that I learned as a young child when things got too intense: I "check out." I guide my mind to a place where I'm no longer feeling, hearing or even aware of what's happening and I stay here for a while. In this place, I'm connected to something that feels like another dimension. I can feel my daughter here with me and I long for her. I want to stay in this space but after some time someone shakes me back to the world and I hear my midwife calling "wake up and push!"

I feel shocked and disappointed as I realize that there is no one to help me. I have to do it all by myself. This was how I often felt growing up during times of stress. I wanted to be joined in this process, I'm worried I can't do it alone. I want to cry and then I want to fight. I quickly mourn the loss of what I had imagined and decide to become bigger, stronger, more powerful, to fight for her, to fight for me, to fight for what I wanted this experience to be versus what society told me it had to be. I pushed so damn hard I tore myself up. I growled like a tiger. Being passive or escaping was no longer possible. I had to be active, to bring in strength that I wasn't sure I had. It wasn't physical strength that I needed, it was emotional, I had to pull away from who I had been into who I really was. I was not only birthing my daughter, I was birthing myself.

She was born and I felt transformed. I looked in her eyes and knew I would do anything for her. At that moment, I decided I would devote my life to her and her soon-to-be brother. I was now Wonder Woman and it was ok to fight. I knew there was a lot of work to do. I didn't want her to not understand her power like I had growing up, to be small, to feel unsafe. Being a psychologist, I knew this work had to come from me. But birth was only the beginning of my therapy. Every cry and laugh along the way awoke me to feelings from my own childhood. As she passed through each age, I also re-experienced that age.

I used to believe I became a mother when I birthed my daughter, but now I understand that parenting starts when we ourselves are tiny as we soak up the lessons, love, emotional patterns and losses that our own parents pass down to us. There is no "blank slate." My daughter and son were born with the stresses and joys I experienced when I was pregnant and all of the emotional patterns and thinking that I may have left unresolved which came from my parents and which they received from theirs, on and on.

Although children are born with their own temperaments, drives and individual traits, we inadvertently pass on our unresolved emotional issues unless we handle ours heads on. We are scared of dogs, the ocean, speaking up, being assertive, etc...so are they. We feel less than, not as good, alone, not beautiful, etc...so do they. And because we realize what we didn't have and what we could have achieved "if only…" sometimes we mold our children into images of our own ideal selves. We send our daughter to singing lessons because we always wanted to sing, push our son into soccer and hope he will go pro as we didn't get to, sign our daughter up for coding class even though she is not interested, on and on. For many parents, they see this as their job: to give their child the opportunities that they didn't have, but we are missing the point of allowing our children to be their own selves. We are also missing the point that in order for them (and us) to really understand what brings them joy and how to make healthy decisions in life, we have to spend time developing ourselves, working on ourselves to get rid of the fears, anxiety, anger, and sadness which have us make the wrong decisions in the first place. Here are just a few examples: the mother who is pushing her son into acting wants to be seen. The father who is pushing his daughter into dancing sees dancers as fit and has low self esteem because he doesn't feel good about his body. The mother who is looking in the mirror and grimacing passes that onto her daughter when she is only 2. The father who gets angry and yells passes fear onto his children and teaches them that they cannot make mistakes so they learn to avoid. Can you imagine what it would be like if we really met our children where they are at? Really, truly allowed them to express their own interests and become who they are meant to be without putting our issues on them? Wouldn't it be great if we honored who they are as individuals and gave them what they need to develop into the best version of themselves?

Our children do not "belong" to us, we do not own them, they are given to us to raise. Since the goal is to help raise emotionally and physically healthy humans, then the job of "parenting" is more about raising *ourselves* than shaping our children. If we can take a breath and look at ourselves instead of trying to mold and sculpt our children into what we feel is perfect, we will not only help our child to hold on to the gifts he or she was born with but also contribute to making the world a more peaceful place.

When we redefine the word "parenting" to include our own personal growth, we set ourselves free of the chains of "parenting" as we know it. We can let go of the idea that we have to raise a perfect child, to be a perfect parent, to "mold" our children into perfect beings who will contribute to society and do no wrong. Not only is this concept impossible but also Egoic; it assumes that there is something intrinsically wrong with our children and that we have to fix them.

The beauty is that when we set ourselves free, we also free our children. It comes naturally. We stop "shoulding" all over them. We stop overreacting on them. We stop seeing them as the living proof of our own parenting ability. It's not our job to "parent" our children, to "do" something to them. It's our job to make ourselves as fulfilled and joyful as possible, to be available for how our children need us, and allow them to be themselves. Children are born joyful; much of the time, it's our interfering that creates suffering.

PARENTING IS A *NOT* A VERB

"Parent" as a verb only entered into common language in the 1970s.[3] Yet we are often fooled into thinking that the more parenting books we read, the more tools we learn, the more we do "what is right" or "what is best" for our children, the more well-adjusted and successful our children will be. It starts before they are born. We follow orders from the obstetrician, then from the pediatrician, then the teacher, the parenting expert, on and on. We are taught to believe that the answers to raising successful kids are outside us, and if we just follow the rules and do what we are "supposed to do," that our kids will grow up happy and healthy.

At the same time, we are in denial that introspection is unecessary and "we turned out fine," so we fly blindly through the years on "intuition," which can be a combination of our heart and our unconscious patterns that have been passed down from generation to generation — some good and others not so much.

Yet almost every parent shares the same fear: we are scared to death of ruining our kids! So we buy whatever it is we are supposed to buy, enroll them in the best classes or schools we can afford, and "prep" them in every way possible from preschool to college. We are so busy making sure we don't ruin them and they are so busy doing what we sign them up for that what really makes the difference for happiness is nearly forgotten.

---

3   Gopnik, A. (2016) *The Gardener and the Carpenter: What the New Science of Child Development Tells Us About the Relationship Between Parents and Children.* New York, NY: Picador.

Bunmi Laditan's book, *Confessions of a Domestic Failure*[4], sounds like comedic science-fiction, but the complex reality of not ruining your kids is today's most common parental stressor:

> Make sure your children's academic, emotional, psychological, mental, spiritual, physical, nutritional, and social needs are met while being careful not to overstimulate, understimulate, improperly medicate, helicopter, or neglect them in a screen-free, processed foods-free, GMO-free, negative energy-free, plastic-free, body positive, socially egalitarian but also authoritative, nurturing but fostering of independence, gentle but not overly pessimistic, pesticide-free, two-story multilingual home preferably in a cul-de-sac with a backyard and 1.5 siblings spaced at least two years apart for proper development but also don't forget the coconut oil. Versus How to be a Mom in Every Other Generation: Feed them sometimes.

I fell into this trap when I first studied psychology, too. I thought that the more techniques and tools I learned, the better psychologist I would be. I studied the most effective treatments for how to reduce anxiety, be happier, eliminate depression, help marriages work, cure ADHD, help children with special needs, etc. Plus, I had more than 3000 hours of clinical experience working with the most extreme cases of schizophrenia, bipolar disorder, multiple personality disorder (now called Dissociative Identity Disorder), abuse, etc. In the end, I realized (and the research confirms) that the most effective way to change people is not in techniques or a particular theoretical style, but through the therapeutic relationship. The evidence is stacked that the therapeutic alliance (the trust and rapport built between therapist and client) is the greatest underlying cause for change.[5]

In the relationship. That's it. The *relationship* – as simple as that! As I grew more experienced in my work with clients and concentrated more on our connection and less on treatment planning, I noticed magic happening! People were transforming quickly! People with chronic anxiety were able to live mostly anxiety-free with 8–12 sessions of therapy.

---

4 Laditan, B. (2019) *Confessions of a Domestic Failure.* Toronto: Mira Books.
5 Reisner, A. (2005) The common factors, empirically validated treatments, and recovery models of therapeutic change. *The Psychological Record,* 55 (3): 377–400.

Change happened faster and faster when I focused more on connection than techniques. Relationships are the key to transformation and personal growth.

Likewise, there is no parenting book, technique, tool, or expert that will ever compare to the power of the relationship you have with your child. *Transformational Parenting* teaches you the psychological tools to grow your relationship with your child, heal your own childhood, and ensure that your child doesn't need to recover from theirs.

Parenting isn't something we "do" to our children. To "parent" is to grow into the deepest relationship you will ever have. There is no other relationship that has the potential to be more connected and more involved than the parent/child relationship. Therefore, the parent/child relationship is one of the biggest growth opportunities that life provides.

Our children are only connected to us for a short period of time. How long they remain connected to us depends on our level of connection. We have a short window of time in which we can have the most impact to transform ourselves and connect with our children. If we are lucky, our children will visit often, but there is no guarantee. We need to understand how precious the time they live with us is. Not all parenting relationships have the power to transform; it's only when there is emotional closeness. Being emotionally connected is the key.

How do you create a close relationship? It starts with freeing yourself from "parenting" and includes healing yourself, because being close and emotionally present requires you to heal your wounds. How much we are able to be connected in the relationship with our children will influence how much personal growth we acquire and how well they develop. In other words, if you accept the task of relationship presence, you will be gifted with deep, life-changing personal transformation. When parents transform, so do their children.

Transformational Parenting benefits parents and children profoundly. No other relationship or experience has the same potential for transformation as parenting does. If we allow ourselves to grow and become intentional in our growth, we receive the gift of our children as our teachers. They learn from us, and we learn from them.

BECOME YOUR OWN GURU

It's time to let go of the idea of a guru, of a singular approach to follow, or other people's rules to live by. If you are drawn to a teacher that is because that person is a reflection of the truth that you see in yourself. When we put thinkers on a pedestal, we limit our own power and potential to manifest brilliance and shine for others in the way that those who inspire us shine for us. True transformation must be made personal. It must be made our own. Personal transformation can certainly be inspired by others, but ultimately, the goal is for you to be your own guru. Don't follow someone else's lead entirely. Allow yourself to guide your transformation authentically.

While this sounds empowering on paper, many of us fall back into putting others on a pedestal while we put ourselves on the floor. I believe this is because we are afraid of our own power. We are afraid that if we admit that we have the potential to follow ourselves instead of others, to break the rules and create our own, to forge our own path...that we will fail and have no one else to blame but ourselves. This is the same reason so many of us do what we believe we are "supposed" to do: we get the education, the marriage, the right number of kids, work a 9–5 job...we've been fed the lie that if we do what we are led to believe is the right path and make the right decisions and just work hard enough that we will be happy. But that simply isn't the case. The unhappiest people I know, some of whom were seeing me for therapy, did everything they were supposed to do but ended up miserable.

I've found that those who make their own rules are the happiest. And, coincidentally, these rule-breakers also aren't very good at following others – they follow their own lead. But this takes tremendous courage. To assess what's available and choose what makes sense for you takes extra work. How do you sift through all of the information? You know you want to be a good parent and want to do things differently than the way you were parented and maybe even differently than other parents you see, but where the heck do you start?

That's what I've done for you. In these pages you will find the most relevant and research-based psychology, child development and parenting literature to bring you the best of what these fields have to offer. I've sifted through the proverbial chocolate box of human psychology and picked out the best ones for you. Your job, if you choose to accept it, is to take it and make it your own.

I've failed if after reading this book you ask yourself, "What would Dr. Johnston-Jones do?" Instead, I want you to ask yourself, "What would the best version of me do in this situation?" And every day, each and every day, if you keep asking yourself that question and keep behaving according to your best self, self improvement will become as inevitable as your children growing older.

You will once again, just as when you were a baby, begin to connect to your intuition and your gut feelings with minimal effort! When you sense something coming up that isn't healed, you will learn to recognize it and face it. Your consciousness will make your children conscious. Your trust in yourself – rather than in a guru, teacher or psychologist – will give you the confidence you need in order to stop playing small. When you practice *Transformational Parenting*, you will not only accelerate your parenting and your relationship with your children, you will see that it also trickles down to the other relationships in your life, including your relationship with your partner, and, most importantly, your relationship with life! It's possible and uncomplicated as long as you let yourself be your own guide and read what's in here with an open heart and an open mind.

PARENTING BEYOND TECHNIQUES

Because everyday situations become opportunities for transformation, you won't need to remember what you read in any book or article. In *Transformational Parenting*, the focus is not on techniques, but on creating more connection. You can also let go of the energy of "not doing" something. I've worked with so many parents who gauge their level of parenting success by whether or not they have yelled. The energy and the distraction caused by "not yelling" takes us away from staying connected to our children. Likewise, parents who haven't yet healed the wounds from the way they were raised have an internal mantra of "I won't do what my parents did to me." The beauty of this is that when parents recognize their pain, they can begin to heal it. The potential for deep connection grows as you heal. And the beauty is that just by reading this book and coming back to it as you need, your awareness will increase and healing will occur naturally.

As you immerse yourself in *Transformational Parenting*, your children will naturally be more respectful and do better in school without having to manipulate them or their environments. The benefit of *Transformational Parenting* is that when you help yourself, you help your child.

STAGES OF THE DEVELOPMENT OF A PARENT

Just as children go through developmental stages, so do we as parents. We are in a parallel process with our children, passing through the stages of life together. Even more powerful, when our children pass through a certain age, we are brought back to that age and reminded of unhealed wounds that we experienced. We are given the opportunity to grow again from that age and accelerate our inner growth exponentially. Often, we are struck with buried pain as our children pass through their ages, knowing that we did not receive what we needed. We are now able to understand the needs of the child from a parent's perspective, and can meet those needs for our children.

After the birth of my daughter, in those quiet days when I was alone and busy holding and nursing this new being, I realized a loss that I didn't know was there for me before I had her. I knew that I was bottle-fed, that my mother was young when she had me, but it wasn't until I was nursing my daughter that I realized the touch and affection I missed out on as an infant. The memory wasn't an intellectual realization, it was somatic, it came from a physical feeling of emptiness and loneliness.

Then, as my daughter grew older, I recalled painful feelings that I wasn't even aware of. It was a recognition that the connection my daughter and I share was different than the one I shared with my mother. Seeing my mother talk to my daughter with less presence and connection validated the feelings I didn't know how to express as a child, a yearning for a deeper connection, to be seen. At first, this consciousness was painful, but I used it to remind me of the importance of really being present with my daughter. For example, when I was a little girl, my mother would talk on the phone for what seemed like forever. It might have been only 30 minutes, but the conversations were after I returned from daycare when I really felt the need to connect. I remember so wanting her to talk to me, to see me, to want to connect with me the way she was connecting with the person on the phone. The recognition of this longing helps me when I am tempted to answer a text or look at my phone when I'm with my children.

It is as if we re-experience our own childhood through our children. The more aware we become, the more we see the effects of our own childhood. So the stages of parent development reflect not only what we need to learn as parents, but also the areas of our childhood that we need to heal as adults.

It can be a beautiful opportunity for us to have empathy for our parents as well. As we struggle with the sleepless nights and constant needs of our children, we can imagine what it must have been like for our parents. Forgiveness becomes easier. Especially if our parents are involved with our children, the relationship can evolve and become more beautifully complex. For example, my father has been able to recreate the joyful playfulness he had with my siblings and I with my own children. When he visits, he sometimes chases my children around the house in bouts of laughter, which he used to do with my siblings and I. In those moments, I am both a happy mother, grateful for my children to have such a loving grandfather, and also a happy little girl myself as I see my own memories acted out in front of me.

In my therapeutic work, I've begun to notice differences between those who have children and those who do not. Often, but not always, people with children are more flexible and willing to work on themselves, which makes them more developed. This isn't always the case, certainly there are adults without children who are incredibly wise. Likewise, there are parents who lack self reflection. However, much of the time, parents are more willing to do what it takes to become the best they can be. There is an intrinsic motivation and urgency that parents have. We know that if we don't "fix our stuff" that we will pass it on to our children. There's a great meme being passed around in social media, I love it so much I almost made it the subtitle to this book. It goes: "Only parenting goal: to raise children who don't have to recover from their childhood."

We know that our children contribute to us as much as we contribute to them. Even from infancy they absorb our energy, and it gets imprinted on them, and vice versa. It's a watercolor approach to growing up; the colors blend, just as the energies and influences do. Not only are they growing up, so are we, both powerfully influencing each other and intermixing energies.

Just as a child develops in stages, there are also stages for parental development. Parents become initiated into personal growth the moment the child is born or even during pregnancy. Every stage of our children's development challenges us to grow and stretch into a stage of personal growth we could not expect before we became parents. We either flex and grow, or we get stuck, frustrated and exhausted. Just when we think we've got the rhythm of parenting down, our children enter into another stage that challenges us to grow yet again! In every age that our child passes through, we have to incorporate the perspective and behaviors which that age demands. For example, the needs of an infant demand more presence. The needs of a toddler demand more faith and trust in the world, and so it continues.

Along the way, remember that during developmental milestones, your child may regress to an earlier stage. What does this "regression" look like? That means children will sometimes behave as they did when they were younger. The most common form of regression in children has to do with becoming increasingly clingy or whiny. However, children can regress in many ways: increased crying, bed-wetting from a formerly potty-trained child, needing to be held more, etc. Regression can also be a symptom of processing stress or something traumatic. Many parents don't know what to do with behavioral regression and fear that all that their child has accomplished and learned is fading away. However, regression is normal and temporary.

Our children will also cling to us when they feel us needing distance, which is very hard! The moment we really need some alone time they will sense it and become more clingy. What a beautiful opportunity to practice faith in them and to not be shaken. A helpful expression to remember during our child's development is "two steps forward, one step back." Child development does not occur in a straight line. When you witness your child showing behavior from an earlier age, don't fret – just take a deep breath and give her or him extra love.

And guess what? We regress too – during big life transitions, stress or when we're undergoing traumatic situations in our life. Interestingly, in psychotherapy, a psychologist can sometimes pinpoint at what age the client had a traumatic experience because some of their behavior is similar to a person of the age their trauma occurred.

Let's now explore parental development in detail: it's paired with Erik Erikson's psychosocial stages,[6] so you can follow along with your child's development.

Parent's Goal When Child is an Infant (up to 1 year)

When a child is born, our parental goal is to let go and accept that life is not in our control. We cannot help but accept this. The dramatic shift that occurs once one becomes a parent is truly life-changing, whether we want those changes or not. I remember before I became a mother, I would hear parents talk about the sleepless nights and how they were too tired to go out anymore. "That won't be what's it's like for me," I thought. Once I became a parent, I laughed at my pre-parent self so many times. All of the things I thought I knew or had control over dissolved. I still laugh at myself for all the ways I thought I would be. I imagined I would be that mother who goes about her pre-baby life as usual, not slowing down, dressing my child in cloth diapers, sweet hand-knit baby outfits, everything organic, the perfect lullaby, the perfect crib, the perfect shoes, peaceful and quiet nights, adventure-filled days. Of course, there is no perfect, she didn't even sleep in her crib. Shoes? What shoes? Hand knit baby outfits? Too impractical. Perfect is not only impractical, it is inau-

---

6 Erikson, E. H., and Coles, R. (2001) *The Erik Erikson Reader*. New York: W.W. Norton & Company.

thentic. To keep this idea of perfection going would be exhausting, and I was already exhausted, so I let go of those fantasies of parenting and embraced the gritty, real earthiness that is infancy.

In many ways, when our baby is born, it's the death of pre-parenting life. In as much as we may be able to embrace the joy of our new child, we also suffer with the death of who we once were and the freedoms we may never have again. There is a natural kind of "postpartum darkness" that most parents experience, when the fantasy bubble gets popped. We must let go of what we thought parenting would be, let go of commitments that aren't absolutely necessary, let go of our life as it was. This realization doesn't always occur right away. Often, it takes years to realize that life will never be what it was, which is wonderful, of course, because our children are amazing, but also difficult to digest. I joke about "my past life" before I became a parent. My life changed dramatically, in ways I could not have predicted, which is true for almost every parent I've ever talked to.

If only we could speak more freely about this loss and be able to share more of the difficulty that is required in this "letting go," I believe we could help prevent some postpartum depression and the emotional and physical isolation that occurs with new parents. Instead of saying "congratulations!" to a new parent who looks like they haven't slept for days, we could communicate something like "Congratulations, hang in there, I know the first year is difficult" to allow the parents authentic expression of their feelings. Many parents feel there must be something wrong with them when they do not feel overjoyed about caring for a newborn or becoming a parent overnight. In truth, mourning the loss of pre-baby life is authentic and natural.

So what about the newborn? Neurologically, a newborn's brain is the most active it will be in his or her entire life. In this tender age of just being born, the **most essential skill for babies to develop is a secure attachment.** That means that your baby needs to bond with you, to know that he or she is safe with you. One of the more common mistakes I see parents make is to be on their phone when feeding their baby. This is a unique time in a child's life as the parent has their full, undivided attention as you feed them. Your baby's eyes lock on you, looking deeply into your eyes, sometimes even their tiny hands reach up to touch your face, connecting to you in the deepest way. This is one of the most essential types of bonding, building a secure attachment that will last a lifetime. It needs to be consistent and repeated. When mothers who are breast-feeding cover their child's face when the baby is nursing in order not to expose their breastfeeding, the opportunity for bonding is reduced, as there is no eye contact. Eye contact is more than nice, it is essential. And you'll notice as your baby is looking into your eyes that they are also reading your energy. If you are anxious, stressed, lonely, etc., your baby picks up on that and it can become a part of them. This starts when you are pregnant and is true throughout your life.

The implications for a child whose parents don't manage their neg-ative emotions are not only unfair and unjust, but also unnecessary. A pure, innocent soul enters the world and becomes tainted with unre-solved negative patterns from their parents. The power of parents' in-fluence on infants is profound. Babies have not yet built up defense mechanisms or energy blocks to be able to protect themselves from the energy of their parents and people who are caring for them. This can be a beautiful time where you pass on feelings of love and peacefulness or a dangerous time where babies take on their parents' anxiety, anger or sadness. But don't worry, you are reading this book so you can help pro-cess your negative emotions to ensure your child doesn't inherit them. Do the work, keep doing the work, and don't forget that everything you feel, so does your child.

As much as regulating anxiety, anger or sadness is essential, so is be-ing attuned to your baby's needs. Babies need to be in close proximity to us to feel safe. Even in 1965, Anna Freud, the daughter of Sigmund Freud, recognized this when she wrote: "It is a primitive need of the child to have close and warm contact with another person's body while falling asleep.... The infant's biological need for the caretaking adult's constant presence is disregarded in our Western culture, and children are exposed to long hours of solitude owing to the misconception that it is healthy for the young to sleep...alone."[7] As much as we are able to

---

7   Freud, A. (1965) *Normality and Pathology in Childhood*. New York, NY: International Universities Press.

have our newborns close and receive as much skin to skin contact as possible, it will help them to develop a secure attachment.

While our goal as parents during this newborn stage is to let go and accept that life is not in our control, our newborns are busy learning to communicate their needs which continues into the next stage of toddlerhood.

Parent's Goal When Child is a Toddler (1–3 years)

During the toddler years, we are consumed with trying to keep our children safe. It may have started during infancy when you would check to see if your newborn was breathing at night. Now you do your best to make sure your child doesn't kill himself by walking. When my son was 18 months old, we were in our new house and it had only one step. We had some friends over and within 90 seconds of me announcing how nice it was not to worry about him hurting himself on steps as there was only one, he came running toward me, slipped and hit his forehead on the corner of the step. Blood everywhere, we rushed to the hospital and to this day he wears a Harry Potter-like scar on his forehead which reminds me to never become too complacent.

So our goal as parents during this tenuous and amazing age is containment: containment of our anxiety, containment of our fear, and loving containment of our child. Have you ever heard a parent scream "Be careful!" or "Don't run or you'll fall!"? Talk about programming anxiety! How many, many times have I thought these statements and had to take a deep breath and calm myself down so I didn't project my fear onto my children? And how many times did my inability to contain my fear result in me blurting something like that out? So you can understand why the developmental stage of a parent with a toddler is to learn to contain anxiety. Chapter 5 delves thoroughly into this essential life skill of containing anxiety. Do you have a child under 3? Feel free to skip ahead to Chapter 5 then start again in Chapter 2 and hang in there! Toddlerhood is a test to regulate your emotions. If we don't regulate our emotions when our children are toddlers, they end up inheriting our anxiety, as anxiety is so present for parents at this age.

Along with regulating our own emotions is the need to help protect our children from the emotions of others. This may mean reducing visits with a family member who is not emotionally regulated or saying "no" to your parents or family members who insist on your child kissing or hugging them for their own validation.

When we ask our child to hug or kiss someone that he or she is not entirely comfortable hugging or kissing, we unconsciously teach her or him to submit against their will which may lead to increased vulnerability. Yet, this act is so common that you'd be hard-pressed even in the most progressive families to find parents who do not force their children to be held, hugged or kissed unwillingly, mostly by innocent relatives who mean no harm, but still, unwillingly.

I was one of those parents when I first became a mother. I was nervous that my friends and relatives would get their feelings hurt if I didn't force my daughter to hug or kiss them when they asked for a hug or a kiss. I knew my daughter had no interest in being forced to hug or kiss anyone when she gave me a look of disdain, backed away or sometimes voiced "no!" At first, I would cajole her, as I thought it would be rude not to, "come on," I would say, "that's your aunt." But I soon realized that to force her to submit her kisses and hugs against her will would not only teach her that others' preferences are more important than hers, but that it was her job to please people (through her body). Oh dear... that was not the message I wanted to program in her.

Others in the field agree; "When we force children to submit to unwanted affection in order not to offend a relative or hurt a friend's feelings, we teach them that their bodies do not really belong to them because they have to push aside their own feelings about what feels right to them," said Irene van der Zande, co-founder and executive director of Kidpower Teenpower Fullpower International, a nonprofit specializing in teaching personal safety and violence prevention.[8]

What we can do to change this is to consider consent for people of all ages. If our child doesn't want to give grandpa or grandma a hug, don't ask her or him to. If everyone is hugging goodbye and your child

---

8   Retrieved from www.lifeaspire.com/7215/why-you-should-never-force-kids-to-give-hugs-and-kisses/

backs away, don't ask her or him to hug goodbye. There is a social pressure to please others and to use children to please. It's time to let go of this expectation and use the idea of consent for people of all ages from newborn to elderly. If you are not sure by his or her body language if they want to be held, hugged, or kissed, then you can ask her or him privately. If your child says no, don't ask her or him again and don't force her or him. Just like we want our high school and college aged children to understand "no means no," we can start teaching them now.

Parent's Goal When Child is a Preschooler (3–6 years)

The preschool age can be challenging and confusing both for parent and child. It's the age of letting go, and also holding on – much like the teenage years. Children of this age must learn a sense of responsibility and ambition that is self-motivated. At this age, parents often make the mistake of bringing in threats and bribes, as it is an age where misbehavior will often rear its head. During this age in particular, parents have the opportunity to lay the foundation for intrinsic motivation. Intrinsic motivation means being motivated to do something because it makes you feel good in itself. For example, hugging a loved one or eating dessert have no external rewards or consequences, they just feel good, so we are motivated to have this behavior. No reward is needed because the behavior itself is the reward.

On the other hand, extrinsic motivation is when we are motivated to do something based on wanting a reward for our behavior or avoiding punishment. Extrinsic motivation is often the primary system used with preschoolers, and it can create problems later in life. For example, a child who grows up always getting a sticker or a sweet for doing positive actions will grow up expecting a reward for something that should happen naturally.

The perfect example of this is "eat your vegetables and then you'll get dessert." Not only are we robbing our children of the opportunity to appreciate vegetables, which can be delicious, but we are taking them away from the present moment and having them focus on something in the future. We are essentially telling them that vegetables are bad, but there will be a reward if they comply.

Extrinsic motivation can also reduce compassion. If our children are overly praised or rewarded for acts of kindness, they are robbed of the opportunity to discover how good it feels to do something kind. Instead, they are trained to focus on "what's in it for me." Often, extrinsic and intrinsic motivation can produce the same behavior and the difference is experienced internally. For example, extrinsic motivation can be studying because you want a good grade, intrinsic motivation can be studying because it makes you feel proud to learn and be good at something. I'm sure you can guess which type of motivation produces happier and more successful children, but learning intrinsic motivation takes time.

Giving a reward or threatening a punishment will often produce an immediate behavioral shift, which is why it's so popular at this age. However, I strongly believe that if we, as parents, can just take some deep breaths during challenges instead of bribing or punishing, our children will come out on the other end with so many more tools to use in life. My son and daughter take such pride in their schoolwork and so truly love learning that even when I tried to encourage them to take time off from school for a Disneyland trip they didn't want to. They receive so much joy from learning new things! Of course, this isn't only a result of allowing intrinsic motivation to grow, it is also a result of great teachers and an open-minded temperament.

During these preschool years, the goal isn't to "teach" internal motivation, but to allow it to grow within your child. You can do this by pointing out, on occasion, the naturally good feelings that come with doing something positive. For example, when you see your child doing something positive on their own, notice it and ask the child to look to their feelings. "I see you've put your dishes in the sink. How does it make you feel to help keep our kitchen clean?" or, "I notice when grandpa was here that you gave him a hug and that made him smile. How did it make you feel to make grandpa smile?" Internal motivation doesn't always have the immediate behavior change that external motivation has so there will be times when you may need to use external motivation, often when you are in a personally desperate situation. For example, your child is repeatedly hitting his sibling or you are running late for a flight. How to do this should be very specific and is discussed in detail in Chapter 7, so please make sure to read that chapter.

So you can see why patience and trust in the goodness of our child are our goals as parents during this preschool age. Doubting that our child will ultimately make the right decision leads us to threaten or bribe which ultimately communicates that we don't trust them and that they don't have the inner resources to do what's right. Having patience and trust in the goodness of our child is essential. Also, Erikson pointed out that essential goals for children this age are to learn how to interact with others as well as plan and achieve goals which both require the development of intrinsic motivation. We want our children to be kind to others because it feels good to be kind, not because they are avoiding getting into trouble.

Preschoolers will also begin to develop ambition, a desire to achieve, which will require hard work. It's so tempting for us to jump in and do things for them, but we accidentally rob them of their ambition when we do this for them. When we do things for them, we also unintentionally communicate that we're not sure they *can* do it themselves, which can also rob them of confidence. If they ask us for help, we can help, but try to be the secondary figure in the job instead of the leader. If parents can allow their preschooler to lead age-appropriate activities, it builds on their foundation for intrinsic motivation and creates pride and confidence.

But there's more to this stage. There's the letting go you need to do... you'll need to reassure yourself as you communicate the message that you believe in your child (because often you will be just *learning* to believe in your child). Allow your child to explore on her own, as long as it's safe. Avoid being over-involved, allow him to work things out on his own. Support your child's choice, even if it's different from your own personal preference. It can be very empowering and confidence-building when your child learns that she can have a say in things that affect her.

This is a good age to offer two choices and let the child choose. For example, instead of announcing "You'll be starting soccer on Monday" you can ask, "Would you rather do soccer or karate?" Instead of "We're having spaghetti for dinner," you can ask "Would you rather have spaghetti or quesadillas?" You can even use the "two choice" method to encourage good behavior. Instead of "Put your toys away," you can ask "Would you rather put your toys away now or in 30 minutes?" Then, set a timer and when it goes off, you can ask, "Do you remember what you decided to do in 30 minutes? It's been 30 minutes...." Instead of "Ok, time to put your toys away now!"

Be available, and provide kind but firm boundaries. More detailed explanations and suggestions for this strategy can be found in Chapters 7, 8 and 9.

Parent's Goal When Child is a Grade Schooler (6–12 years)

At this stage of life, your child will frequently compare himself to his peers, and likewise, you also will feel the pressure to "do what the other parents do." Your child may sulk, "Pauls' mom lets *him* play Fortnite!" or beg, "But Julia gets Doritos in *her* lunch!" or whine, "Why can't you be like Malik's parents!" Therefore, our parental goal is to create and maintain family rhythms, family traditions and family values at this age. Family rhythms include the day to day movement of your family such as what time you all wake up, when do you eat together, play together, when do you go to sleep, etc. Rhythms should be consistent and structured. Children feel comfort and security when there is consistency in their schedule. Even with older children, maintaining a consistent bedtime, wake time, and meal times are so very important. It's amazing how much can be prevented when children are simply fed and well-rested consistently. Here are a few tips for school-age children from the National Sleep Foundation.[9]

---

9 Retrieved from www.sleepfoundation.org

School-age children:

- Need 9-11 hours of sleep, with deep REM sleep to process stress from their day away.
- Benefit from going to bed at the same time every night, even on the weekends (ideally before 9pm).
- Should not be watching TV or playing on their iPads or phones close to bedtime.
- Benefit from a bedtime routine such as reading a book before they go to bed. They love special time with you!

Also essential is to create rhythms around the use of tech. Here is what I recommend:

- Manage the dangers of too much tech and it's negative effects by having tv, phone and video games allowed on weekends only.
- When in the car, make that a time for family conversation. Don't make phone calls or have phone conversations with your child in the car. Likewise, during family meals, put your phone and laptop away and have screens off. Use mealtimes as an opportunity to make eye contact and connect. You'll learn more about this in Chapter 7.
- Talk to your child about appropriate online conduct. They may be exposed to things you don't want them to be unless you tell them how to be safe online.
- Put away screens at least an hour before bed. The blue light that devices emit stimulates the retina and decreases the brain's production of melatonin, which makes falling asleep more difficult.
- Protect your child from violence and adult references in movies, tv, websites and video games they watch and play by censoring what they watch! Sometimes PG is really like R!

Planning family rhythms is important because if you don't plan them, they will happen for you, and the rhythm may not be healthy. Without planning rhythms, mornings are often chaotic, your family free time is be taken up with tasks you didn't plan to do, bedtimes become a power struggle, and children feel disorganized which increases their chances of misbehavior. The key is intentionality – choose that which you most wish for your family and create your rhythm around that goal. For example, if you wish for peaceful bedtimes, make sure you manage your own frustration by getting into a quiet, peaceful energy and your children will follow. Also, you can eat dinner at least two hours before bedtime and do something quiet (and avoid screens) at least an hour before bedtime. If you would like to make sure your child has time with you, plan for it, otherwise the busyness of life may interfere and it will not happen. You'd be surprised at how regular one to one time with your child will often eliminate behavioral issues. Chapter 8 is entirely devoted to this subject. Other questions you can ask yourself for creating intentional family rhythms include:

- When does your child have one on one time with you?
- When do you get into nature together?
- How do you spend your free time together?
- What family activities do you do together during the week?
- How can you do more activities together?
- Is there an activity that you enjoy that you can do regularly with your child? Exercise? Art? Movies? Sports?
- When does your family eat sweets? (If this is planned, there will be less asking/begging. For example, on the weekends, we eat desserts, but not during the weekdays).

The more you can create healthy rhythms and habits for yourself and your child, the easier day to day life will become. Family rhythms and guidelines around use of technology, bedtime, what happens during meals, family meetings, when you spend one on one time with your child, etc. will help everyone in your family feel at ease and go with the flow of the family rhythm.

Family traditions are essential, too. Not only do they create anticipation, but they become the basis for a foundation of good memories. At this age, your children are old enough to participate in deciding what family traditions they would like to have. Sit down with your children and brainstorm together what traditions can work for everyone and when you can begin to implement them. For our family, since we love to travel, we allow the children to choose many of the travel destinations. Our tradition is that when they turn 10 and 15, they each get to choose the travel destination. We have many more simple traditions such as making grandma's cookies at Christmas, having family dance parties, and more. Our children cherish these traditions and we are working on their involvement in co-creating more traditions together.

When it comes to family values, you'll find that creating a list of values is often easier than implementing them. You may find that "love of reading" is on your list but when was the last time your family sat down and read together? You may find that "a peaceful home" is on your list, but out of exhaustion and overwhelm find yourself yelling at your children or spouse. To engrain positive family values, you yourself must model them. Just as with family traditions, family values are also great to come up with together as a family. Remember: all ideas count. Support your child's choices, even if different from your own. You can find Family Traditions and Family Values templates to complete with your family at www.TransformationalParenting.co.

Parent's Goal When Child is a Tween (9–12 years)

The term *tween* comes from the English preposition "between," which is a position between two extremes, and is also similar to the word "teen." It first appeared in 1987 in an article in the magazine *Marketing and Media Decisions* to differentiate a market formed by a young middle tier possessing "its own distinct characteristics and capabilities."[10] While Erickson doesn't have a stage for tweens, I thought it as essential to include because, as any parent who has a child this age knows, it is a different stage. Perhaps in the 1950s when Erikson wrote his stages of psychosocial development there was no need for another stage, but in the 2000s there certainly seems to be.

The tween age often comes with a tidal wave of unwanted cultural influence. This is often the age that, unless extremely careful, we can lose

---

10   Hall, C. (1987) Teen Power: Youth's Middle Tier Comes of Age. *Marketing and Media Decisions*, 22, pp. 56–62.

our children to social media. It used to be common understanding in psychology that the teen years were when peers become more influential than parents, but I would argue that the age of peer influence is even younger, and now can start as young as 9. As parents, one of our most important goals is to create boundaries that preserve our family values. For most families, because screen time means exposure to content that is much more mature than the child's age, it means filtering out what the child is exposed to, maintaining firm boundaries when it comes to the pressure of saying yes to your child because other children are participating, and being aware of what's out there.

For example, my son is almost 10. Most of his friends play a first person shooter video game which he wants to play so badly. We explained to him in an age-appropriate manner about how the brain gets used to whatever it sees and how we never want him to get used to seeing people hurt, even if those people are video game characters. He is definitely out of the social loop in that area, as a lot of his friends come to school Monday morning after having played hours and hours of this game over the weekend. But he has found other ways to connect with his friends. It can feel like a tsunami wave of culture is trying to wipe out your family values, but resist the temptation to give in.

Parent's Goal When Child is a Middle Schooler (12–14 years)

While our middle school-aged children are beginning to ponder the existential questions of "Who am I?" and "What do I want to do with my life?" it's our job to provide them with the freedom to try on different answers to those questions. When parents place too much pressure on their children to perform or direct their child's interests, a child will likely miss out on the essential learning for this age. It's important for parents to allow children to try on roles and keep their parental anxiety in check. In other words, our primary role at this stage, just as in the toddler age, is to come to terms with our anxiety and preconceived notions of what we hoped our child would become and allow them to be who they think they may want to be. They need the freedom to be able to explore this without our issues coming up. Chapter 5 will walk you through this in detail and not only will you learn tools to let go of anxiety about what your child will or will not become, but also anxiety about life in general.

The Western Myth of Teen Disconnection

Our children are only connected to us for a short period of time. How long they remain connected to us depends on our level of connection with them. Some children begin to distance themselves when they are babies, some in elementary school. The age they begin to distance themselves is largely based on how connected we are to them. In Western culture, we have come to expect that pre-teens and teens will distance themselves. I used to think that it was part of human development for teens to disconnect emotionally in an extreme way from their parents but now I realize that it's a cultural myth. While there is a lot going on with them neurologically and hormonally, culturally we impose negative standards on this age. Just mention the term "teenager" and you'll get sighs and eye rolls from most adults. In India, for example, many teens remain as connected to their parents as they were as children. In America, parents unconsciously disconnect from their teens. The teens become more independent, after school activities and friends have them in the house less and slowly the relationship fades, and because of this Western myth of disconnection we accept this distancing and disconnect ourselves. Some of this disconnection is natural but a lot of it is unnecessary. At a time when our teens are going through some of the most confusing and challenging experiences of their lives, it is our job to hold on no matter how hard they try to push us away.

The happiest families I know are connected to their teens. They are not necessarily as involved as they were when their children were in elementary school but they remain involved nonetheless. They host teen parties. They know their teen's friends, they use any and every opportunity to talk to their teen, and they snuggle and hug them every chance they can get. Although teens will not want to sit in our lap and snuggle us as they did as toddlers, they may be willing for us to put our arm around them when watching a movie, to massage their back and shoulders or feet, or to hold their hand.

Parent's Goal When Child is a High Schooler (14–18 years)

The high school years with our children remain as essential as the others. Often, parents make the mistake of being less involved at this stage – the sheer height and adult-like appearance of your teen will undoubtedly have an effect on your subconscious, making you treat your child differently whether they are ready for that or not. But in these last stages of parenting actively, our final goal is to trust yet remain connected.

When our child is in high school, our job is to back off and allow them to fly. If you are too strict they will rebel, if you are too lenient, they will disconnect. The advantage is that they are beginning to come into adulthood so your communication can be more sophisticated. If your teen is acting out, it's important for parents to communicate their responsibility instead of blaming the teen: "I would have liked to be there for you in the way you wanted. Can you share with me what you need from me?"

Let go of the temptation to control your teen. The less punitive you are, the more connected they will be with you. You'll want to maintain good boundaries. The teen years are most likely the closing of the window where we have a real opportunity to connect. Once they go off to college the window is mostly shut – you can still get in, but you need to knock first and they may or may not let you in. For many children, this is true in middle school as well.

Developmental Goals of Children (by Erik Erikson) and Parents (by Jennifer Johnston-Jones)

Child's Age	Goal for Children[11]	Goal for Parents	What can help parents to achieve their goal when their child is this age
Infancy / Baby 0–1 years	To learn to trust based on consistent availability and their cries being responded to	To be present and emotionally available for your child, let go of pre-parent life and focus on bonding with your child	• Let go of anything non-essential • Study mindfulness • Don't be on your phone when your child is breastfeeding • Hold your baby: skin to skin contact is essential • Sleep whenever you can!
Toddler (1–3 years)	To begin to learn to do things on their own (autonomy)	To regulate your own emotions, understand the meaning behind toddler meltdowns, let children do things for themselves	• Learn positive discipline techniques • Keep practicing mindfulness and patience
Preschooler (3–6 years)	To learn a sense of responsibility and ambition, interact with others, plan and achieve goals	Be available, provide kind but firm boundaries	• Allow your child to explore on her own as long as it's safe • Avoid being over involved • Allow them to work out things on their own • Support your child's choice • This is a good age to offer two choices and let the child choose

---

11   Hayslip, B. Jr., et al. (2006) Developmental Stage Theories. Chapter in: M. Hersen and J.C. Thomas (eds): *Comprehensive Handbook of Personality and Psychopathology*. Hoboken, New Jersey: Wiley.

Child's Age	Goal for Children[11]	Goal for Parents	What can help parents to achieve their goal when their child is this age
Grade schooler (6–12 years)	The child compares himself to his peers often in this stage. If issues occur at home or school, feelings of inferiority can set in	Create and maintain family rhythms, family traditions and family values	Support your child's choices, even if different from your own
Tween (9–12 years)	Erikson doesn't have a tween stage	Resist the temptation to control	Maintain firm boundaries, while being aware of external influences (social media, etc.)
Middle schooler (12–14 years)	From ages 12 to 19, Erikson discusses the need to answer the questions "Who am I?" and "What do I want to do with my life?"	Connect. Keep your anxiety in check	When parents place too much pressure on their children to perform or direct their child's interests, a child will likely miss out on the essential learning for this age. Important for parents to allow children to try on roles and keep their parental anxiety in check
High school age (14–18 years)		Trust yet remain connected	Remain connected and resist the temptation to control

As you can see from the chart above, the child's developmental goals are in line with a parent's goals. If a parent doesn't focus on mastering their developmental goals, it can make it difficult for the child to pass through their own developmental goals. For example, a parent who is anxious teaches their children that the world is unsafe so their children may have difficulty passing through their search for independence and finding their own place in the world. At the same time, it can be extremely difficult to accomplish our parent goals such as "resist the temptation to control" or "regulate your emotions" without working on our personal growth. If only simply knowing we need to regulate our emotions would actually help us regulate our emotions.... Yet, the reality is learning emotional regulation and letting go of the need to control, letting go of anxiety, anger and sadness is a process, not a goal one can just check off a list. That is why we need to work on ourselves to help our children become the best they can be.

IF YOU WANT YOUR CHILD TO CHANGE, YOU MUST CHANGE YOURSELF

In essence, if you want your child to change, you must change yourself. Allowing ourselves to open our heart and be vulnerable to personal growth is a journey that we can take with our children to become the best version of ourselves together. Growing with our children is an exciting and wonderful opportunity that allows parenting to be a gift rather than a burden. Many don't realize that unless you actively work on personal growth, you will unconsciously teach your children all of your learned habits. Without your active awareness, your children will take on your unconscious fears and unhealthy patterns. They will unconsciously incorporate your feelings of rejection, loneliness, and anger into their psyche.

Let's be honest, just because we are adults doesn't mean we have our act together. I know no one, including myself, who has it together all the time. Perfection is not the goal here, awareness is. It's important to recognize that anytime we feel discomfort, upset, anxiety, fear, or any of the negative emotional states, it is because we need to heal something within. By simply noticing things and knowing you want to change that trait, you will begin the process of breaking down the dam. So, let's admit, most of us are just kids in adult bodies and it's time to raise ourselves.

Transformational Parenting helps us see that our children help to raise us. By recognizing our reactions to their behaviors and being aware of our internal goings-on, parent and child can effectively work together to develop into our best selves. Can you imagine what the world would be like if all adults took full responsibility for their personal development? It may sound unrealistic, but I strongly believe, and most experts in human development will agree with me, that the most effective way to co-create a peaceful and (dare I say) joyful world is to actively work on ourselves. As we know from psychological research, there is no better way to do so than in relationships...and the most powerful relationship we can potentially have is with our children. We must heal ourselves and prioritize our relationship with our children. Simply by being willing to resolve issues that resulted from the way we were parented, and becoming more conscious of what we need to work on by noticing how we are triggered by our children, powerful change will occur.

We've inherited our parents' unhealed wounds, and it's our job to make sure our children don't inherit ours. Along the way, we can not only prevent the negative but we can improve the trajectory: raise yourself along the way, and in the process create more joy and peace in your family and future generations. Change begins with you.

CHAPTER 2

DEPROGRAM

"We need to deprogram ourselves. I know for sure that you can't give what you don't have. If you allow yourself to be depleted to the point where your emotional and spiritual tank is empty and you're running on fumes of habit, everybody loses. Especially you."
– Oprah Winfrey

Programming starts from the moment we are born and continues throughout our lives. The well-meaning remark "what a pretty little girl" can program us into feeling that we are only worthwhile if we are beautiful. Crying as a young child and being ignored can program us to feel that we don't deserve to be seen. Being told "don't cry" can program us to feel like our authentic feelings are unacceptable, even if we are in pain. Music we hear that tells us how to act, movies we see that show us how our relationships should be and what we should look like, advertising that programs us to believe that if we are not perfect we will not be loved...on and on it goes. Wanting to be loved and accepted, we mold ourselves to the will and comfort of those around us, to the messages of the music and movie producers, to the advertisers and corporate manipulations often prohibiting the true expression of our soul.

This creates a world where most of us are running on harmful programming, running on language and ideas of fear, of "fitting in," of pleasing others in order to feel safe, or following the false roles our parents created for us and their parents created for them. Therefore, in order to begin to uncover our true self and realize the freedom of being able to be who we really are, we need to start with deprogramming: to deprogram the limited thinking of what's possible. Just like a computer with a glitch, we need to reboot, to clean out the viruses in our internal software that have been passed down from our parents by their parents and by society's fears and limited beliefs that keep us small.

Most of us are programmed to have a limited mindset, to think small. It's unconscious and gets passed down from generation to generation. One of the most powerful things we can do is to reset what we think is possible, to eliminate self-limiting beliefs...the "shoulds" we tell ourselves: I shouldn't do that/this, be this/that way...I should be like her/him, do this differently, etc. We need to eliminate the "I'm not _____ enough." We tell ourselves: I'm not smart/pretty/funny/courageous/talented/etc. enough." Shaming gets us nowhere fast and doesn't help anyone.

There are five primary harmful programming themes that most of us need to deprogram. The table below shows these themes as well as the Transformational Messages we can replace them with in order to free ourselves and our children to a life of possibility. Then, we'll break down these themes together one by one.

Harmful Programming	Transformational Messages
What happened to you is who you are.	You can become your best self regardless of what happened to you.
We don't deserve good things to happen to us.	Good things come to those who believe they deserve them.
Life is what happens to you.	You create your own reality, your own life.
A "purpose" has to be an incredible world-changing task.	"Purpose" can be as simple as having a deep relationship, a loving connection or creating something you're proud of.
Parenting is exhausting and depleting.	Parenting is sacred work which can fill your soul.

YOU CAN BECOME YOUR BEST SELF REGARDLESS OF WHAT HAPPENED TO YOU

One of the most important layers that we have to peel off and deprogram is the belief that what happened to us is who we are. If you were traumatized or experienced rape, incest, abuse, neglect, violence…if you grew up very poor or were not paid much attention to, if you grew up in a household full of yelling and stress…even if you felt too much pressure or were not seen for who you are, you likely developed a survival response.

Sometimes, you will see that what is now holding you back is what helped save you in the past. Let me tell you the story of Dr. Felitti, a San Diego physician working in an obesity clinic. He was tasked with asking background questions of all new patients. Being an obesity clinic, these background questions included how much the patient weighed at a certain age and the age of their first sexual experience. During one intake, Dr. Felitti was nervous and instead of asking, "How old were you when you were first sexually active?" he asked, "How much did you weigh when you were first sexually active?" The patient, a woman, answered, "Forty pounds." The woman burst into tears, adding, "It was when I was four years old, with my father."[12] Dr. Felitti realized she was discussing sexual abuse and that she had literally built a shield of obesity around her by overeating. It helped to save her from further abuse in the past but now was killing her. This history of abuse connected to obesity is not unique.

Dr. Felitti realized there may be a correlation, even a causation, between childhood trauma and medical issues and began his study called the Adverse Childhood Experiences study. The first study[13] was done in 1998 and since then tens of thousands of people have been studied further, confirming the relationship between adverse / stressful childhood

---

12   Retreived from https://acestoohigh.com/2012/10/03/the-adverse-childhood-experiences-study-the-largest-most-important-public-health-study-you-never-heard-of-began-in-an-obesity-clinic/

13   Felitti, V.J., Anda, R.F., Nordenberg, D., Williamson, D.F., Spitz, A.M., Edwards, V., Koss, M.P., Marks, J.S. (1998) Relationship of childhood abuse and household dysfunction to many of the leading causes of death in adults: The Adverse Childhood Experiences (ACE) Study. *American Journal of Preventive Medicine*, 14: 245–258.

experiences and chronic disease. Of the more than 17,000 people studied, most had more than one adverse childhood experience. Examples of adverse childhood experiences include abuse, neglect, and parental substance abuse. There is a common myth that adverse childhood experiences only happen in impoverished communities or communities with less education but, "The ACE Study participants were average Americans. Seventy-five percent were white, 11 percent Latino, 7.5 percent Asian and Pacific Islander, and 5 percent were black. They were middle-class, middle-aged, 36 percent had attended college and 40 percent had college degrees or higher. Since they were members of Kaiser Permanente, they all had jobs and great health care. Their average age was 57."[14] This study and the research that came from it is changing the way we look at health, parenting, school systems, chronic disease, and more. We've known that abuse and neglect hurt children, but now we know that experiences such as being teased, going through a stressful time, having your parents get divorced, getting yelled at and more seemingly benign experiences can also hurt them. If there was ever a reason to change – this is it. Listen up:

There is a direct link between childhood trauma and mental illness, chronic disease, doing time in prison, and work issues such as absenteeism. But that is only true when the trauma is untreated. Let me repeat: if something bad happened to you, you don't have to have it affect you if you do the personal growth necessary to heal.

You see, what happens to us when we are children becomes our adult lifestyle unless we actively bring consciousness into healing ourselves. Children with stressful homes or who don't have a basic foundation of safety grow up to have chronic disease. Unless healed, it becomes a way of living, constantly being in a flight, fight or stress mode. So just like the obese woman who unconsciously overeats to protect herself from predators, you may have behaviors that used to serve a purpose that no longer do.

---

14 Retreived from https://acestoohigh.com/2012/10/03/the-adverse-childhood-experiences-study-the-largest-most-important-public-health-study-you-never-heard-of-began-in-an-obesity-clinic/

Perhaps you once needed to be hyper alert to avoid being yelled at by an emotionally unstable parent. Over time, that hyper alert trait which saved you in the past may have developed into a neurological pattern of anxiety or hypertension. Perhaps you were around a lot of fighting in your home between your parents, and you learned to need hardly anything because there was so much going on. Perhaps you were around a parent who was constantly stressed out so you learned to take care of others before yourself…as children dependent on our parents these responses help us survive homes that are not peaceful. More often than not, however, this turns into patterns of behavior that are toxic to us as adults.

Yet, thank goodness the brain is flexible. We can transform that anxiety into a state of normal awareness. We can transform that depression into a state of appreciation. We can transform your tendency to put yourself last into a mindset that allows you to be deserving, too. We discuss how exactly to do this in Chapter 4. For now, it's important that you allow your identity to evolve beyond what you needed to be to survive as a child. You are more than your response to a situation. You are more than the label that your parents and others gave you (athlete, smart, pretty, funny, annoying, hyper, shy, etc.). You have the power to become and experience exactly who and what you want in life. You can become your best self regardless of what happened to you.

GOOD THINGS COME TO THOSE WHO BELIEVE THEY DESERVE THEM

It used to be said good things come to those who wait. But waiting never quite gets you the good things. And the truth is, sometimes, even when we get those good things, we push them away because we don't feel we deserve them. Or we don't recognize them as good, or we don't know how to actually accept them. Until you begin to see that you deserve those good things, it's pretty hard to have them.

Think of a time in your life when you got exactly what you thought you wanted. For example, your dream job is offered to you, with everything you wanted, the pay, the benefits, the time off. Everything. In the beginning, it's amazing! You can't believe your luck.

And then the doubts set in. You begin to wonder when they will figure out that they gave the job to the wrong person. You make a mistake. You're certain that mistake will end this dream job and possibly your career. You hope they don't notice. Your days get more and more difficult, until eventually you make it come true and you lose the dream job.

This sabotage isn't your fault. You aren't trying to do it. In fact, I would guess that you do everything you can think of to have it not happen. It has nothing to do with luck or ability. It's just the little voice that was developed and cultivated during your childhood: "You'll never be enough." "What makes you think you deserve that?" "Who do you think you are?"

If you stop for a moment, and listen for it, you'll hear it. It comes from all the negative things that were said to you in your formative years. Even if you had a great childhood, it wasn't perfect. You were criticized or made an example of by someone – a parent, a teacher, a friend, a relative.

So how do you become someone who deserves the best stuff? How do you get to be that good parent who deserves a great relationship with their children?

It starts with knowing that sense of undeserving is there. When the sabotage is completely subconscious, you don't even know it's happening. As it is revealed, it has less power over you.

Have compassion for yourself as you begin to open up to that part of you that thinks it is undeserving. Yes, there is pain there, but we're here to explore it together.

Here are a few ways you can begin to feel more deserving.

- Forgive yourself for all the ways you've sabotaged yourself unconsciously.
- Allow yourself to be messy – perfection doesn't equal deserving.
- Give yourself space to process the feelings that come up when you get something you've been wanting.

- Set your bar a little lower – you don't have to meet anyone else's unreasonable expectations.
- Embrace the resistance that naturally comes up – don't fight it. Remember, that which you resist, persists.

As you begin to feel more deserving, you'll see that you can have the things you've always wanted. People will treat you better and life will become easier overall. It's the signals that we send others that we are not always aware of which tell others if we are comfortable with ourselves or not. When we are uncomfortable with ourselves, others feel uncomfortable around us. When we feel undeserving, others respond unconsciously to us feeling that we are indeed undeserving. I don't expect that just by reading this you will feel more deserving. I only hope in this chapter that you become more aware. In later chapters in the book you'll work through healing and determining your identity beyond emotional reaction, and you will begin the process to feel deserving.

YOU CREATE YOUR OWN REALITY, YOUR OWN LIFE

No one else has the power to create your reality but you. You are the author of your existence. So many of us live life in the passenger seat, not realizing that we are supposed to be driving! We "let life happen to us" instead of creating the life we really want.

What you believe and think is what your reality is. The subconscious mind possesses the power to manifest physical reality from thought. Every object and circumstance in this world is representative of a mental thought. *All that now exists was once imagined*! Isn't that incredible? Someone created the chair, the mattress, the sailboat. Someone created the idea of 9–5 workdays, of holidays, of careers. Someone created the idea of how you should dress, what you should look like...such is the power of the mind. You also get to invent, to create, to design the life you want. But in order to partake of this incredible powerhouse of creation that you are, you must be able and willing to experience within yourself – in your mind – that which you wish to manifest. Thoughts become things when you *feel* them, and are able to impress them upon the subconscious mind, which will then take over. Your brain responds most powerfully to emotions. To move beyond what happened to you and toxic behavioral patterns, we need to get excited about something… big emotions whether they are positive or negative are what are the most influential to us. How do we get excited? We realize the truth: that we can create the life we wish to live.

Instead of life happening to you, you have the power to happen to life. You literally create your own reality. For each and every experience you have, you have an unconscious and a conscious emotional reaction which guides your internal state and colors your experiences. In Chapters 4, 5 and 6, you will learn to bring these unconscious feelings to the surface, to identify areas that need healing, and to depersonalize events. Instead of feeling overwhelmed with trying to mitigate and change the outside world, you can create a calm and loving internal world so that no matter how much your toddler tantrums or how many times your teen shouts "I hate you!" you can maintain an inner state of serenity, calm, and executive functioning so that you can create exactly the internal environment you desire. You'll learn a broader interpretation of life's challenges and not only see challenges as opportunities, but actually grow from them. Once our inner world becomes healthy, very few things can upset us. There is no luck; life does not happen to us. We create our own luck; we happen to life!

Create Your Own Reality

While I was giving a parent education workshop about the importance of filtering media for children, one of the parents had been on his phone most of the time and was not participating. Suddenly, when I was discussing how we create our own reality he perked up. I was grateful to have his attention. He looked at me quizzically and stated, "But why would we shelter them from reality? Shouldn't we expose them to 'the real world'?" I was so happy he brought this up because it's a common response and the way most of us were raised: the myth is that there is a "real" world and it is hard and tough and we need to toughen up our children to prepare them for this awful world. Many of the parents I worked with used to think this way when they spanked their kids, that they had to "toughen them up" to make sure they didn't end up in jail or a drug addict or worse. In doing so, parents tear at the relationship between them and their child and ironically make their children even more vulnerable to addictions, poor health, and crime, as spanking and fear-based discipline creates relational trauma. This is such a common trap that limits our ability to truly experience life. It is exactly the kind of thinking that gets us locked up in an unconscious "it happened to me" and "I'm surviving and just doing the best I can" mentality. The consciousness behind this thinking implies that the world is what it is and we are powerless to change it or to influence it, and the only way to survive it is to understand it as best as you can and outsmart it.

My response was simple: "What is 'the real world'?" I asked him. He looked at me like I was crazy. "Is your world less 'real' because you live in Malibu than those who live in South Central Los Angeles or Syria?" (Long pause, no response). "There are multiple realities. Your Malibu reality is just as real as my friend's reality from his impoverished gang-infested neighborhood. The 'real world' is whatever you create, whatever you make it. And many of my friends in that impoverished neighborhood are happier than my wealthier friends in Malibu. Reality is subjective. What you are experiencing right now will be very different from what she (pointing to another parent in the workshop) is experiencing, but that doesn't make either of you wrong, it just means that there are different truths for everyone." He nodded and made eye contact with me for the first time in the entire workshop and stopped looking at his phone for the remainder of the time.

It's one of our biggest cultural myths, and it's become a cultural habit. We unconsciously participate in the false belief that there is one universal truth and that we are victim to it. Most of humanity is spending their one precious life unconscious, reacting instead of creating, acting as a victim instead of a manifestor. There is an entire corporate machine built around this consciousness fueled a little by greed but mostly by more unconsciousness that contributes to massive consumer mentality: overspending, taking more than we need, throwing away things and relationships when they appear to be broken when only a simple fix is necessary because it appears so easy to just get another one. And most of our decisions are not really decisions. They are reactions, jerk-reactions to a survival mentality. You're just trying to keep living.

I encourage you to release this mentality, to untangle yourself from this web of collective unconsciousness, to escape the Matrix. Break the cycle and stop participating in this cultural habit of powerlessness. Instead, engage in powerful intentional living. This requires really knowing what you want. What do you want? What is your hesitation? Many people say they do not know what they want, but what they really mean is they don't know how to get what they want. The Ego steps in and unconsciously tries to protect you from disappointment so it interrupts your dreaming. Take a minute and think about something or an experience that you've always wanted. It may be something material like a new car or a house near the beach or something relational like a stronger bond with your partner or to find true love. Most likely, your Ego stepped in even before you finished reading the sentence and came up with reasons why that would not work for you. It's trying to protect you by keeping you from dreaming. It confuses disappointment with death. One way around this is to become connected to what excites us...to what we want.

What Do You Want?
As parents, we become resigned to putting our own needs last and then we forget what we want in life. Then life gets busy. We get busy working, paying bills...changing diapers turns into making lunches and driving to and fro, by the time you get to bedtime, you become happy just to watch a movie before bed. Life can go on like this for years and then what? You've forgotten to pay attention to what you want, to what brings you joy. Some people live their whole lives like this. Doing so can eliminate your life force, your mana, or state of flow.

But identifying what it is you want from life is often not as easy as it sounds. Because you've been on autopilot for so many years, you've probably lost your way a bit when it comes to imagining the possibilities for yourself. Or, your limiting beliefs may get in the way of your mind allowing you to dream. Here are Celeste's and Ravi's examples of limiting beliefs. See if you can relate:

Celeste: Celeste used to have so many dreams. After she became a mother, she limited her dreams more and more to the point where, when I was in session with her, she could not even pinpoint what it was that she wanted. She was used to putting herself last for the sake of everyone else's happiness. When there was a plate of cookies, she would take the broken one, telling herself that she didn't really care. When she needed new clothes, she rarely purchased the clothes she really liked and instead purchased only clothes that were on sale. When her children needed something, she would stop whatever it was she was doing and help them. When her husband needed something, she would do the same. In her 40s, she had lived a life for others and now realized that unless she made a change, the rest of her life would be led the same way.

Through our work together, Celeste realized that what she wanted most was freedom. Freedom to go where she wanted to go, when she wanted to. Freedom to explore the world and enjoy being alive. As a child, she was given the message that her job was to make her mother happy. When she was married, she thought her job was to make her husband happy. When she became a mother, she thought her job was to make her children happy. All along, she was longing for the freedom to make herself happy. But as a mother, she had a hard time imagining that freedom. How can a person be truly free when small ones rely on you? Celeste's limiting belief was "I want to be free, but I can't because I'm a mother."

Ravi: Ravi's yearning was to be seen. As a child his parents were not around much and he was also an only child so he was alone a lot. He spent a lot of time alone in front of the television, alone in front of a video game screen and alone in the house. He was a bright kid and taught himself computer programming at a young age. He went on to create a video game company. One day, his company was sold to a large corporation and he had his first experience of being seen. A large newspaper did a story on him and he felt not only validated, but proud. Ravi struggled for years as to why he felt so good when he was given attention.

Through our therapeutic work, he was able to connect his need to be seen as a child with his need to be seen as an adult. However, Ravi thought that being seen was Ego-based. "I shouldn't be wanting that attention," he would explain to me. "There must be something wrong with me." And if you only witnessed this one dimension of Ravi, you might agree, but Ravi was not Ego-based, he was kind, compassionate, generous and the opposite of a narcissist. Yet, he felt conflicted because he experienced joy and excitement when it came to being known as being the best. And as his psychologist, I saw his issue as being clouded by unnecessary shame. Yes, there were reasons why he craved this validation, but ultimately it gave him joy. In the end, the work was not around learning to *not* be validated, but around being ok with enjoying the validation. Ravi's limiting belief was "I want to be seen but I can't because that would be Ego-based and selfish."

We all have limiting beliefs, and it's essential to deprogram them. One of the easiest ways to get back on track and to re-discover what you want is to follow that which makes you excited. Feeling excited and joyful is a much more accurate compass than monitoring your thoughts. Thoughts are often clouded with unhelpful programming, whereas excitement and joy cannot be denied.

Exercise: What do you want? WHY do you want it?
What makes you feel excited? What brings you joy?

List 30 things that make you feel excited or joyful. The first few may come quickly and the last not as much, but it's important that you try to complete all 30, as we often forget what makes us excited or we're unconsciously following someone else's dreams.

1.＿＿＿＿＿＿＿＿＿＿＿＿＿＿＿＿＿＿＿＿＿＿＿＿

2.＿＿＿＿＿＿＿＿＿＿＿＿＿＿＿＿＿＿＿＿＿＿＿＿

3.＿＿＿＿＿＿＿＿＿＿＿＿＿＿＿＿＿＿＿＿＿＿＿＿

4.＿＿＿＿＿＿＿＿＿＿＿＿＿＿＿＿＿＿＿＿＿＿＿＿

5.＿＿＿＿＿＿＿＿＿＿＿＿＿＿＿＿＿＿＿＿＿＿＿＿

6.＿＿＿＿＿＿＿＿＿＿＿＿＿＿＿＿＿＿＿＿＿＿＿＿

7.＿＿＿＿＿＿＿＿＿＿＿＿＿＿＿＿＿＿＿＿＿＿＿＿

8. _____

9. _____

10. _____

11. _____

12. _____

13. _____

14. _____

15. _____

16. _____

17. _____

18. _____

19. _____

20. _____

21. _____

22. _____

23. _____

24. _____

25. _____

26. _____

27. _____

28. _____

29. _____

30. _____

Now that you've listed things that make you feel good, you'll have more of a sense of what you want. However, to help you further investigate, go to the places that make you feel good, to get inspired. When I work privately with clients, I encourage them to make an inspiration book. Some people use Pinterest for this, but you can also use a journal. You'll want to include anything that inspires you, makes you feel excited, enthusiastic or joyful. Here, I've also incorporated some teachings from the book "*The Law of Attraction*" by Esther and Jerry Hicks which is similar to what we know creates change in psychology.

It can be helpful to imagine how you want to get what you want, but no need to be too specific or not specific enough. Anything you imagine that gets you excited is a sign that you are in the right direction. You will know if you are imagining just the right way if you will feel positive emotion. Don't fall into the trap of questioning how it will happen or the details or you will begin to feel doubtful. This wisdom has been passed along through time, as that which people are the most passionate about is created.

You may find yourself thinking or saying things such as "I'd love to _____ but _____." However, when you say "I want it **but...**." you kill the possibility of this manifesting. The more you think and speak of what you want, the faster it will come.

It's not good to be patient, for that implies that things take a long time and they don't have to take a long time. They only take a long time when you have doubts.

When you know what you want and you're ready for things to happen, focus your attention on something you really want and at the same time experience strong positive emotion. But, you cannot have underlying doubts or fears about your wish; you must be confident in your desire. It's essential to focus on that which you want; if you get distracted, it may not happen as easily.

Focus completely on your imagination. Get inspired by what you have seen that you wanted and create it anew! Don't limit yourself to what you remember of your own experience. You will know when you are on the right path to imagining when you become excited!

But beware: when you think of the life you desire, make sure to frame your goals in the positive. The unconscious mind does not understand "no" so when you say, "I don't want to do something," you are telling yourself that you want to do something. For example, instead of "I don't want to be fat," you can say "I want to be healthy."

Another way of saying this is that any energy or thoughts that you put into thinking about that which you don't want, fuels that which you don't want. Instead think of what you do want and focus on what you do love. Don't dwell on your troubles, difficulties, or illnesses. The subconscious mind by its very nonselective nature accepts all your feelings associated with troubles as your request – and worst of all, proceeds to make them your experience in the world of your material reality. The subconscious mind responds to suggestions. You can reprogram your subconscious mind so that it goes on its accustomed role of autopilot with intentional thoughts which help you realize your goals.

THE TRUE MEANING OF "PURPOSE"

We are the only species that gets caught up in the existential dilemma: Why am I here? What is my purpose? Animals walk the earth unburdened by such neuroses. Think of a dog, just happy being alive. You may wonder why such joy is not as easily accessible to us. As a psychologist I've spent many hours contemplating this. Why are we so grandiose thinking we need a "purpose" in the first place? Perhaps the real truth is that we are here to survive and procreate, just like our animal friends. But that's simply not true. There is much more to the story, and much more to humans than surviving and making babies. And it's true for animals too. Think of your dog who finds his greatest joy when you are giving your full attention to him. Even undomesticated animals experience pleasure when in relational states.

When we acknowledge our need for a deeper purpose and make it a priority, we prioritize our relationships and live life intentionally. As parents, our most important relationships are with our children and involves our awareness of how we influence our children (and how they influence us). Thus, *our highest purpose as parents lies in our relationship with our children.*

You may hear the word "purpose" and think you need to come up with an altruistic life-calling reason for your existence. "I'm here to make the world better, to cure cancer, to serve humanity…" We overdo the idea of purpose. So if we don't have a grand and lofty meaning to our lives, it is easy to feel inadequate. We have our Ego to blame. We want to feel important, like there's a reason we are special, like without us, the world would not be the same…. But the truth is that authentic "purpose" is much, much simpler than we make it out to be. Let me explain....

My favorite psychiatrist isn't Freud, or even Jung (though he's my second favorite), it's Viktor Frankl, a holocaust survivor who came along about 20 years after those two grandfathers of psychology and chose to focus on purpose and meaning. He has become famous for teaching people that regardless of what suffering they experience, they can choose their own inner experience and that purpose is derived through finding meaning. Frankl explains, "We can discover this meaning in life in three different ways:

(1) by creating a work or doing a deed [creating something is a way to find purpose];

(2) by experiencing something or encountering someone [love is a way to find purpose and may in fact be your purpose]; and

(3) by the attitude we take toward unavoidable suffering" and that "everything can be taken from a man but one thing: the last of the human freedoms – to choose one's attitude in any given set of circumstances."

Frankl emphasized that realizing the value of suffering is meaningful only when the first two creative possibilities are not available (for example, in a concentration camp) and only when such suffering is inevitable – in other words, he was not proposing that people suffer unnecessarily.

In other words, you can find meaning and therefore purpose through the process of creation or through love. So you can see the simplicity of purpose. Not sure what your purpose is? Create and Love, it's that easy! And preferably do them together! Can you think of anything in life that embodies the ideas of love and creation more than raising children? Our highest purpose lies in our relationship with our children.

Many find that adding to love and creation in other ways fills them as well. Whether your form of creation is starting a company, writing a blog, painting a painting, or cooking a meal, you are finding meaning and purpose...fill that with love and you've got it! Yes, you'll probably make the world a better place if you do these things together but don't put that kind of pressure on yourself, please! Just enjoy what you create, make sure it brings you joy and doesn't become an obligation and you're all set! And remember the word "practice" when living purposefully because sometimes it won't come easy. Just keep on getting in there to create, to love...practice makes purpose!

What will you create this month?

_____

_____

_____

Practicing Purpose

During the late afternoon, we often have a slump in energy. Some of us (guilty!) use sweets or coffee to try to compensate for this energy drain. But even better than sweets or coffee is being able to increase your natural energy through practicing purpose. Do you know what I mean by "natural energy?" It's the energy we feel when we are really excited about something, the energy we felt as a child when we played and laughed, the energy we still sometimes feel when we're going on a trip or really anticipating something. But this energy isn't dependent on the food we eat or how much or little sleep we have, this energy comes from serving our soul.

Do you know what I mean by "practicing purpose?" Having a deeper understanding of the true meaning of purpose to create and love and use this perspective in every activity you participate in will naturally fuel you without caffeine. It's less of an action and more of a mindset. It's choosing to see the world through a lens of love and creation. It's creating your life based on what you love. It's in this power that you will be fueled with a calm, healthy purposeful energy that isn't reliant on the needs of the Ego such as external validation, having the "right" clothes, career or traditional success.

The most essential shift to go from just living to transforming your life into the life of your dreams is understanding the power that comes from creating your life instead of letting life happen to you. Which is so important, I want to emphasize it again. Most people let life happen to them. When they are looking for work, they look for jobs that are available instead of thinking of what job they want and talking with the businesses that may hire them, or creating their own job. When they are looking for love, most often take the best of what they find instead of envisioning their perfect partner first. When they are looking for happiness, they look toward things or experiences instead of thinking about the feelings they want to have. In essence, they experience what comes to them instead of intentionally shaping what comes to them. Not only do we underestimate our power but we don't even realize we have any power at all. And the more we practice purpose, the more our soul will be filled, and this powerful and exciting energy will come more frequently without having to look for it through sweets or coffee.

Tear Up the Report Card

When you were a kid, that report card could make you feel great, or it could show your failure to everyone who looked. And truthfully, you probably didn't care as much about your report card as others did. That piece of paper could get you in good graces or in the dog house.

It's easy to carry that mentality into your adult life, measuring your achievements and failures against some standard that you didn't create for yourself. You're probably not aware of all the ways you measure yourself against that standard. You compare your looks, your income, your car, your clothes, your kids...the comparisons and judgements are endless.

Go ahead now and rate yourself as you would when you are judging yourself.

Here's an example:

Category	Grade	Why?
Appearance	B	Weight, wrinkles
Health	B-	Could do better
Parenting	D	Yelling too much
Relationships	C	Need to spend more time with hubby
Career	C-	Not loving it
Wealth	C	Need to save more

Now you go ahead and write.

Your Report Card:

Category	Grade	Why?
Appearance		
Health		
Parenting		
Relationships		
Career		
Wealth		

Fortunately, as an adult, we no longer have to arbitrarily rate ourselves against others, we get to set our own standards. Now, let go of those grades, those judgments. Let go of judgments on that report card. Instead, ask yourself these three questions:

1. Am I striving?
2. Am I learning?
3. Am I kind to myself?

Life is rarely balanced. You'll find yourself excelling in one area and needing improvement in another area. This doesn't mean you're "less than" or "below average," it means you're learning. Allow yourself to be the best you can be, in a relaxed manner. You can't be your best when you are stressing about trying to be perfect. The idea of perfection takes away from the ability to be authentic. You can begin to examine what your own standards are for your achievements and behavior. To begin to do so, you can start with changing your mindset.

CREATING A GROWTH MINDSET

When you try something new and you aren't good at it, do you want to give up, attributing the failure to something about you ("I'm not good at sports, I never was artistic, I'm not a good dancer") or do you do it anyway? As you approach a challenge, are you more apt to try harder with things you think you can do instead of things you think you can't? Me too. Growing up, I was praised for my academic and artistic skills and was afraid to fully engage in sports. A lot of my own self-labeling ("I'm just not a sports person") and others' labeling ("She's just not that competitive") kept me away from a life of would-be enjoyable experiences and limited my capacity to fully use all of me instead of just my mind. This avoidance of trying new things and challenges that you think you're not good at is called a "fixed mindset." As the famous psychologist Carol Dweck says, "Most of us suffer not just from a fixed mindset but a fixed lifestyle." It keeps us in a little box and truncates our full potential.

What is something that you avoided trying for fear of not being good at it or failing?

_____

_____

_____

_____

Is this something that you are still curious about? If so, what are some steps you can take to make it happen?

_____

_____

_____

_____

When we have a fixed mindset, a lot of self-doubt comes into play and also a great fear of failure to make attempts (which also shows up as procrastination). The fixed mindset says "Are you sure you can do it? Maybe you don't have the talent." The cure for this limited fixed mindset is what Dweck coined as the "growth mindset." Yes, there's still fear of failure but with a growth mindset, there is willingness to try. The growth mindset answers the fear of not being able to do something with

"I'm not sure I can do it now, but I think I can learn to with time and effort."

A fixed mindset also creates limited identity development, the false belief that if you fail that means you're a failure. No one wants to consider themselves a failure so generally attempting challenges is avoided. As a psychologist, I can tell you that a fixed mindset can also be a recipe for depression and can accentuate anxiety.

Wondering how to raise a child with a growth mindset? Use Transformational Communication. We'll go over this thoroughly in Chapter 9. Language is programming and the more you use effective language, the more you and your child will develop a growth mindset. Also, you need to make sure to model this willingness to try new things and to do things that you are not necessarily good at.

So, how to encourage a growth mindset in yourself? Here are some tips from Dweck[15] herself:

Step 1. Learn to hear your fixed mindset "voice."

Step 2. Recognize that you have a choice.

Step 3. Talk back to the fixed mindset "voice" with a growth mindset voice by encouraging effort.

Exercise

Use this activity[16] to help you think about incorporating your own growth mindset into activities where you have a hard time seeing personal improvement. Consider how your attitudes about your own strengths and challenges are influencing messages you share with your children.

In three of the boxes, write or draw a skill, or something you are good at. In the fourth box, write or draw something that you don't think you are good at, and would like to improve on. For example:

15   Dweck, C.S. (2012). *Mindset: How you can fulfil your potential.* London: Robinson.
16   Retreived from https://oregonask.files.wordpress.com/2015/12/nurturing-growth-mindset-in-adults.pdf

Good at: SINGING	Good at: GARDENING
Good at: RIDING MY BIKE	Would like to improve: CHESS

Now your turn. Write or draw three things you are good at and one thing you would like to improve about yourself:

Good at:	Good at:
Good at:	Would like to improve:

Now take a moment to write a little more about what you're good at and why.

I'm good at:

_____

How I developed this skill, ability, etc.
1._____
2._____
3._____

I'm good at:

_____

How I developed this skill, ability, etc.
1._____
2._____
3._____

I'm good at:

_____

How I developed this skill, ability, etc.
1._____
2._____
3._____

I'd like to improve at:

_____

How I can develop this skill, ability, etc.
1._____
2._____
3._____
4._____
5._____

After doing this exercise, how do you believe you can improve?

_____

_____

_____

_____

In this activity what steps did you take to nurture your own growth mind-set?

_____

_____

_____

THE ADDICTION OF "BEING BUSY"

"Life is what happens when you are busy making other plans."-Unknown

Ever notice notice that "busy" has become the default response to "how are you?" People used to respond with "fine" or even the automatic "good, thanks." But now the response is more frequently, "busy." The disease of busyness has hit epidemic proportions. How many people have you come across that would describe themselves as "not busy?" Can you think of anyone with a calm demeanor where you feel truly relaxed in their presence? Chances are you are lucky if you can think of one or two of those people – most of us run around like chickens with our heads cut off. We've come to accept rushing as a part of everyday life. We rush to get out the door, we rush to appointments, we rush back home…. We are so busy "being busy" that we are too tired to play with our kids, make love to our partners, and connect with friends. So our kids grow up without us noticing because we didn't spend enough time with them, our intimacy fades, and we have lovely friends who we hardly ever see. Our busy lives distract us from our happiness. We've become so accustomed to rushing and the habit of being busy that we forget there's an alternative.

Here's the truth about being busy: being busy is almost always a disguise for anxiety, we use it on an unconscious level to distract ourselves from core fears. And "being busy" and anxiety have become a habit.... It is estimated that anxiety affects about 1 in 13 people worldwide. Anxiety is especially prevalent in Western cultures. For example, in the US, it is estimated that between 18% and 30% of young people have severe anxiety, making it the most prevalent mental health issue in the country.

So, why has being busy become so common? From a psychological perspective, we consider the benefits of unhealthy mindsets to understand why they perpetuate. For example, someone who is anxious has the advantage of avoiding certain things that make them uncomfortable. Being busy benefits us in many ways. It makes us feel important. There is an inherent belief that busy people must be very important. In fact, many people unconsciously handle feeling insecure with busying themselves. Internally, this distracts them from the fear of being unloved and externally it sends a message to the rest of the world that they are important. So, while their inherent need is to connect and receive love, their anxious busyness keeps them from doing exactly that.

Being busy also distracts us from the things that we may not want to deal with. It can provide us a way to avoid an uncomfortable emotion – just as depression does. In fact, busyness and depression have a lot in common (more on that later) and often people make themselves busy to avoid feeling anxiety, sadness or depression. It's a culturally sanctioned defense mechanism, also known as sublimation, the expression of socially unacceptable feelings or thoughts in socially acceptable ways.

Being busy provides us with a biological adrenaline rush which can be addictive. It patterns itself in our brains and then we crave it just as we've all developed addictions to our smartphones. It's one of the Western world's greatest vices. Dr. Robert Holden, author of *Happiness Now*, puts it perfectly: "We are too busy to be happy. We have confused adrenaline with purpose."[17]

When we are locked in a system of busyness we have less access to the biological feedback loops that our body sends to let us know that we

---

17   Holden, R. (2007) *Happiness Now.* Carlsbad, CA: Hay House.

need to change something. The gift of slowing down is that we can be more aware of our physical and emotional needs.

Have you ever experienced a time in your life when you had to work really long hours and then when that wasn't necessary any more it took your mind a while to calm down? I remember when I was in graduate school at one point I was working three jobs and driving all over Los Angeles to do so. It doesn't feel like an exaggeration to say that 30% of my awake time was spent in a state of anxiety…. Once that wasn't necessary any more, I kept running on that anxious energy. That sense of urgency led me to be extremely productive but my work lacked soul, and so did I! I'm 44 now and for the first time in my life I am learning the power that comes from not filling my every hour. Part of the reason why this book took me so long to publish is because I had an incredibly difficult time sitting down doing one thing for that long of a time. I would fidget and struggle with what the buddhists call "monkey mind" where I would get distracted every 30 seconds. To be perfectly frank, I still need to work on this. I think about the kids and adults I work with who actually have ADHD…if my mind gets distracted in a blink, I can only imagine what that neurological distraction would be!

I remember this little girl I worked with who was diagnosed with ADHD. She was also processing her parents' divorce. We had a great connection and she loved working with me as much as I loved working with her. We were making great progress but when I would visit her at school I could tell that she was overstimulated. One of her body's ways of dealing with this overstimulation was to not make eye contact. Indeed, from that experience, I was reminded of the power of eye contact. Just by looking someone in the eyes, the distracted mind is softened. So, she and I began to simply make eye contact. It slowed both of us down and grounded us. Later I taught her mindfulness techniques to cope in such a busy classroom and also encouraged the teacher to modify the classroom on behalf of all the children to make it less overstimulating. Sometimes teachers, just like parents, feel that more is better. Unfortunately, there is no real "multitasking" and environments and lifestyles that are too busy simply have us all feeling like we have ADHD.

So, How Do We Let Go of the Addiction to "Being Busy?"

If you have a child under 7: this will be easy as all you have to do is follow their lead. Instead of rushing your children, give ample extra time when you need to be punctual. In our house, we used to start the bedtime ritual a full hour before bedtime because sometimes the bath would take 40 minutes as they revelled in the joy of bubbles, snuggling would be 20 minutes as we gave in to the tender moment. But this didn't come easy, or naturally. There were times when it was very difficult to follow their lead, and when our children wanted us to lay with them until they fell asleep and it would take 90 minutes for them to fall asleep while we had to lay there silently, we felt like we were going to go stir crazy! I would remind myself of the need of this little soul and the hours we were apart during the day and allow myself to peacefully surrender. Sometimes I would use this time to meditate and, when I was present enough, I simply basked in the moment as I knew it was temporary. I'm not necessarily advocating that you go to this extreme, but the message is that when your child goes slow, follow their lead and slow down too.

Have you ever tried to walk somewhere at a regular pace with a young child? They get distracted by beauty and wonder...the snail on the sidewalk, the yellow flower, the puddle of rain. They are reminding us what we once knew – that appreciating beauty and nature increases happiness and relieves the need for a life spent rushing around. I have some friends who devote themselves to nature, camping in the wilderness, going on long nature hikes, regularly swimming or surfing in the ocean – all without wifi – and they are some of the few who live with the least amount of busyness and are often the happiest. Yes, it's correlated!

If you have a child over 7: you will likely have to take the lead. At this age, they've picked up on many of our nasty habits including busyness. Years of distracting them when they were younger with a phone or iPad, years of seeing you rushing out the door and yelling at them to hurry up, has most likely primed the palate for your child to follow this anxiety-ridden mindset. But don't feel guilty – not only is guilt an incredibly wasted emotion as it doesn't accomplish a darn thing, but it is very common and a part of our cultural disease. Finally, be careful not to overschedule your children (even teens). Overscheduling our children creates anxiety in them and also in us. When we can't be still or sit in quiet, it is a sign that we are too busy.

Find Your Meditation

Even though we know it is so good for us, some of us, myself included, do not make the time to meditate regularly in the traditional way. Sitting down for twenty minutes and focusing on my breath and letting my thoughts go is wonderful. I do it when I can, but I'm certainly not doing it daily. Perhaps one day I will find my peaceful groove, but often, it feels like something else on my "to do" list. In the meantime, I revel in places of quiet and stillness. For me, and many others, meditation can be found in stillness. In quiet walks (leaving the phone at home), in silent cuddles holding my children as they drift off to sleep, in nature, in places of worship, in sitting and staring out the window, even in driving with no music or audio book, just allowing my mind to wander. This stillness can also be a form of meditation. Such stillness can also improve creativity and your immune system functioning. In Chapter 10, I share with you some rituals you can bring into your family that include stillness. In the meantime, think of times in your day that you can insert stillness and quiet. Maybe it's doing the dishes, before everyone wakes up in the morning as you prepare for the day, or walking the dog (or yourself) in the evening. Remember to leave the tech behind so you will not be interrupted. Find your meditation.

When would be a good time to insert more stillness and quiet into your day?

_____

_____

PARENTING IS SACRED WORK

"Changing More Than Just Diapers" – Moms Rising Slogan (www.momsrising.org)

Not only is raising children one of the greatest achievements in life, it is sacred work that deserves to be honored. Our society takes for granted that parents will just do all that work quietly and without acknowledgment. Raising children is often a thankless job, void of acknowledgment and respect, yet full of judgement and criticism. Society judges parents and criticizes every time a parent does not meet their standards.

And yet no one would make it to adulthood without a parent, someone who was willing to bring that child forth from their body. It takes beauty, strength and courage to raise a child. To meet every challenge, whether with grace or not. To stand when all you want to do is collapse in a heap on the floor.

There is no society without your work as a parent. A study at Oregon State University showed that good parenting can have a positive impact on multiple generations.[18] David Kerr, the author of the study, explained, "Positive parenting is not just the absence of negative influences, but involves taking an active role in a child's life....We see now that changes in parenting can have an effect not just on children but even on grandchildren." It takes work and focus to raise children well. Take time to honor yourself for your commitment and your hard work.

_____

18 Retrieved from http://oregonstate.edu/ua/ncs/archives/2009/sep/positive-parenting-can-have-lasting-impact-generations

Not only do you deserve it, but if we all honor ourselves and respect each other, perhaps there is hope for parenting being respected as the sacred, essential work it is.

FOR MOTHERS: DEPROGRAM WHAT IT MEANS TO BE A MOTHER

Almost every woman I know, including myself, has fallen into "The Mother Trap." Locked between our vision for ourselves as women, society's need to put us "in our place" and the realities of the endless needs of children, we end up confused, exhausted, and unsure or even unaware of how to take care of ourselves. Unlike fathers, whose identity beyond the family is socially acceptable, mothers regularly fall into the trap of taking care of everyone else before ourselves. Even those coupled with the most thoughtful partners find that we put ourselves last. There are, of course, obvious reasons why: not only does society endorse us putting ourselves last, but we love our children so deeply that practically all we can see is them. I remember when my children were infants, I had a hard time making eye contact with anyone else. I was completely lost and infatuated by their hypnotizing gaze. Truth be told, I still get lost in them.

Why do we put ourselves last? It started when we were little girls: we were taught to please others, to serve others, to make others happy first. Yet, all we wanted, and still want, is to be seen for who we are separate from having to give to or please others. We yearn to be acknowledged and to not be alone. If you have found yourself giving too much, over-extended because of all you do for others, it's a red flag that it's time to heal. It's time to expand your identity from needing to be accepted by others to just accepting yourself. Symptoms of this are pleasing behaviors which often receive a lot of external validation and praise.

The phrase "take care of yourself" is often spoken but rarely practiced. Women in particular, and especially mothers, regardless of culture, put themselves last and the needs of everyone around them first. The needs of young children are limitless and can easily surpass the resources of the adults who care for them. Young children's needs are constant: physically, emotionally, and spiritually. Many caregivers of young children even find going to the bathroom in private a challenge. One mother of three describes, "I cannot remember the last time I used the toilet without a little one on my lap or in the bathroom with me." Indeed, with so much love and so many needs, it is easy to lose sight of taking care of yourself.

As any parent or caregiver who cares for children full time can attest, the mandate to "take care of yourself" is not so easily accomplished. All too often, token and temporary breaks are mistakenly considered solutions. On occasion, mothers and caregivers voice their overwhelming feelings and are responded to as if the problem is easily solved; "why don't you take a nice walk, get a massage, relax a bit?" As any mother or caregiver knows full well, the problem does not have a simple solution.

The problem is a complex, multigenerational and multicultural epidemic. Caring for children is not given adequate value and those who care for children full time are not given adequate emotional or financial resources to do so. The economics of the United States has left families working harder than ever. Many cannot even afford childcare. For those who can afford childcare, the anxiety surrounding leaving the children is immense as standards for childcare are often so low that they cannot be sure that their children are safe. Husbands, despite taking a more active role than ever in parenting, are often working more than full time so they cannot be relied upon to take up the slack if a mother or caregiver were to integrate more of a balance into her life by having more personal time. In all, women who care for children are entirely exhausted. One mother explained, "I cannot remember the last time I had a full eight hours of uninterrupted sleep." Another mother admitted to showering only once a week. A daycare worker disclosed being so tired after caring for other people's children all day that when she went home to her own children she only had enough energy to watch television with them.

Young children's physical needs are overwhelming. In any given day, they must be fed, cleaned, bathed, carried, wiped, diapered, groomed, held, and rocked, then fed, cleaned, bathed, carried, wiped, diapered, groomed, held, and rocked all over again. Additionally, unlike former generations, young children must be watched constantly. There is no safe place for them to run and explore alone in fields. In parks, one must constantly be hypervigilant as to a child's safety, and for many children there is no outdoor time at all, save for a small plot of concrete called a playground. Therefore, parents and caregivers are often faced with the necessity of attempting to help a child release her energy indoors and the results are often inadequate. Adults caring for young children often collapse into bed at the end of the day only to be awakened a few hours later for a nighttime snack.

In addition to the physical challenges of childcare, the psychological challenge of childcare is especially trying because the job of caring for children, whether paid or not, is clearly not honored in our society. Caregivers and mothers feel that they are treated as second-class citizens. Indeed, for those who are paid, they receive some of the lowest wages in the country, often earning barely over minimum wage. Instead of viewing child care as caring for the future of humanity, it is seen as inferior work. I believe that if childcare was more respected and held more status in society, that it would balance the grueling physical demands to create a more rewarding and enriching role. Unfortunately, despite the fact that women are the primary force shaping the future of humanity, our roles are not respected so we can easily become stressed, unfulfilled, and lose sight of caring for ourselves.

When women are asked what they do for a living, many respond, "I'm just a mom." The phrase "just a mom" is used to describe women who care for their children as their primary role. I've also heard women respond "just a grandmother," "just a babysitter," even, "just a daycare worker" when asked what they do for a living. Many women use this phrase to describe themselves without realizing the unconscious negative note the word "just" implies. Further investigation into the semantics of the phrase undoubtedly implies "less than" and does not command respect.

Indeed, caring for young children is challenging. Yet, for some odd reason, discussing the challenges of caring for young children can be taboo. While it is socially acceptable to discuss how wonderful a baby's skin feels, it is frowned upon to discuss the exhaustion of caring for young children. Mothers and caregivers are not socially permitted to discuss the truth. This taboo, this tendency for society to frown upon the reasonable complaints of childcare, leaves mothers and childcare workers feeling unsupported, alone, and worse, hopeless.

The golden opportunity is to use the time of caring for children as personal growth. To envision exactly who we want our children to be and become that ourselves. Many parents I work with feel that it is "too late" for them so they invest their dreams into their children. Not only are they wrong (it is never too late as long as you are still alive), but it can be a curse for the child to try to live up to their parent's unfulfilled wishes. Instead, we must muster the courage to have hope for ourselves, for our dreams, to know it is not too late to become the person we most want to become: the best version of ourselves.

CHAPTER 3

BECOME THE ADULT YOU WANT YOUR CHILD TO BE

"Parenting is a mirror in which we get to see the best of ourselves, and the worst; the richest moments of living, and the most frightening."
— Jon and Myla Kabat-Zinn

Your child is a reflection of everything about you; your light and your shadow, your strengths, your fears, your passions…. In essence, your child is your mirror. If you truly want your child to be happy, take the job of making yourself happy as seriously as your paying job. Instead of putting your wishes, dreams and energy only into your child, become the adult you want your child to be. There is no better way to teach your children to have authentic success, to be resilient, to be kind, to enjoy life, to have high emotional intelligence…than to do so yourself. We are programmed to a certain reality by the family we grow up with. By making our own healing a priority, we free our children of the unconscious chains that bind them to the pain of the past and allow them to grow into healthy, authentic and, with any luck, joyful humans who are full of life.

Do you love yourself? Do you appreciate your gifts? Your beauty? Your light? Do you love yourself as much as you love your children? I think I can count on one hand those who do. I'm still working on this myself. This inconsistency between our love for ourselves being less than the love for our children creates two major problems for our children. First: they are aware of this (sometimes the awareness is not conscious) and since they see themselves in our image, they wonder that something must be wrong with them if we do not love ourselves fully. Second, if you're not thrilled about what you've got going on inside, you may unconsciously avoid spending time with your child in order to avoid "messing them up". There are so many parents who don't feel good about themselves and fear that their child will grow up to be just like them, so they don't spend time with their children. It's usually not a conscious decision. Very few people wake up and think to themselves, "I'd better stay away from Joshua so he doesn't turn out like me," but it happens all the time. Parents busy themselves, they have a lot of friends over so there's less one on one time with their children, they become over-involved in sports, and in after school activities so they feel involved, but there is no alone and quiet time to deeply connect.

This is what I believe happened with my mother. She had a tough childhood and a lot of emotional issues that she didn't heal by the time I came around when she was 24. When she was around, she wasn't around...she would be doing something without me that I couldn't share. And she wasn't around much. I grew up fast, and the bond between us was never fully established. Because she had unhealed wounds, she would lash out at me which would make me distance myself even more. She wished we were closer, but during my childhood she wasn't around much. Of course, I have positive memories and I love her, but truthfully I don't feel love for her like a mother...more like an aunt or a cousin. It's one of the reasons why I am so compelled to share this information and one of the reasons I left my high profile job at a hospital when I became a parent. I wanted to be available to my daughter in a way that my mother was not available to me. The parent-child relationship has a window. If you're not around when they are growing up, there is a high chance you won't be able to make up for lost time when it's convenient for you.

People usually can clearly state what they don't want to happen, what they don't want to be like as a parent, but it's reactionary. The pendulum swinging in the opposite direction is a reflex of trauma. For generations, humans have been going back and forth with being overly permissive or overly punitive to try to make amends with their experiences as a child. Unfortunately, knowing what you don't want to do doesn't really get us to where we want to be. Just because you know you don't want to be a sewage tank engineer doesn't help clarify what career is right for you. This is why we can't just "not do" what was done to us as children or to do the opposite; we actually have to process our experiences so that our unconscious mind and primitive part of our brain isn't running the show. We can begin with unraveling our story.

UNRAVEL YOUR STORY (HOW TO NOT REPEAT WHAT WAS DONE TO YOU)

Like a spool of thread that has been so twisted and knotted that you can't even unwind, our stories bind us. They trap us into limited identities, limited roles, and limited (often small) concepts of our authentic self. Our childhood interpretations of stressful, traumatic, painful or lonely situations become our template for living, unless we unravel them. What we tell ourselves (or don't tell ourselves) about our experiences creates our reality. Healing doesn't have to be complicated. One of the primary ways to heal is simply by acknowledging our pain while expanding on our story with our adult perspective. We can have compassion for our abuser and still be set free from fear of being victimized. We can grow out of the limiting labels we were given and become the joyful, healthy person of our own making. When we review our stories with the intention of acknowledging and releasing our pain, it allows our heart to open to healing, creates empathy so we don't accidentally repeat what was done to us to our children, and allows us to receive the lessons we are meant to learn.

Unless you unravel your story and heal your pain, you may unconsciously replicate the pain that you experienced as a child, because your denial of your own pain has you pass on the pain to the next generation. Without acknowledging the pain we suffered, we close ourselves off, repeat generational trauma, and unintentionally recreate the wounds that were passed down to us by our parents (and likely their parents before them and so on).

One of the best ways to get motivated to change is by recognizing our anger, sadness, or the unfairness of a situation. So, in order to help you unravel your story, here are some of the most common painful childhood scenarios in the hopes that you will see yourself in some of them.

If you avoid learning of others' suffering, perhaps you haven't been able to see your own suffering fully. If so, this section will be especially helpful to you. You may see yourself in one of the stories. If you find yourself wanting to skip this section, chances are you probably tend toward denial. No judgement. I myself certainly lived very happily in denial for years. It was my children's authentic laughter and tears as well as the courage of my therapy clients to express their pain that had me realize I had more work to do. It's an ongoing process. Just bear with me and know I empathize with you along the way. Open your mind to see if any of these stories stay with you. Chances are, there's something there to unravel.

The Child Left Alone

Even if you were deeply loved and knew it, if your parents were away from you during most of your waking time, you probably fit into this category. Many children of single parents or children raised primarily by one parent will fall into this category because most of the time the parent who you were raised by had to do it all alone. Even though you knew you were loved and saw how hard your parent worked to help you have the best life possible, she or he was most likely not around. This left you having to cope for yourself, to reduce your needs, to depend only on yourself, to "suck it up."

Tara wasn't neglected, she wasn't abused, her parents were just...busy. Tara's parents were divorced. She only saw her father during the summers as he lived in another state, and her mother worked full time. She saw her mother for 30 minutes in the morning before she got on the school bus and for an hour in the evening before her bedtime. She got to school early, stayed as late as the after care program was open and didn't participate in sports or enrichment activities as she had no one to drive her. She had to learn quickly how to do things for herself and often felt guilty for her mother's exhaustion. She felt jealous of her friends whose parents came to see the school plays and events as her mother couldn't get time off work.

The Emotionally Neglected Child

John lives in a beautiful home with an ocean view in Malibu. As a child, he was a good student, a star athlete and had an enviable life. But inside, he feels empty and unmotivated. When he shares about his childhood, the development of this emptiness becomes clear. His parents were wealthy and lived a grand life, but John was left out of it. As an only child with very social parents, he was at home alone a lot. When his parents were home and had dinner with him, he was rarely asked questions with the exception of "How are your grades?" or "Did you win the game?" Their response to his attempts at requesting praise and acknowledgment were "That's nice," or "good," nothing else.

When they had visitors, he was often taken off guard when someone would ask him something about himself. Most of the time his mother would answer for him and cut him off. By the time he was 3, he learned that he didn't have a voice. Even his attempts at tantrums didn't evoke anger from his parents. They would just leave him in his room and lock the door. Sometimes the housekeeper would come in to calm him, but sometimes not. He was raised by nannies and sent to boarding school. At boarding school, his parents didn't visit; there was always an excuse. John would see other parents hugging their children. Sometimes he would feel angry or jealous, but as he got older he just detached from his emotions entirely. As a 43-year-old adult, he can't remember the last time he cried (he thinks maybe he was 6) or the last time he got excited or even angry. The emotional neglect he suffered left him feeling invisible, leading a life where he felt only half-alive.

If John's story resonates with you, it's important that you recognize the wound that neglect creates. Even though John had his physical and financial needs met, and he leads what many would consider a fortunate life, the emotional neglect he experienced as a child must be acknowledged in order for him to ensure he is emotionally present for his children (and himself).

The Child Who Was Pressured Too Much

Myann's parents immigrated to the US before she was born. The reasons for their move was not that they didn't want to stay in their country, but that the ability to work and make enough money to live on was nearly impossible. They wanted a better life for their children. When they got to the US, they worked very, very hard and were treated with much discrimination and racism. When it was time for Myann to enroll in school, her parents feared that she, too would be treated poorly and worried that if she misbehaved she would be even more discriminated against, so they were very strict with her. They also insisted that she receive only the highest marks. They believed that in order for Myann to succeed, she must be absolutely top of her class. After school, they made her practice piano and do school work until dinner, then after dinner, they made her practice piano more. She was not allowed to socialize on the weekdays or to participate in sports. Myann did everything her parents asked of her, motivated by guilt for their struggle and fear of their disapproval. She went to the college they wanted her to go to, even became a lawyer because they told her that's what she should do. Now in her 50s, Myann is miserable. She despises being a lawyer and realizes that for her entire life, the pressure she received to be the perfect child had led her to being a miserable adult. In therapy, she is working on saying "no" and, for the first time, discovering what actually makes her happy instead of what pleases others.

The Child Who Lived in Conflict

Olivia's father said "hate" a lot, especially about her mother. Olivia's parents were divorced when she was three and her entire life she experienced nothing but conflict. It was in the air she breathed, at the dinner table, at bedtime, everywhere. Even as an infant, before her parents were divorced, there was so much yelling and screaming that Olivia's attempts at tantrums were largely ignored. "Take care of your kid!" her mother would yell. "No, you take care of YOUR kid!" her father would retort. As you can imagine, Olivia quickly learned not to make things worse and became the perfect child. Straight As on every report card, star athlete, teacher's pet, would always do her chores without being asked. Even as a teenager, she didn't cause problems.

But inside she was aching, yearning for a safe place. She began to smoke marijuana at a party, which dulled her a bit, then she experimented with cocaine and liked how it kept her thin. At the same time, she began to force herself to throw up after eating something unhealthy so she wouldn't gain weight. After, she'd feel empty and calm which was a rare feeling. Around this time, her parents began to give her a lot of compliments on how pretty she was. But there was still a lot of screaming in her home and a constant tension. Olivia couldn't control the chaos in her home life so she tried to control the chaos she felt inside by controlling what she ate. She developed an eating disorder and as an adult is working on processing the need to let go of feeling perfect or in control in order to feel safe.

The Child Who Came from a Mentally Ill Household

London's mother hasn't been diagnosed, but everything London has described to me about his mother sounds exactly like mental illness. London's childhood was extremely chaotic behind closed doors. In public, his mother put on the perfect face. At home, she would find dishes in the sink and come within two inches of London's face yelling, "you are so selfish, you don't care about me. Don't you see what you do to hurt me every day?" Tearful, London would apologize profusely and go to clean the dishes. If the neighbor visited in the middle of this scene, London's mother would answer the door with a smile. "Come on in, so good to see you."

London did have his brother to help. Sometimes, he and his brother would hide in the closet when they heard their mother in one of her "moods," fearful that she would scream at them. London noticed that when his mother screamed at them, her appearance changed dramatically and her face looked like a different person. She was "sick" a lot too. She would spend all day in bed, and London was expected to take care of her. He would make her meals and bring them to her. Eventually, his mother started asking him to stay home from school so he could help her. The school would call and his mother would answer, "Oh he's sick and won't be able to come in today," although London was feeling perfectly healthy.

His father would witness the abuse and not say anything. Eventually, when London was in high school, his father left his mother and he was left to live with his mother and brother alone. That was when his mother began to threaten suicide on a regular basis. He would witness her control her outbursts in public but at home see her rage. Most of the rage was directed toward his father, but sometimes the rage was directed toward him and his brother.

When he went to college and took his first psychology class, he began to recognize some of what his professor was describing and realized his mother was mentally ill. Since then, he has been trying to get her to go to therapy, to get some professional help. Her response remains rageful, "there's nothing wrong with me, how dare you!" He was entangled in a web of simultaneously fearing her and feeling the need to take care of her. Every weekend, every holiday, he would drive 200 miles to visit her; he really believed his visits were necessary so she wouldn't kill herself. London is now 33 and his mother still subtly threatens suicide. "I'm not sure if anyone loves me; what's the point of living," she says.

London came to see me in therapy as he is trying to figure out who he really is, who he could be if only he had been allowed to be himself and to grow up without fear. He's learning the important lesson that just because someone gave birth to you doesn't mean that you are obliged to have a relationship with them. If only his mother had healed her wounds, she would have been able to have a relationship with her sons and to release her anger.

London now has kids of his own, and he's very conscientious to handle his mental wellness. Because of his childhood, he is easily triggered by his children. He finds himself angry at how ungrateful they seem. At the same time, he finds himself wanting to support them, although he is not sure how. He spent so much of his life caring for his mother's emotional needs that he doesn't yet know what his own are.

If you resonate even a little with London, you will benefit from learning to listen to your own truth and freeing yourself of obligations. Live by your truth and don't let others tell you what you should be doing. Because it wasn't safe for you to be authentic, you will need extra practice as an adult. With authenticity you will begin to develop your intuition as well.

These experiences are not unique. The National Association on Mental Illness estimates that 1 out of every 5 people (or approximately 18.5%) in the US experience mental illness and 1 in 25 experience serious mental illness that interferes with life functioning. Most mental illness goes undiagnosed and results in people trying to self-medicate their pain through alcohol or drugs. A majority of the time, mental illness is born from trauma, abuse, or neglect. So, if you grew up in a household that lacked stability, didn't feel safe, or where drugs or alcohol were the norm, there is a likely chance that you have a family history of trauma. In Chapter 4 I will review some healing that will help.

The Child of Divorce (with Conflict)

Josh's parents were divorced when he was just a baby. In his infancy, there had been a lot of yelling and screaming in the house. His cries for attention competed with the constant fighting of his parents, and from a young age he learned to make himself small. His father angered easily. Josh can remember when he was 8 leaving his backpack at home while driving to school and his father screaming at him so loudly that he had to cover his ears (even as an adult, recalling this scares him so much that he has tears in his eyes). He quickly learned to be a "good boy" as to never upset his parents. However, nothing would upset his father as much as hearing his mother's name. Josh lived with his father and saw his mother every other weekend and part of each summer. Josh's mother called sometimes, but Josh's father became so angry when he heard Josh answer the phone and respond meekly "Hi, Mom" that he pretended to be unhappy to receive his mother's calls. Eventually his mother stopped calling.

Josh's father hated his mother and said so (in front of Josh) ever since he can remember. He shared with Josh how awful she had been to him before they were divorced. Josh felt torn. Of course he loved his mother, but since he was a child, he assumed everything his father said was true. When he saw his aunts and uncles they would talk about how much he was like his mother. But Josh didn't want to be like his mother. His mother must be a monster.

Over the years, his father continued to say awful things about his mother in front of him, and Josh and his mother grew apart. When Josh would stay with his mother on the weekends, he would lock himself in his room and listen to music because he wasn't sure how to be around her. When Josh's mother remarried and his stepfather had a son of his own, Josh felt certain that his father must be right. The conflicting emotions of the fear his father had created of the image of his mother along with the jealousy he felt toward his step-brother sent him further apart from his family emotionally. Josh grew up thinking that since everyone said he was so much like his mother, and his father said that his mother was so awful, there must surely be something wrong with him.

When Josh was 38, he came to therapy for the first time. He wasn't happy and felt like there was something so wrong with him, he could never get married or find someone to love him. After a few weeks in therapy, Josh was able to uncover that he had internalized the negative talk about his mother from a young age to be negative talk about him. It was his father that had something wrong with him, not Josh.

In this example, we learn that unresolved feelings about the child's other parent can be internalized by the child. Even when parents disguise their upset about the other parent and don't share the dislike in front of the child, the child still senses it. This is why neutral (even positive) feelings about the child's other parent are so essential. Being a child in the middle of a divorce (especially one with conflict) can be extremely scarring. In your own parenting, if any of this example resonates with you, your lesson is not only to be authentic but to handle conflict peacefully. Transformational Communication (Chapter 9) would likely be especially beneficial to you.

There are many more common childhood stories. Psychologists understand that our childhood stories become our template for living unless we unravel the stories we are tangled in. What is your story?

Exercise

In order to create lasting change, we have to recognize our pain and use the pain to motivate us, not to replicate (even unconsciously) the behaviors that were done to us. In this exercise, take a moment to tap into a painful childhood memory from any age. It may be a memory that you have pushed aside and haven't thought of in years or one that comes to you often. There is no right or wrong. You will benefit as long as recalling the story evokes emotion.

What is your story? What happened?

_____

_____

_____

_____

_____

_____

_____

_____

_____

_____

_____

_____

_____

_____

How old were you?

_____

_____

_____

_____

_____

What feeling did you experience then?

_____

_____

_____

_____

What feeling do you experience now?

_____

_____

_____

_____

RAISING CHILDREN IS THE BEST OPPORTUNITY FOR SELF-IMPROVEMENT

One of the most beautiful but also the most challenging aspects of the parent-child relationship is the everyday nature of it...there is no break. There is not much alone time to pull yourself together in the moment... you have to have your emotions in control to be able to not react when your child drops an emotional bomb on you.

Nearly every person has an aspect of his or her childhood that they wish could have been avoided. The most common issues I hear tend to include parental abuse, sibling abuse, stranger abuse, emotional abuse, trauma, illness, and premature death. However, even an issue such as loneliness or being teased can have a profound effect on one's development. To cope with distress, humans create ways of protecting themselves, also called defenses. These defenses were once productive ways of responding in the midst of distress, but can become detrimental and limiting to the cultivation of happiness and joy once the distress has gone.

First we will take a little trip back in time – to childhood. As we all know first-hand, the way we were raised directly influences the way we care for children. Being aware of what triggers us can help our ability to understand when the response is more about our childhood than about the child. In order to ascertain your triggers, we will go through a regression exercise, an exercise in free association which will require you to write the first thing that comes to your mind. Do not censor yourself and please do not attempt to make things sound pretty. Just write the first thing that comes into your mind as you complete the sentences below.

Ever since I was a child

_____

_____

_____

Mother was always

_____

_____

_____

What I needed from mother and didn't get was

_____

_____

_____

Father was always

_____

_____

_____

What I wanted from my father and I didn't get was

_____

_____

_____

The bad thing about growing up is

_____

_____

_____

Now, please take a moment to write a bit more. The goal remains to free-associate, that is, do not think about what you are going to write, just write, and do not concern yourself with punctuation or spelling. To truly obtain effective results from the exercise requires you to let go of barriers of how things appear and instead to let your soul speak.

Describe yourself as a child:

_____

_____

_____

_____

List the first painful childhood memory that comes to you:

_____

_____

_____

_____

How does your father feel about you?

_____

_____

_____

_____

_____

Give a description of your father's personality and his attitude toward you (past and present):

_____

_____

_____

_____

_____

Give a description of your mother's personality and her attitude toward you (past and present):

_____

_____

_____

_____

_____

In what ways were you punished by your parents as a child?

_____

_____

_____

_____

_____

Do you punish your children in the same way? Why or why not?

_____

_____

_____

_____

_____

Were you able to confide in your parents? Why or why not?

_____

_____

_____

_____

_____

Did your parents understand you? Why or why not?

_____

_____

_____

_____

_____

Did you feel loved and respected by your parents? What did they specifically do to make you feel this way?

_____

_____

_____

_____

_____

Thank you for having the courage to honestly begin to evaluate your childhood. The exercise is not designed to be an evaluation, but instead, a tool to assist you in reflecting on your experiences. Based on the information you provided, please summarize here your three most difficult aspects of your childhood:

1. _____

_____

_____

2. _____

_____

_____

3. _____

_____

_____

These three memories that you have listed influence your perspective on life. It is essential to be aware of these and acknowledge them. These memories, and all of the tens of thousands that you carry with you, influence your decisions, your behavior and your feelings. Simply by acknowledging painful memories we take one step closer to decreasing the power they have over us.

Sigmund Freud, the father of psychology, coined the term "Projection." It is the tendency to project your own undesirable feelings or emotions onto someone else, rather than admitting to or dealing with your own unwanted feelings. In other words, if you're feeling angry, you may think that your husband is feeling angry because being angry makes you uncomfortable. I believe that projection also occurs in adults' interactions with children. The feelings that we adults have for children are influenced directly by the way we feel about ourselves. Specifically, it is most likely that the very things that you find most troublesome or irritating with children are the very same qualities you consciously or unconsciously dislike about yourself. Now, please list three behaviors that your child has done that made you feel uncomfortable or that you disliked:

1. _____

_____

_____

2. _____

_____

_____

3. _____

_____

_____

Do you also dislike these qualities in yourself?

That is the beauty of Transformational Parenting! You see the connections, the psychology of raising children. The incredible learning opportunities available every day! What a gift for us and our children that when we feel anger or disappointment in our children we can understand that it is something that needs healing in ourselves. And this understanding will, in its very nature, lead to growth, insight and freedom to be your authentic best self, to live life fully and embrace the gift of lessons along the way.

I AM WHAT I CHOOSE TO BECOME

"I am not what has happened to me. I am what I choose to become." - Carl Jung

Do you agree with the Swiss psychoanalyst Carl Jung, who said, "I am not what happened to me, I am what I choose to become"? The idea is romantic and mostly true if we actually "choose to become." "Choose to become" is one of the core tenets of *Transformational Parenting*. Not only do we recognize that no one but ourselves is responsible for our feelings, but we also recognize that no one but ourselves can create who we are *if* we are intentional about healing our past.

Unfortunately, most of us forget about the "choose to become" part and therefore end up being what happened to us! The small doubt that you had as a child about if you are lovable grows into a lifestyle of avoiding relationships. The emotional neglect that you suffered that once created resilience now makes you lonely. The lack of authentic care that you received that made you excel at everything you did now has you feeling empty and purposeless.

Unless we consciously heal what happened to us, and *everyone had something* happen to them, we remain locked into an identity of our past where we have little control over our lives. We develop an unconscious (sometimes even conscious) mindset that has us blaming others or making others responsible for our happiness. What power we unconsciously give to others! Are you wondering if you fall into this trap? Do you feel that if only people behaved differently toward you that you'd be happier? Do you find yourself frustrated or angry at people on a regular basis? Then, you share the mindset that others are responsible for your happiness. But don't fret! This is a cultural issue all over our Western perspective. Just by reading this that will shift for you...read on my friend...

My favorite book in the whole world is by a psychiatrist who survived the Nazi concentration camps. He has become famous for teaching people that regardless of what suffering they experience, they can choose their own inner experience. He writes, "everything can be taken from a man but one thing: the last of the human freedoms – to choose one's attitude in any given set of circumstances."[19]

The book is *Man's Search for Meaning* and the author's name is Victor Frankl. From his experiences during his time in the concentration camps, he created Logotherapy, which is considered one of three schools of thought in psychology. The other two being Freud's will to pleasure and Adler's will to power. "Logo" means "wisdom" in Greek and Logotherapy is based on the idea that people are driven not by pleasure or power, but by meaning. While I believe we are driven by a mix of power, pleasure, and meaning, the idea behind choosing our attitude is powerful. In fact, the lens in which I practice psychology, called "Positive Psychology" which views people from a place of strengths and virtues

---

19 Frankl, V.E. (2006) *Man's Search for Meaning.* Boston: Beacon Press.

instead of pathology, is a child of Logotherapy. Positive psychology uses meaning and purpose to help create a positive mindset.

Where I disagree with Frankl is his belief that people are either "decent" or "indecent." I'm sure that if I survived a concentration camp, I would be comfortable calling people "indecent" as well. Yet in my nearly 20 years giving therapy I've worked with many people who society would consider "indecent." I worked with a man who murdered his wife, another who molested his daughter, and a woman who purposely burned her children's hands on stoves. I see what Frankl calls "indecent people" as "unhealed people." These are people whose painful childhood experiences were left unhealed. I believe in the inherent goodness of people and that we were all born good. Of course, these are extreme examples, but I want to remind you that our definition of "indecent" changes from generation to generation.

For example, I was punished by being hit with a belt...now this is illegal. Do I believe my father is indecent? No...but I do believe if he had healed himself and risen above the place of fear and anger he was experiencing at the time he would not have hit me. He was just doing what was done to him and what he saw other parents at the time doing. Were you spanked or hit? Were you yelled at? Were you made to feel ashamed or that you had to be perfect? I haven't met one person who can answer "no" to all of these questions. We can forgive, we can have compassion for our parents who did the best they could, and for their parents who did the best they could. But the onus, the responsibility to "choose to become," is on us. We are in a time where we have a true collective consciousness, where information is almost as easy to access as breathing, and we have almost all of the information in the world available to us at the tips of our fingers, so we can no longer say "we didn't know..."

We get to "choose to become" all of the things we didn't receive and even to move beyond a place of healing and into a place of vision! Can you imagine what we could create if we all accelerated our consciousness to heal and became the best version of ourselves? We have the awesome opportunity to accelerate the healing of our generation, to accelerate the development of the human race, and to parent consciously. We can't allow ourselves to replicate what was done to us because it was programmed into us...the spanking, the guilt trips, the shaming, the anger directed at children, the busy life (the life of anxiety)...it has got to go. Unless we are completely honest about our subjective childhood experiences and begin to heal them, we will become "what happened to us" and keep unintentionally repeating to our children what was done to us.

Why do I say "subjective"? Because "truth" is always subjective. "Truth" is largely unimportant when it comes to healing, anyway. What matters is the emotions felt. Many well-intended people refuse to verbalize their negative experiences because they believe they must have exaggerated the memory and feel guilty about it or don't believe it's relevant or important. This happens often with victims of abuse...they question whether what they remember is completely accurate and so don't want to dig around in those murky waters of negative memories. But accuracy is not what is important to heal; to heal, one must acknowledge the feeling that was felt.

Probably the most important step in becoming a healthy adult and especially a decent parent is being honest about the pain we experienced as children. Sometimes our love for our parents, or fear of not being loved by our parents, created a kind of emotional mutism as we learned from a young age the danger of speaking a truth that isn't complimentary. And often, we withhold our negative experiences to protect ourselves. We fear that if we talk or think about negative memories, that it will drudge up too much and cause problems that we won't know how to handle. And we worked so hard to "resolve" those bad feelings – we don't see what good can come from thinking about them again.

All of these reasons can cause us to place our memories in the deepest locked vault of our mind where they slowly grow into a system of denial.

Every once in awhile, I come across someone who claims to have had the "perfect childhood." It only takes a few questions to reveal that under that mask of perfection lies guilt, shame, or fear...and denial. Denial and minimization ("it wasn't that bad") are tempting seducers for sure... like dessert versus vegetables. It just tastes sweeter and easier, but in the end we pay for it.

I also have to watch my own need to minimize. I had compassion for the pain my mother experienced as a child. When some of that pain was recreated in me, I forgave her quickly but then didn't acknowledge the pain that I had left to heal. I minimized my pain out of my love for her, and it was easier not to feel the uncomfortable feelings that came along with the pain.

Think of a time when you minimized something that happened to you and write about it...why do you think you minimized that?

_____

_____

_____

_____

_____

_____

_____

_____

_____

_____

_____

_____

_____

_____

_____

_____

_____

_____

So now we begin the process of unraveling our stories, removing the old bandages and denial and minimization that no longer serves us...we begin to allow ourselves to heal by telling our story.

CHAPTER 4

HEAL YOURSELF

"The wound is the place where the Light enters you."
— JALALUDDIN RUMI

W hat if you had to choose between healing yourself or damaging your child? Guess what? You do have to choose. And if you don't make a choice, life will choose for you.... I don't mean to scare you, but as a psychologist I know this to be true. Unless we make a conscious effort to heal our wounds, they will be passed onto our children. In fact, research has shown that emotional pain is passed down from generation to generation unless there is an effort to heal. Even if we think we don't have anything to heal, when we find ourselves fearful, irritated or stressed out it is a sign that there is healing to do. In other words, unless we detox all of the unhealed wounds that we have inside, our children will take them on, and possibly their children too. Emotional healing is is one of the most important responsibilities of being a parent and one of the greatest gifts we can give our children.

No human enters this world with a clean slate; even before they are born their potential is limited by what stresses their mother. Babies in the womb respond to our stress as if it were their own and our stress from driving in traffic or an argument with our spouse can mimic life or death to the little fetus inside as it becomes filled with stress hormones. This doesn't change after they are born, or when they start to walk, or when they start school, or even when they enter puberty! Our pain becomes theirs.

Our unhealed pain grows into regular stress, frustration, anxiety, depression or apathy. Apathy is often overlooked and is a huge issue. It's the "zoning out" in front of television or social media, the disconnect we feel from each other and our dreams, and the zombie-like state most adults function in during their day to day.

Sometimes the pain we feel is overwhelming for our children and they learn that to be healthy they need to avoid us. They will stop making eye contact, and stop spending time with us. In fact, this is what often happens during the teen years when teens begin to separate from us. Yes, our children are craving independence and there are hormone surges but also they begin to understand how our unresolved issues are impacting them. When you take responsibility for healing your wounds and prioritize your relationship with them, you will find your connection stays strong even during these teen years of change.

THE MYTH OF "TIME WILL HEAL"

Contrary to popular opinion, regardless of your age, whether you are in your 20s or 70s, time by itself will not "heal" the pain of a childhood left unhealed. In fact, the longer you live without acknowledging and healing your pain, the more it will grow into other issues such as the diminishing enjoyment of life, reduction of compassion and empathy, self-neglect, addiction of some kind, dissociation with what's going on in your body, even chronic illnesses.

When we ignore the pain we suffered, time buries the pain or creates defense mechanisms to move on, but that is not healing. I've worked with many adults over 50 who still suffer when thinking of their childhood. Even worse, many adults have lived in denial of their pain for so long that they are easily triggered and have created a false persona of who they are in order to avoid feeling further pain.

MAKE HEALING A PRIORITY

What happened to you in the past no longer has to have an effect on you. You can be free of the scar and let go. Devote yourself to the tools in this book. What's presented in this book is, in my opinion, the best of what psychology has to offer in terms of healing. It's like having the wisdom from all of the best psychologists, therapists, and spiritual teachers in one room to guide you. If you choose to be in therapy or participate in a *Transformational Parenting* group when you go through this process you will find your healing becomes accelerated as well (information for how to start your own *Transformational Parenting* group is at the end of the book). When we can connect with other people's experiences it helps us unlock our own.

Because we have been coping with unhealed and often unconscious wounds, we are often unaware that we need healing. We have done such a good job at hiding our own pain that we fail to recognize that we even have pain. We go about our busy life hurrying from one place to the next and lose our ability to be aware of our pain. We get headaches, sugar cravings, have trouble sleeping and think this is all a part of being an adult. Our culture teaches us that headaches are to be expected, just take an aspirin. Cravings are a part of life…. Trouble sleeping? There's a pill for that too…. In fact, just mention any physical symptom and there's a pill for that. We've come so far away from recognizing that physical pain is emotional pain manifested and that emotional pain left untreated turns into physical pain that we've come to expect that being medicated is normal.

There's great power in recognizing that many physical symptoms (tension, headache, sugar craving, trouble sleeping, etc.) are a sign that you may have an emotional wound that needs healing. Simply go into any drugstore and you'll see evidence of our country's tendency to medicate instead of heal. Professions are built on treating symptoms of wounds instead of healing the wounds themselves.

By recognizing the connection between physical and emotional pain, you will build awareness of your need for self-care. Your headache will no longer be just a headache that you seek aspirin for. A headache will tell you that you need to rest, you need to slow down and perhaps you need a good cry or to reach out and ask for help.

The American Academy of Pediatrics recognizes the need to address childhood wounds. They published a paper called the "Adverse childhood experiences and the lifelong consequences of trauma."[20] In it they wrote, "Many people can identify a person in their lives who struggles with a chronic illness like heart disease, diabetes, or hypertension. Most people also know someone who struggles with mental illness, substance abuse, or relationships in general. Traditionally, the health care system would point to high-risk behaviors such as poor diet, drug use, or a sedentary lifestyle as the primary causal factors. Questions for patients have focused on 'What's wrong with you?' rather than 'What happened to you?'" A 1998 study from the Centers for Disease Control and Prevention (CDC) and Kaiser Permanente is leading to a paradigm shift in the medical community's approach to disease. This study of more than 17,000 middle-class Americans documented quite clearly that adverse childhood experiences (ACEs) can contribute significantly to negative adult physical and mental health outcomes and affect more than 60% of adults.[21] This continues to be reaffirmed with more recent studies.

If you need more motivation to heal yourself, remember that regardless of how much you love your child, if you don't heal your pain, they will grow up with the same pain. Generation to generation, the unconscious pain gets passed down. In psychology and psychiatry we recognize this as a biological basis for illness. The grandmother who was abused by her father passes on her fear to her son who develops a sleeping disorder and passes his fear to his daughter. His daughter is diagnosed with an anxiety disorder which is treated with medication and she grows up thinking that this fear-based living is simply life. So you can see how pain gets passed on from parent to child again and again. Unless you recognize that you need healing, you will continue to pass on the cycle of pain from previous generations. There is ample research on this phenomenon, called intergenerational trauma, where families can trans-

---

20 www.aap.org/en-us/Documents/ttb_aces_consequences.pdf
21 Felitti, V.J., Anda, R.F., Nordenberg, D., Williamson, D.F., Spitz, A.M., Edwards, V., Koss, M.P., Marks, J.S. (1998). Relationship of childhood abuse and household dysfunction to many of the leading causes of death in adults: The Adverse Childhood Experiences (ACE) Study. *American Journal of Preventive Medicine*; 14: 245–258.
Anda, R.F., Felitti, V.J., Bremner, J.D., et al. (2005) The enduring effects of abuse and related adverse experiences in childhood: A convergence of evidence from neurobiology and epidemiology. *European Archives of Psychiatry and Clinical Neuroscience*, 256 (3): 174–186.

mit trauma from one generation to another. "The people at the highest risk of trauma and those with the most difficulty working through it have experienced their own trauma but also have come from a family where there was a trauma in their parents and often in their parents' parents," says Stephanie Swann, PhD, LCSW, a private practitioner who owns and operates the Atlanta Mindfulness Institute. "Where trauma has been untreated, what is fairly common is that the untreated trauma in the parent is transmitted through the child through the attachment bond and through the messaging about self and the world, safety, and danger."[22]

We have become disconnected from our bodies, disconnected from our pain. Most of us are so dissociated from the real needs of our bodies that we have a hard time recognizing what the needs even are. When we are tired, we watch more television. When we are thirsty or hungry, we snack unhealthily. When we are lonely, we go to social media instead of calling on a friend. And when we have a headache, we take an aspirin instead of allowing ourselves to rest.

So, how do we reconnect with our needs? How to know if we need healing? How do we recognize if a pain is emotional or not? One of the easiest ways to connect to the wounds that need your attention is to do a body scan. You quiet your mind and check in with your body to assess tension and discomfort. Below is an excerpt from University of California Los Angeles's Mindful Awareness Research Center, which also has free audio downloads to help you with a body scan.[23] Or you can read this text to yourself. And as you read, do a mental body scan.

Body Scan

Begin by bringing your attention into your body. You can close your eyes if that's comfortable for you. You can notice your body seated wherever you're seated, feeling the weight of your body on the chair, on the floor. Take a few deep breaths. And as you take a deep breath, bring in more oxygen enlivening the body. And as you exhale, have a sense of relaxing more deeply.

---

22 Coyle, S. (2014) Intergenerational Trauma — Legacies of Loss. *Social Work Today*, 14 (3): 18.

23 http://marc.ucla.edu

You can notice your feet on the floor, notice the sensations of your feet touching the floor. The weight and pressure, vibration, heat. You can notice your legs against the chair, pressure, pulsing, heaviness, lightness. Notice your back against the chair.

Bring your attention into your stomach area. If your stomach is tense or tight, let it soften. Take a breath. Notice your hands. Are your hands tense or tight. See if you can allow them to soften.

Notice your arms. Feel any sensation in your arms. Let your shoulders be soft. Notice your neck and throat. Let them be soft. Relax. Soften your jaw. Let your face and facial muscles be soft. Then notice your whole body present. Take one more breath. Be aware of your whole body as best you can. Take a breath. And then when you're ready, you can open your eyes.

Use body scan and "breathing into" to heal. Notice when you are triggered. Notice where you have tension, where you have stress and breathe into that tension, when you inhale, breathe in healing, and when you exhale, breathe out tension, stress and any emotions that do not serve you. The time is now. You only have a short time to heal your pain so that you can raise not only an exceptional child, but an exceptional you. What has happened to you in the past no longer has to have an effect on you (or your children). You are a unique and wonderful being with so much to share with the world, but you must heal in order to fully come into your potential. This body scan is a first step. You can do the body scan when you are falling asleep at night, upon waking, whenever you have a quiet moment. Every day will be different and your body will begin to share more information with you as you begin to pay attention to it.

ACCEPTING YOUR IDENTITY AS A PARENT

I sometimes still can't believe I'm a parent, I've been one for more than 14 years but I sometimes waver in denial, especially in the mornings or when it comes to packing lunches (again). Then there's the aging denial: How can I be this old? Who is that old lady in the mirror? (But I digress, that's another book!) I've found that I'm not alone: the transition into accepting yourself as a parent takes time...and is full of challenges. I'm not even talking about the day to day of parenting. I'm talking about the fact that your life is no longer just for you. I'm talking about the fact that you are responsible for not only keeping a small human alive but doing your best to help them learn life skills that you yourself are still learning! Let me repeat that: we are still learning what we are expected to teach! If that isn't overwhelming enough, then there's the constant tick-tock timer in the background of when you need to transition into your parent self and pick up the kids: your free time is extremely limited by childcare. Much of the difficult process of parenting and a lot of postpartum depression can be attributed to this feeling of helplessness; the feeling that our life is no longer ours to command.

We sometimes give in and lose ourselves in our children, feeling out of control. It also doesn't help that it is not culturally acceptable to share the difficult feelings that occur when raising children. This leads to feeling isolated or that there must be something wrong with us. Especially when we first have a baby, no matter what we read, we can never be fully prepared for the overwhelming physical and emotional neediness of an infant. Because we fear being judged, and the judgement is real, we often share only a part of what we are going through, if at all. Parenting can be hard, lonely, and lacking reward but it doesn't have to be. Many parents, especially mothers, can become overwhelmed with their new role and lose much of who they were before they became parents. We can forget who we are! In order to not get lost in the role of "mother" or "father," you'll need your own life – that's called differentiation.

WORK ON DIFFERENTIATION

I have found the concept of differentiation to be essential not only as a parent, but as a wife as well. But what is "differentiation?" The term came from Murray Bowen, an acclaimed psychiatrist who offered an alternative to the individualistic Freudian view. Bowen's Family Systems Theory involves looking at the family as a system and the individual as part of that system. The Bowen Center for the Study of the Family defines a person with a well-differentiated self as someone who:

"...recognizes his realistic dependence on others, but he can stay calm and clear headed enough in the face of conflict, criticism, and rejection to distinguish thinking rooted in a careful assessment of the facts from thinking clouded by emotionality. Thoughtfully acquired principles help guide decision-making about important family and social issues, making him less at the mercy of the feelings of the moment. What he decides and what he says matches what he does. He can act selflessly, but his acting in the best interests of the group is a thoughtful choice, not a response to relationship pressures. Confident in his thinking, he can support others' views without being a disciple or reject others' views without polarizing the differences. He defines himself without being pushy and deals with pressure to yield without being wishy-washy.[24]

On the other hand, a poorly differentiated "self" is someone who depends so heavily on the acceptance and approval of others that they either quickly adjust what they think, say, and do to please others, or they dogmatically proclaim what others should be like and pressure them to conform. Relationships such as the parent-child relationship, spouse-spouse relationship, and many of the most intimate relationships are especially vulnerable to poor differentiation. You may have experienced a time when you got lost in someone: at first it's romantic, then suffocating. Lack of differentiation can sometimes stem from receiving the message in childhood that authentic feelings are not okay and can often be passed from generation to generation. Someone with a poorly differentiated self often looks like a people-pleaser, but poor differentiation can come in many forms. For example, bullies depend on approval and acceptance as much as those who change who they are depending on who they're with to please others. Even those who rebel extremely may be poorly differentiated as he or she pretends to be a distinguished "self" by opposing the opinions of others. Having a poorly differentiated self is not a mental health diagnosis – don't worry! It's quite common. However, it does indicate that you need to work on yourself.

One of the most important psychological shifts one can make in any relationship is to differentiate. Not only is differentiation essential for parenting but it is also one of the top predictors for a happy married

---

24 https://thebowencenter.org/theory/eight-concepts/

life. Being differentiated means you take care of your own emotional needs, don't expect others to make you feel happy, don't feel guilt or resentment, you can express yourself freely without having to "protect" others, and you allow children to be themselves.

To work on improving your differentiation, let go of your expectations of others, work on finding your own identity and remember who you are separate from the people you are closest to. Because this book is about parenting, we will focus on how to differentiate from your children, but I also encourage you to differentiate from your spouse or partner. The benefits are profound: one of the most common struggles I've seen couples come in with during couples therapy over the years is the frustration with feeling a lack of freedom. Differentiation solves that and much more. Now back to the relationship with your children... differentiate by allowing them to be themselves.

Allowing Children to Be Themselves

Perhaps one of the most difficult tasks of parenting is to truly allow children to be themselves. We love them so deeply, invest so much of ourselves in them, and want them to be happy so very badly that it becomes very hard to allow them to behave in a way that is different than what we hope for them. So much of how we interpret life occurs subconsciously. We often make decisions without really thinking about it, and then project those decisions onto our children. Sometimes, these decisions that we have made for ourselves, that we then hope for our children, become the way for our own needs to be met, rather than allowing them to learn what their own needs are. This is a lack of differentiation and it happens at one point or another to almost every parent I know, including myself. For example, I always loved theater and being onstage. It gave me confidence, poise and helped me figure out what role I took in school. When my son decided that he was not into theater at all and did not even want to try it – had absolutely no interest – it killed me. I made him enroll in an after school theater program and (no surprise) he hated it. He went for most of the program because I was just hoping he would come around but he remained steadfast. It was not him. I had to let it go and let him find his path. I haven't pressured him again but it's hard for me...when the posters go up in our community about auditioning for the next play I worry about what he's missing out on. But I have to remind myself: it's not him, it's me. It's not my job to put my decisions or likes on him...he finds his own path. There are a hundred more examples of this. I'm sure you have your own as well.

Seeing children for who they are, not our projections of them, is essential. We must allow our children to be who they are instead of extensions of ourselves. When we are discouraged, the temptation to use our children to feel a sense of worth is strong. The danger of using children to complete us is that it only serves our own needs, and does not allow them to find their own way. It can be challenging to know when we have wandered off and gotten caught in our own unsatisfied needs. This is why one of the best gifts we can give our children is to focus on our own personal growth.

HOW TO DEAL WITH OTHER PEOPLE

You've woken up in a great mood. The sun is shining, your child runs to you and gives you the best morning hug. You're feeling great! On your way to take her to school, you pull up to a stop light. The person in the car behind you honks with irritation because you didn't immediately drive when the light was green. Then, that person races in front of you and swears at you while showing you, and your daughter, their middle finger along with an ugly glare. Then, you pull up to the school and begin talking to a parent you don't know well who decides to tell your daughter that her outfit is "interesting." Then later on the way home you get pulled over, for no apparent reason. Then you go home and your partner yells at your daughter, and your daughter has a full-blown meltdown and decides to tell you that she "hates you." While this day may be exaggerated, the examples are common. So often in life other people seem to ruin our positive feelings. And of course, people can be cruel, unkind, or even worse.

But what if you could have compassion for a bully, feel sorry for the driver that flipped you off, even have sympathy for a murderer? I learned this skill over the years as a psychologist as I listened to those people's stories and their traumatic childhoods. You don't have to be a psychologist to grow your compassion toward others – you just need to understand that all babies are born good and it's trauma, abuse and neglect that mutate their spirit and produce the behaviors you witness. And here's another motivator: increasing your compassion for others increases your personal power. By not reacting to others' behavior and simply allowing them their own reality, you don't need to take things personally – because they aren't!

When you find yourself having a negative reaction to someone, take responsibility for your own thoughts and feelings and see it as an opportunity for growth. You'll find that the most annoying people can be the best teachers. The most challenging people are constantly testing us; your emotional response is your report card. Did the gossipy mother get on your nerves? The lesson is not that she should stop gossiping (although we hope that she will do her own inner work to release that behavior), but that you need more work to not let it affect you. Did your spouse leave the laundry on the floor again? Again, the lesson for you is not "What can I do to help him get his laundry in the bin?" but rather "How can I not let his bad habits get to me?"

Others cannot alter your emotions unless you invite them to through thought. Throughout the day we have countless opinions, our Ego is busy chatting us up, telling us what it thinks of this person or that object, even the weather can send some people into a bad mood! It's what we think about most often that becomes our reality, and if you find yourself on the negative dominant side of thinking, your future will reflect that.

The cure to negative thinking does not have to be complicated. Simply pay attention to your thoughts. Someone was rude to you? Observe it, work to find compassion for that person, and don't think of it again. Is that someone rude to you on a regular basis? How lucky you are! You have a chance to have a lot of practice at this! And remember to LOVE the practice! You may even eventually find yourself amused by the behavior of this person (rude behavior can become a free comedy show). You can work further on letting go of negative thinking patterns in Chapter 5.

And what about your loved ones who are suffering? Your mother? Your aunt? Your brother? Your father-in-law? This is where it gets tricky, but you must also allow them to have their own experiences. You may certainly make yourself available for them and let them know you are here to help them should they ask for it, but do not make their pain your own. Do not make their drama your drama. It's so very hard when people we love are suffering. What other people choose does not hinder your own choices. If you pay too much attention to the choices they are making, your own emotional composition will change and you will end up taking on their suffering unnecessarily.

The exception to this rule is with your own children (as long as they are still children). In fact, it's your role to help them shape their reality. Not only is it your role to help them create a positive reality, but if they are suffering, it's a sign that you also need to change your reality. Our children simply mimic our perspective. If your children are suffering, you need to put your attention to your own personal growth and hop to it!

To allow yourself to be as you are and to allow others to be as they are is as important to emotional health as eating vegetables is to your physical health. That means to release yourself from judgment. Most of us judge ourselves more than we judge others. We are our own worst critic. Again, this comes from our Ego. Our Ego is deathly afraid of change, so it traps you into thinking that you are "less than" and feeds off of artificial praise and the illusion of traditional success. By allowing yourself to create your own reality you also need to allow others their own reality. This is a powerful lesson and will save you time and negative emotions.

You must also be aware that you can create your world as you want it to be and others can create their world as they want it to be. Their choices don't threaten yours. Diversity is important. All of our perspectives make up a collective reality, but we don't and shouldn't try to participate in everyone's reality or to change others' realities. I am not recommending that you remain neutral in important human rights and political strivings, only that you allow and have an inner peace and lack of judgement/anger about those different perspectives. When we learn to allow others to be themselves, it gives us freedom to be ourselves and contributes to our own immense personal growth as well as that of those around us.

NEUTRALIZING NEGATIVE EMOTIONS

Every day, even every hour, we can experience an incredible variation in emotions. They can flash in and out within seconds; from guilt to gratitude, to anger, to fear, to disgust and pride and many more. Research shows that we are experiencing some kind of emotion 90% of the time. A study of more than 11,000 people found that the most common emotions reported are joy, love and anxiety.[25] Joy is the most common (that makes me happy)! In fact, for both men and women, positive emotions were experienced more than 2.5 times more than negative emotions. Yet, it seems that the negative emotions are what we recall the most; they stay with us and can become burdensome. Although we waver from minute to minute in our emotional state with positive and negative emotions, it's the negative ones that hold our attention the most.

---

25 Trampe, D., Quoidbach, J., and Taquet, M. (2015) Emotions in everyday life. *PLoS ONE*, 10(12): e0145450. http://doi.org/10.1371/journal.pone.0145450

This was most likely developed from a need to survive. By focusing on stressors, our body remains more alert and therefore we were more apt to survive a potential threat. As most humans are actually experiencing more positive than negative emotions, recalling mostly the negative ones can create an unhealthy focus.

You see, every emotion is connected to an action or inaction. For example, experiencing anger and joy helps people take action. Feeling fearful exaggerates the danger of taking a risk. Feeling disgust has an interesting response: it makes people want to throw away or discard their belongings, even when the source of feeling disgusted is unrelated to the situation at hand.[26]

So you can see how, unless we are self-aware of our emotions, unless we are conscious of our feelings, desires and what is actually motivating us, we can get lost or stuck in life as we are pulled this way or that by our emotions. I'm not recommending not feeling our emotions: feeling emotions, even negative ones, is one of the gifts of being human. And being aware of what's going on inside allows us to comfortably communicate our needs to others. But when we are in emotional pain, or just plain irritated, we will need to bring ourselves to a neutral state so that we don't inadvertently hurt another with our feelings. Since our children are so good at making us feel big feelings, one of the greatest tools you will come across is how to neutralize your negative emotions.

First, become aware of your body. When our brain is flooded with stress hormones, it's nearly impossible to be logical, but becoming aware of how our body is feeling can help us to connect our physical symptoms with our emotions. For example, many people have jaw tension when they have unreleased anger or headaches when they need more joy and levity, stomach aches when they have anxiety, and so on.... Simply sit for a moment and close your eyes, do a body scan to assess which areas of your body are tight and breathe into those parts of your body.

Second, release your body. Should you notice tension in your jaw or shoulders, for example, take a deep breath in and when you exhale, let go of that tension in your body. Give your mind a moment of calm in

---

26 Lerner, J.S., Li, Y., Valdesolo, P. and Kassam, K. (in press) Emotion and decision making. *Annual Review of Psychology*, 66.

your inner storm. Whether it be for two breaths or 30 minutes, just let your mind and body be without judgement.

Next, release your mind. Now that your cortisol levels are reduced, you can take a moment to help your mind let go. This will help you more clearly identify what you are needing, which will help you become less triggered in the future. See each of your thoughts as a balloon you are holding on to. Now let each thought / balloon float away. Allow yourself the blank space in-between thoughts and breathe a breath into that space.

The next step is to notice what you are feeling and needing: Now that you have some physical and mental clarity, you can more easily identify what you were feeling and what you are needing. What exactly *are* you feeling? Sometimes what at first seems like anger is actually sadness. Sometimes what at first seems like frustration is actually exhaustion. Many emotions mask other emotions. They come in layers, like an onion. The more you practice this, the more you will be able to peel away the reactive emotions and get to what you are needing, your core emotion. Try not to overthink it…. If you were feeling angry, sad, or afraid, name the feeling, then identify what you are needing (to have a moment to myself, to have safe relationships, to have kind communication, etc.)

Last, decide what you want from yourself right now. Rather than focusing on what you want others to do or to change, determine what you can do right now for yourself to change your situation. Unhappiness arises when we try to change another's behavior, even if it's our children's! Instead, focus on what you can do to get your needs met even if it's something as simple as taking 5 minutes of alone time in the bathroom. It's important that you create an action that you can do immediately.

The more you practice neutralizing negative emotions, the easier it will come to you. When I first began, it would take me 5–10 minutes, now I can manage the whole process in about a minute. I've worked with many, many people who didn't think they would ever be able to neutralize their negative emotions and every single one of them was able to do so. For more on this, be sure to thoroughly read Chapter 5, which covers how to let go of negative feelings when they become habits (such as anxiety, depression and frequent anger).

Neutralizing negative emotions is a kind of meditative practice. You'll find the more you do it, the easier it will be. What works for me is to practice it when I need it. However, a lot of the people I work with practice it before they even experience negative emotions. Because emotions come in and out so quickly, even when you're feeling neutral already, you can probably find a negative emotion or tension hanging on in your body and mind somewhere and neutralize it, let it go. Especially if you have regular negative emotions, a daily practice can be very helpful. But actually, anytime you neutralize negative emotions is helpful. At first it will be clumsy and you may think you can't do it. Stick with it. Keep trying. You'll find it can be a life-changing tool.

PAIN IS RELATIVE

The basic needs of childhood (to feel loved, to feel safe, and have all physiological needs met) are rarely met consistently by any parents. Even the most loving and present parents often cannot meet all of their children's needs. Therefore, almost every human experiences childhood pain no matter how wonderful their parents were. Whether the childhood pain was abusive or not, it's more accurate to call it what it is: pain. Unhealed pain produces unhealthy results. Let me share an example.

Jonah was born with everything a child could ever want or need. His parents were wealthy and he grew up attending elite private schools, wearing the finest clothes, participating in many extracurricular activities, receiving extra help from tutors, and enjoying the perks of a full-time chef. He had a nanny who loved him very much and did her best to take the place of his parents, who were often away. Jonah's suffering was silent. Even as a baby, when his mother would hold him, it wasn't for very long and his nanny would be called to "take the child."

He felt this distancing even before he could speak. As he grew older, he did everything children do who yearn for authentic love: he tried to please his parents at every opportunity by excelling at school, sports, and any endeavor he was engaged in. When he was a baby, his pain was more conscious as he would express disappointment in not being held by his parents. As he grew older, his disappointment became unconscious as his spirit strove to keep him going. Also, his suffering wasn't socially permitted. How could a guy that has everything have trauma?

He compensated at an early age by attaching to his nanny. When he was conscious of the lack of physical touch and the complete lack of presence in his life, when he had the lead in the school play and his parents weren't there, he turned to her. When he got into middle school, however, his nanny was let go. He realized that without her receiving a paycheck, there was no one to love him. He suffered deeply, but because his quiet suffering had been so consistent for so many years, it was mostly unconscious. He grew into a man who was emotionally distant and couldn't connect with others. His relationships were transactional – he was always looking for what people could do for him. His pain was silent, but it was pain nonetheless.

Everyone has pain and everyone has trauma. Just as in the example above, Jonah experienced a "small 't' trauma" while holocaust survivors experienced a "big 'T' trauma." I'm trained in EMDR (Eye Movement Desensitization and Reprocessing) which is considered a best practice treatment for PTSD and other traumas. I was trained in this special therapy with Laurel Parnell, who differentiates between "small 't' trauma" and "big 'T' trauma." She explains

> There are a wide range of clinical applications for EMDR. It's for anyone with a "big-T" trauma, which are the kinds of trauma that lead to post-traumatic stress disorder, like war or horrible accidents—anything that causes flashbacks, nightmares, anxiety, or hypervigilance. It's also good for clients with "small-t" traumas, which all of us have. These are traumas that create a narrow view of ourselves and what we can do in the world, like humiliation, shame, or not feeling seen or understood. It's also the accumulation of hurts we experienced as we grew up. Working with these requires more skill on the part of the therapist, but it's possible.[27]

---

27 EMDR: An Indispensable Tool for Trauma Therapists An Interview With Laurel Parnell (2018) Retreived from www.eomega.org/article/emdr-an-indispensable-tool-for-trauma-therapists

When I was learning how to do EMDR, I was paired with an older man in his 70s. He was extremely soft-spoken, so much so that I could barely hear him speak. He was also slouching and was not making eye contact with anyone. Even when he sat across from me, he was barely looking at me, just at the floor. Our trainer asked him to think of a traumatic memory. He described "not finding a partner." I thought to myself, how is this trauma? Sad, but not traumatic.... I wondered how I was going to practice EMDR on such a topic. However, within a 90 minute session, EMDR helped him to connect to a memory that he hadn't recalled in his life before. He recalled being a little boy of 4 or so and being downstairs while his parents were fighting. Then, all sorts of other memories came up: none were abusive, mostly memories related to a child being afraid and not understanding what was going on. During the process, big tears came up and at some points when recalling early memories, his voice even sounded like a little boy. I was in awe of the process yet still wondering, "how is this all related to him not having a partner?" Then, at the very end of the session, he was able to identify that he felt it was his job to take care of and protect his mother. Also, that this job was so big that he would need to devote himself to working very hard so he would have enough money to care for her. That revelation opened up beautiful healing tears and at the end of the session, he sat up straight, looked me straight in the eyes and with a strong voice said "Thank you." For next five days I saw this man change his disposition from shy to confident, from soft voice to loud voice and he was seen! He was getting noticed by others, making his voice heard. I bet when I see him again, he will have attracted a girlfriend, as he wished.

You see that pain is relative. Trauma is relative, too. I've worked in one of the poorest neighborhoods in the country, South Los Angeles, for nearly 10 years and also in one of the wealthiest neighborhoods in the country, Malibu and Pacific Palisades, for about the same amount of time, and I can tell you that all people struggle and suffer emotional and physical pain. All people deserve our compassion and healing. You deserve compassion and healing, too.

Emotional and physical pain is a funny thing. The irony of pain is that the more you feel pain the more you feel pain. So, if you allow minor pain to go on, to only treat the symptoms and not the problem, when something else comes along, you'll feel it more. For example, if you keep treating your headaches with aspirin instead of looking to get more rest or drink more water, or whatever is the root cause of your headaches, when you skin your knee it will actually hurt more than if you weren't having chronic headaches. And when you get angry or upset, it will feel more extreme emotionally as well. We cannot ignore pain or mask it with pain medication or with alcohol, drugs or screens. The only way through pain is to go into it and cure the root. Otherwise, every emotional and physical experience you feel will become more and more intensely painful.

YOUR RELATIONAL STYLE

In our early years, we learn how safe we are in the world or how unsafe the world is. When we are babies, we cry and hope to be fed, changed, and comforted but it doesn't always happen that way. As we grow, our needs evolve and become a little more complex. The need to belong, to be validated, to be loved unconditionally, to be seen and heard for who we are, to find meaning and significance, to not live in fear, and to have consistent emotional and physical safety are basic human needs. Not everyone is born with parents or caregivers that are able to meet these basic needs, so many of us grow up being unsure if the world is safe. However, if these needs are met, babies grow up to have a strong bond with their primary caregivers and develop what's called a "secure attachment," which is a psychological term for knowing the world is safe. This, as you can imagine, is one of the most important psychological lessons one learns: am I safe or not? Can I be myself or not? Will my needs get met or not? In order for a human to have secure attachment, a parent must be able to manage their stress, respond to their baby's cues, and successfully soothe their infant. When parents soothe their children from uncomfortable feelings such as worry, fear, anxiety or sadness, the child learns the world is safe.[28] Unless these basic needs are met, children develop a certain perspective on the world and on relationships that has a profoundly negative effect on health and relationships.

These attachment styles persist into our adult years and affect how we interact in relationships. Not everyone grew up feeling safe and loved unconditionally. It doesn't take being abused to create an unhealthy attachment style. Sometimes parents and caregivers that are simply emotionally unavailable can also create unhealthy attachment styles. Sometimes children are lucky and when their parents can't be available to them emotionally or physically, they may be raised by an emotionally present adoptive parent or grandparent or another family member. But unfortunately, this is not always the case.

Attachment styles are extremely important because they establish the basis for all of our future relationships. Learning about healthy attachment and bonding is an essential parenting tool. Often, unhealthy attachment is passed on from generation to generation, frequently tied to intergenerational trauma. It's important to remember when you are trying to figure out which style most fits you that through loving and healthy relationships, we can all grow into a Secure Relational Style regardless of how we grew up and even how we are now. Here are the different kinds of Relational Styles; which one reminds you of yourself?

If you:

- often doubt yourself
- depend on others' approval
- fear rejection and being unloved
- are needy and over-interpret others' actions under stress

then you probably have an Anxious (aka Disorganized) Relational Style. This often results from being raised by anxious parents/caregivers. You thrive being around people and don't like being alone often. You connect well with others but care too much about what they think of you. Your strength lies in your ability to relate to people. You would

---

28   Retreived from http://oregonstate.edu/ua/ncs/archives/2009/sep/positive-parenting-can-have-lasting-impact-generations

benefit from scheduling regular times to see friends and family. In addition, sharing what you feel vulnerable about will help you feel less alone. If you are:

- very self-reliant
- less comfortable with emotional expression and emotional intimacy
- shutdown or opt to leave relationships under stress

then you probably have an Avoidant Relational Style due to being raised by unresponsive, distant, or depressed parents/caregivers. While you certainly can get a lot done on your own, you err in doing too much without asking for help. This can lead to burnout or being overwhelmed. You tend to "not get too attached" to things and can easily leave a relationship if it is not working. Sometimes, projects and relationships that are not working for you are left too soon before they are given a fair chance. Your strength lies in your ability to problem-solve. You would benefit from working on achieving your goals and exploring your inner motivation.

If you:

- desire warmth but get uncomfortable with intimacy
- if your partner is avoidant or anxious
- find yourself avoiding intimacy but also craving it deeply

then you probably have an Ambivalent Relational Style from being raised by inconsistent parents who were sometimes loving then sometimes harsh or unresponsive. Your childhood was likely a mish-mash of different styles, either your parents were divorced and had different parenting styles or they clashed while married. Because of this, however, your strength is adaptability. You could benefit from a clear, consistent schedule and clear communication skills.

If none of these fit you, chances are you have a Secure Relational Style. Do you find yourself mostly:

- at ease with emotional intimacy
- valuing closeness
- generally having long stable relationships
- able to ask for help under stress?

Then you probably have a Secure Relational Style, lucky you! This means that you are comfortable with emotional intimacy and tend to have long-term relationships. You are good at getting your needs met and your relationships tend to be balanced. You create great loyalty in those who work with you. You could leverage this loyalty to motivate people. Your strength is that you know when to ask for help.

ATTACHMENT AND BONDING

The concept of Relational Styles is derived from Attachment Styles, related to the caretaking a child receives in childhood. In the 1950s, psychologist Harry Harlow's experiments with rhesus monkeys showed baby monkeys void of relational connection will have permanent physical and psychological damage. In Harlow's initial experiments, baby monkeys were separated from their mothers at six to twelve hours after birth and were raised instead with "surrogate" mothers made either of heavy wire or of wood covered with soft terry cloth. The baby monkeys could choose between the cloth mother doll without a nipple for food or the wire one with a nipple for food. But even when the wire mother had the nipple for nourishment and the cloth one did not, the baby monkey spent a greater amount of time clinging to the cloth surrogate. They chose softness over nourishment.

Around the same era, psychiatrist John Bowlby studied attachment in children and found that infants have a universal need to seek close proximity with their caregiver when under stress or threatened. Bowlby discovered that without a caring mother or caregiver, or having a neglectful one, children had significant decreases in intelligence, as well as increases in depression, aggression, delinquency, and lack of empathy for others.

There is an entire subset of psychologists that study attachment and the benefits of having and consequences of not having a meaningful person or caretaker. The quality of attachment has a critical effect on development, and has been linked to various aspects of positive functioning, such as psychological well-being.[29] Again and again, psychology has shown the expanded interpretation of "survival" to mean "relationships." One of the core premises of this book is that purpose is relational and that parent–child attachment is essential for psychological well-being.

Psychologist John Bowlby, the first attachment theorist, described attachment as a "lasting psychological connectedness between human beings." Bowlby believed that the earliest bonds formed by children with their caregivers have a tremendous impact that continues throughout life. I agree and you'd be hard pressed to find any psychologist who doesn't. I share this important research with you to solidify the importance of prioritizing your relationship with your child.

The central theme of attachment theory is that parents who are available and responsive to their child's needs help the child establish a sense of safety and security. There is a lot of research on attachment theory and we know it creates the basis for our understanding of relationships and our view of the world. There are four different attachment styles:

1. Secure attachment where the child believes his / her needs will be met as a response from a quick, sensitive and consistent parent / caregiver (usually mother). The child typically is happy, secure and explorative of her environment.
2. Avoidant attachment occurs as a result of the parent / caregiver being disengaged. The child has a subconscious belief that his needs will probably not be met. He typically has a tendency to be emotionally distant and not explorative.
3. Ambivalent attachment is as a result of the parent / caregiver being inconsistent (sometimes sensitive and sometimes neglectful). The child learns that she cannot rely on her needs being met. She is anxious, insecure and angry.
4. Disorganized attachment is a result of the parent / caregiver being extreme, erratic, frightening to the child, intrusive or even passive. The child responds with behavior that is depressed,

---

29 Bowlby, J. (2008) *Attachment*. New York, NY: Basic Books.

angry or passive and unresponsive as he feels severely confused and with no strategy that his needs will be met.

In sum, the first and foremost goal of parenting consciously is to prioritize the relationship with your child above all else. Your child needs to know that you put them first and to know that no matter how they screw up that you will love them unconditionally. They also need to know that you can handle yourself in spite of the storm that they bring with them. But the good news is that you don't need to pretend that you have it all together. Being authentic with your child about feeling overwhelmed, or making a mistake and then apologizing, can help heal wounds you may accidentally create when navigating the rocky storm of raising a child.

I was deeply loved but developed an avoidant attachment style. My parents were divorced when I was young. As was more common in those days, primary custody was given to my mother who was struggling financially. As such, she simply wasn't around much and my brother and I spent a lot of time in childcare centers with the most well-intentioned and kind teachers, but never had the consistency of caregiving. Our mother also struggled with managing her stress so we often learned to rely on each other or ourselves to cope. What developed in me was an "I don't need anyone" and "I can do it without you" attitude. I was afraid of getting too close to people for fear of being let down so I avoided emotional closeness. I let a few people in but mostly kept others at bay. On the outside, I was performing very well, high grades, awards, and accolades. But on the inside, I didn't allow myself emotional intimacy and, although I didn't know it at the time because you never know what you never know, looking back now I see how lonely I was.

Now here's the next (and very hopeful) part of the story...I fell in love with my husband and, though it took me many years to let down my guard, I learned to trust that my needs are important too and that I didn't have to do everything on my own. I had what we psychologists like to call a "reparative experience." My relationship style went from Avoidant to Secure.

That's not to say that at times of stress my primitive brain doesn't get triggered into fear of needing someone...true love requires vulnerability and awareness around expanding your heart instead of creating walls around it.

So, even if you're like me and grew up with an unhealthy attachment, new relationships can be reparative and can open our hearts again.

And of course, there are memories from our childhood that we can't seem to shake. Memories and experiences that occur before we can speak and therefore have such a powerful effect on us that they are often mistaken as temperament traits or psychological disorders.

Do you sometimes experience:

- an inability to concentrate
- some difficulty regulating feelings of anger, fear and anxiety
- self-loathing
- aggression
- risk-taking?

These are often indicators of unhealthy attachment. What to do about it? Read on...

HEALING TRAUMA

When people think about trauma, they often think of people who have experienced war trauma or extreme physical abuse. However, trauma is relative and can manifest in many forms. There can be trauma from an intense birth, trauma from a medical procedure, trauma from being left alone as a child, trauma from being teased or bullied, trauma from seeing someone being teased or bullied, trauma from growing up in a family with no structure, trauma from growing up in a family that was very strict, and on and on. Trauma can take as many forms as there are humans to experience it. Unless healed, its effects can create limitations on living a full life. Often, one doesn't realize that they need to heal trauma until they learn the symptoms of trauma.

What are the symptoms of trauma? One of the primary symptoms of trauma is dissociation. Dissociation is when your mind takes you to another place in order to find safety. It can be as simple as "spacing out" or having a hard time being present. Dissociation can also feel like not being fully alive, as if you are a bit numb. The more extreme manifestation of dissociation is Dissociative Identity Disorder, characterized by two or more distinct personality states, often a result of child abuse.

As for me, I didn't realize I was dissociating until I learned more about trauma in the last eight years. Even though I had a PhD in psychology and was a licensed psychologist since 2004, my training did not include being aware of the less obvious forms of dissociation such as not feeling fully alive or "checking out." Ever since I was a little girl, I would "check out" when there was intensity around me. I kind of went into a zone; I would stare into space and my senses would diminish. The noises were less loud, the yelling faded. I didn't do it on purpose, it just happened when things got intense. Then, sometimes, as an adult, I would find myself a little numb; I wasn't feeling things as intensely as I thought I could. My laughter could be infrequent and I would find myself too serious. I envied my friends who could just laugh and be at ease in the world. I didn't always feel this way, though. Sometimes, I would find myself able to belly laugh and be beautifully present. After my children were born, I was able to be more and more present. Their constant needs as infants helped ground me. It was difficult to learn to be present and I am still working on it, but I welcomed the learning experience.

Do you dissociate? Do you ever daydream, lose touch with your surroundings, or "check out" of where you are? Do you ever feel detached from your body or mind? Do you ever feel as though you are outside your body watching events happening to you? Do you ever feel as if things or people in the world are not real, or feel detached from your surroundings? If so, you are not alone and you can learn how to become fully alive again.

If you are unsure, you may think back to an intense experience and how you handled it. Since one of the most intense experiences someone can have is childbirth, think about how you handled the intensity of labor and crowning of the head. Did you "check out" and go to another place or did you remain in the moment? Did you arrive to the hospital or birthing room full of fear and anxiety? Did you plan to be medicated to avoid the pain? You can see how telling labor can be. If you dissociated during childbirth, there's a good chance you dissociated before in your life and also a good chance you experienced some kind of trauma.

I was able to see the personal growth that being a mother gave me between my first and second child when I compared the birth experiences of the two. I "checked out" during part of the birth of my daughter. It is what I had always done during intense experiences and I thought it was a good coping skill until I realized I had to be present when it was time to push. It was the years with my first born that helped me learn to be more and more present. Therefore, during my son's birth, I was present the whole time despite the fact that he arrived a whopping 10 pounds, birthed at home with no medication. Being present in the moment remains an area that I know I most need to work on.

Dissociation leaves people not being able to fully take in what is happening in the present and leaves them not feeling fully alive. Of course, if you began to dissociate as a child, you may not remember what it was like to feel fully alive. With the habit of dissociation you are angry less, but also you laugh less, and experience less joy. In essence, you are numb. Sometimes feeling numb may make you feel ashamed or guilty, like when you are informed of the death of someone and don't quite feel sad, or when you experience numbness at a birthday party or other celebratory event. Because you don't often feel truly alive, some brains respond by sending you back to where you did feel alive, to the traumatic situation, as in flashbacks or other times that you can recall feeling angry. I believe people who anger easily and often are simply responding to their somatic urge to feel alive due to unhealed trauma.

The response to trauma that is based in flashbacks is often worse than the original trauma, as the feelings may come unexpectedly. You may feel afraid or tense and can't explain why. You may be easily angered or agitated. On the other hand, some people just blank out and dissociate. When you look at the brain in this state under a brain scan, almost every area of the brain shows decreased activation.

In this section, I bring in the work of Bessel Van der Kolk, considered the world expert on trauma. Dr. Van der Kolk explains that healing from trauma involves four steps, summarized here:

1. Learning to become calm and focused.
2. Learning to maintain that calm and focus.
3. Learning to be fully alive and engaged.
4. Not having to keep secrets from yourself, including about how you survived.[30]

It can be helpful to understand the neurological response to stress, explained by Dr. Van der Kolk. The amygdala, which he refers to as the "smoke detector" of the brain, is there to identify whether "incoming input is relevant for our survival." It is assisted by the hippocampus, which relates new experiences to past experiences as a measure of memory and emotion. The amygdala signals danger by releasing stress hormones such as adrenaline and cortisol into the body which increase rate of breathing, heart rate, and blood pressure preparing us to fight or run away (flight). And then there's the medial prefrontal cortex, which he refers to as the "watchtower." The medial prefrontal cortex is in our frontal lobe, just above our eyes. It interprets what is happening and can sometimes allow you to make a conscious choice, but in the case of people who have experienced trauma, often the amygdala can overreact which has us also overreacting.

Neuroimaging research shows us that humans experiencing intense anger, fear or sadness have reduced activity in the frontal lobe, in particular the medial prefrontal cortex, which means they respond intensely as if they were unsafe in ordinary situations. A noise may startle, a touch may feel abrasive, or they may "check out" and freeze.[31] You can change this threat detection system either through the reptilian brain using touch, movement and breathing or through the medial prefrontal cortex by modulating messages.

30 Van der Kolk, B.A. (2014) *The Body Keeps the Score: Brain, mind and body in the healing of trauma.* New York, NY: Penguin Books.
31 Van der Kolk, B.A. (2006) Clinical implications of neuroscience research in PTSD. *Annals of the New York Academy of Sciences*, 1071: 277–93.

Healing trauma requires "being truly heard and seen by the people around us, feeling that we are held in someone's mind and heart. It requires feeling comfortable with feeling what you feel, to know what you know without questioning and to feel full ownership of your mind and body."[32] In the past, mental health practitioners would understand healing of trauma through a lens of needing to release the feelings and would attempt to do so with talk therapy, or retelling the story. Now we understand that when trauma occurs, the memory can also become locked in the body. Unfortunately, recalling the memory and understanding why you feel strongly about it often does not heal the trauma.

Neuroscience research shows us that the healing occurs when we interface with the emotional brain. Opening the past may retraumatize you further if you are not managing your emotions in the present. Therefore, to begin in the healing of trauma requires starting with learning to regulate your emotions in the present. Also, because traumatic memories are highly somatic (recalled in the body as much as the mind) mind-body therapies can be highly effective.

---

32 Van der Kolk, B.A. (2014) *The Body Keeps the Score: Brain, mind, and body in the healing of trauma.* New York, NY: Viking.

Here are some research-based ways to start:

1. EMDR: short for Eye Movement Desensitization and Reprocessing. In my clinical experience, I have not seen anything as effective as EMDR. It has been extensively researched and considered the gold standard treatment for trauma. It should not be done virtually, but in person with a licensed clinician. I've seen dramatic changes and healing after only a few sessions and find also that the client leaves feeling empowered instead of overwhelmed. EMDR healing is believed to be similar to what the body does naturally during rapid eye movement sleep when a person processes stress. EMDR includes "allow[ing] experiences that are causing problems to be 'digested' and stored appropriately in your brain. That means that what is useful to you from an experience will be learned and stored with appropriate emotions in your brain, and be able to guide you in positive ways in the future. The unhealthy emotions, beliefs, and body sensations will be discarded. The goal of EMDR therapy is to leave you with the emotions, understanding, and perspectives that will lead to healthy and useful behaviors and interactions."[33]

2. Neurofeedback:[34] this is the training of the brain function by using painless brain wave sensors to observe the brain while the person is performing a task, usually on a screen, such as a video game. The brain gets rewarded on the game when it moves to more appropriate patterns. In addition to trauma, I've also seen it work very well with inattention and anxiety.

3. Yoga: by regulating the body, you regulate the mind. A regular practice of yoga has been shown to help heal trauma.[35] Other forms of body movement that are likely also effective include martial arts, Brazilian capoeira, and certain kinds of dancing.

---

33 https://emdria.site-ym.com/page/120
34 Fisher, S.F. (2014) *Neurofeedback in the Treatment of Developmental Trauma: Calming the fear-driven brain.* New York, NY: W.W. Norton & Company.
35 Van der Kolk, B.A., et al. (2014) Yoga as an adjunctive treatment for PTSD. *Journal of Clinical Psychiatry,* 75 (6): 559–565

However, there hasn't been enough research to call these other modalities effective yet.

4. Mindfulness: the research on mindfulness practices to help with self-regulation is immense. When someone is traumatized, they become disconnected from their body sensations and thoughts. Mindfulness helps bring us in touch with our inner world. It helps us practice self-regulation so we are less likely to go into fight, flight or freeze states.[36] Practicing mindfulness has been shown to help in depression and chronic pain,[37] as well as decreasing cortisol levels, blood pressure and helping the immune system.[38]

In the US, one of the most traumatic situations in recent history was on the morning of Tuesday, September 11, 2001 when terrorist attacks occured in New York, killing almost 3000 and injuring more than 6000. After the attacks, one of the primary treatment centers' psychiatrists conducted a survey of 225 people who had escaped and asked what had been the most helpful in overcoming the effects of their experiences. In order of effectiveness, the survivors listed: acupuncture, massage, yoga, and EMDR.[39] I find it interesting that talk therapy was not listed. Traumatic events are hard to put into words and appear to be remembered with our bodies and through imagery.

In addition to these helpful interventions, healing trauma requires releasing shame and secrets. Keeping secrets can kill us from the inside and solidifies the feeling that there is something wrong with us. This deep feeling causes one to isolate, which makes healing impossible. Some of the most powerful healing in therapy occurs when clients re-

---

36 Kabat-Zinn, J. (2013) *Full Catastrophe Living: Using the wisdom of your body and mind to face stress, pain, and illness.* New York, NY: Bantam Books.

37 Hofmann, S.G., et al. (2010) The effect of mindfulness-based therapy on anxiety and depression: A meta-analytic review. *Journal of Consulting and Clinical Psychology*, 78 (2): 169–183.

38 Davidson, R.J., et al. (2003) Alterations in brain and immune function produced by mindfulness meditation. *Psychosomatic Medicine*, 65 (4): 564–570.

39 Dr. Spencer Eth to Bessel A. Van der Kolk, March 2002. From Van der Kolk, B.A. (2014) *The body keeps the score: Brain, mind, and body in the healing of trauma.* New York, NY: Viking.

lease all of their secrets. The relationships that you have may not be as healthy as they need to be; many of your closest relationships may not know all of your secrets. However, it is not necessary to share all of your secrets with all of your close relationships in order to heal.

It will be helpful to share as many of your secrets as you are comfortable with, which is why one of the most effective ways to accelerate healing is to work with a licensed therapist. Licensed therapists have a very strict confidentiality code and are bound by legal and ethical guidelines to preserve the secrets and stories of their clients. Also, a licensed therapist is trained and tested in the tools most effective for personal growth. Finding someone who has the appropriate experience and also who is a right match can often be daunting. Stay away from Cognitive Behavioral Therapy (CBT) when you are healing trauma. I use CBT to help my clients with phobias and some anxiety-related disorders so long as there is no history of child abuse. When there has been any physical or emotional abuse or neglect in the past, I find that attachment-focused therapy and EMDR are much more effective in these cases. You'll also want to make sure that you "click" with your therapist. Not only should he or she have the right training, license and experience, but you should like them and enjoy their company.

The body is profoundly impacted by traumatic experiences. While this is a newer area of research, when working with clients to help them process and heal trauma, I often recommend body work such as massage and craniosacral therapy. These tools are a great addition to accompany the inner work of therapy.

I am often asked whether I recommend medication to help manage the effects of trauma. My general view of medication is that is can be a helpful band-aid to treat symptoms when absolutely necessary, but for most people it should only be used in the short-term as it will help numb the symptoms but does not cure the root of the disturbance. It also takes away the opportunity to learn self-regulation and retrain the brain.

CHAPTER 5

FEELING GOOD: HOW TO LET GO OF ANXIETY, DEPRESSION AND ANGER

"Just when the caterpillar thought the world was ending,
he turned into a butterfly."

– PROVERB

I've yet to meet a parent who wasn't anxious, depressed or overwhelmed with frustration at some point. Being a parent in itself is enough to trigger overwhelming feelings. I know almost no one who is completely at ease with being responsible for someone else's life. The immense responsibility that comes with parenting can turn even the most relaxed person into an anxious one. So, if you're feeling anxious, depressed or angry please know you're not alone!

Yet, the beauty and gift of parenting is that we get to use this challenge as an opportunity to grow. As we look into our children's eyes and see them growing so very quickly, we are reminded of the urgency of taking care of our own emotional needs as we see the effect that our own unhealed wounds can have on them. I'm often asked "What if I can't heal my anxiety or depression? What if there is no solution to my anger? Will I pass it onto my child?" The unfortunate answer is: most likely. These unresolved feelings will either get passed on to your child, or your child will have to develop a way to deal with your emotions that will most likely limit him or her in other areas of their life. That should be incentive enough to be open to change, yet sometimes resolving these overwhelming emotions can feel, well, overwhelming. But, don't worry! There is nearly always a solution to anger, anxiety and depression.

Anxiety, anger and depression have a lot in common and often stem from unhelpful thinking patterns. Treating anxiety, anger and depression requires a combination of changing these thoughts that are no longer helpful, being aware of associated physical responses, and then modifying our behavior based on our modified thoughts. This may sound like a lot to handle, but it doesn't have to be. I'll walk through it with you step-by-step.

Because our thoughts give rise to emotions, not the other way around, it's incredibly empowering (and also effective) to learn to manage your thoughts. As a result, you will be more equipped to manage your feelings and behaviors.[40] This work can be done on your own, but most find it helpful to have a therapist to help you along the way. We've listed some of our favorite therapists at www.rootsnwings.org, and you can go to www.psychologytoday.com for a more broad list. I would also recommend the following books for treating anxiety and depression: *How to Deal With Anxiety* by Drs. Kannis-Dymand and Carter, as well as *Feeling Good: The New Mood Therapy* by David Burns. If your anxiety, anger or depression is interfering with daily life, you will get the best results if you work with a therapist directly.

In this next section, I will begin helping you change your thinking and offer specific tools for handling anxiety, anger and depression. You can start with the general section on changing your thinking and then feel free to skip to the section that is relevant to you.

---

40   Beck, J.S. (1995) *Cognitive Therapy: Basics and beyond.* New York, NY: Guilford Press; Chapter 9.
Greenberg, D. and Padesky, C.A. (1995). *Mind Over Mood: Change the way you feel by changing the way you think.* New York, NY: Guilford Press; Chapters 5, 6, and 7.

CHANGE YOUR THINKING, CHANGE YOUR LIFE

Sadness, Anger and Fear (Anxiety) have a purpose. They are trying to communicate something to you. These negative emotions arise because you need to do something about it – to change the source of pain that is causing you to feel that way. In fact, anger usually comes from sadness that has been ignored for too long or a feeling of being unfairly treated. Anger can fuel change. Feelings of sadness often come up when one needs to slow down and go deeper in their feelings, while fear/anxiety propel you to manage your thoughts. As tempting as it is, beware of the tendency to deny or avoid these negative emotions by trying to cover them up with food, alcohol, tv or social media. While these behaviors may provide immediate short-term relief, they will ultimately make things harder in the long run.

Let me share with you the story of Sophia, a brilliant and hard-working woman. In high school, Sophia studied very hard and earned high grades, a trend that continued through college. While high achieving on the outside, Sophia often felt overwhelmed, sad, anxious and would sometimes become angry at seemingly small things. However, because she was so good at achieving, she landed a great paying, corporate job after college. She kept on doing what she thought she was supposed to do, hoping the day would come when she would get a break to relax a bit. To cope along the way, she began a habit of watching tv for a few hours each night before falling asleep, overcome with exhaustion. As the years went on, she needed more coffee to cope, especially in the afternoon when her physical and emotional energy was at its lowest. She would often use food as a reward for herself. Most days she would permit herself to eat a fast food meal or to enjoy a chocolate bar.

Upon becoming a parent, Sophia felt filled with joy; however, she felt even more exhausted at work. When she would come home after a long day, she would often find herself frustrated and angry at her daughter during bedtime. As is age appropriate for a two-year old, it would often take her daughter almost an hour to get to bed at night. Sophia found her patience quickly dwindled as she became more exhausted. She never yelled at her daughter but inside found herself reciting the all-too-familiar mantra "Go the f**k to sleep!" Her daughter grew older, but the anxiety, exhaustion and anger Sophia experienced didn't go away. She kept on working hard, doing all of the things she was supposed to do, all the while coping with tv and junk food. After a few years, as you can imagine, not only was Sophia overweight, she was also addicted to sugar and tv. Her daughter had learned to be careful not to make mommy mad (her daughter didn't feel emotionally safe around her). Sophia came to me at last and we were able to receive her emotions and learn to understand what they were trying to communicate to her for years. Her anxiety was telling her to let go of a career that paid well, but didn't allow her to have a life. Her anger was telling her to get off of her toccus and change something already! Her tv and sweets addiction needed to be replaced with something that actually gave her joy. Finally, we discovered her sadness to be subconsciously linked to feeling that she must be a failure. After all, she had done exactly as she was "supposed" to do yet felt joyless and unsatisfied. She participated in the Transformational Parenting program and was able to see things with a new perspective while making changes along the way. She is now self-employed, and while she lives in a smaller house, she is actually able to enjoy spending time with her daughter. She even has some free time!

She turned off her cable service so that she could no longer watch tv shows, except from her computer, which cut back her tv binging significantly. She replaced her afternoon junk food "fix" with an afternoon walk instead. Most importantly, she learned to listen to the messages her emotions were trying to send. Sophia now practices meditation at night when she is in her daughter's room waiting for her to go to sleep, instead of being annoyed that the process is taking too long. Sophia was lucky enough to escape the common trap of internalizing her emotions.

Lark, on the other hand was not so lucky. Lark had been feeling anxious for so many years that she started to think of herself as an "anxious person." She eventually came to describe herself that way to others when explaining why she "couldn't" participate in certain social activities. Eventually, she placed more limitations on herself and her anxious feelings became exaggerated. What started out as her mind and body trying to communicate a need for change turned into a lifestyle of avoidance and making herself smaller. Precisely because she had brainwashed herself into believing that she had an anxiety disorder, she got one. In therapy, a lot of the work I needed to do with her surrounded letting that programming go, and letting Lark be someone who experiences feeling anxious, versus being "an anxious person." Do you see the difference?

There is a powerful distinction between saying that you "experience anxiety (or depression, or anger)," versus believing that you "are an anxious (or depressed, or angry) person." It's essential to recognize that the negative emotion is not who you are. We tend to overanalyze and internalize our emotions. If we feel sad for a long time, we "are" a depressed, anxious or angry person. Our thoughts and our words become our programming. When we make our emotions a trait, our mind and body responds as if we are permanently disadvantaged. But when we are careful with how we describe ourselves and use temporary descriptions such as "feeling," "experiencing," or being "in a mood," it opens up the mind for an internal change. When we make our negative emotions a state instead of a trait, we can find the freedom to change and move beyond the negative emotional state.

Change Your Thinking By Breaking the Habit of Negativity

Breaking the habit of negativity is an essential step as negative thinking often becomes an unconscious habit. Anything we say over and over again becomes our programming, like a hypnosis. It's important to give yourself no more than five seconds to experience a negative thought and then let it go. Our negative thoughts are similar to the mind of a small child in that they are often susceptible to distractibility. You can use this to your advantage! When you catch yourself in a negative thought pattern, you can use tools such as music or exercise to take your focus away from the pattern. Physical action is an essential tool to help the mind and body break free of the cycle of negative thinking. A dear friend of mine found great salvation in running. Although I don't relate to his joy of running at all, he credits his running to helping him break free from moments of emotional breakdown. When we are physically engaged, we gain feel-good endorphins and somatic healing that comes from being active. Our thoughts tend to be more focused on the present when you are able to move your body. I've yet to find anyone who can do sit ups or push ups while engage in overthinking at the same time.

Singing, while less active, can be just as powerful a tool. When you sing an emotional song with a loud and passionate voice, you'll also likely stop your negative thinking pattern. Another tool that works is to think about something you are grateful for instead of the negative thought that's percolating around. Funny enough, it's extremely difficult to experience gratitude and negativity at the same time. For me, just jumping from the negative thought to thinking about something I'm grateful for is challenging, so it helps me to write it down. I find that writing makes the "gratitude" exercise more tangible and my thoughts become more convinced to pay attention to the positive instead of the negative. I'd recommend writing over typing as there can be neurological benefit to writing, especially in cursive.

Breaking the habit of negativity can be very hard, I won't fool you. In fact, as I write this today, I am currently "in a funk," as I call it. My energy is low, my focus is tending to be directed toward the negative. Smiling or laughing seems not only exhausting, but completely inauthentic. I've been feeling this way for a few days, but thanks to my profession, I know that I'm in a "temporary shadow state". I use the word "shadow" as coined by Carl Jung himself to describe a dark state, the side that's almost always with us but that we sometimes forget is there. I also know that this sadness I'm feeling is trying to tell me something. I realize I have been ignoring an unpleasant truth about a family member and my sadness is likely connected to the loss of what I imagined could have been, but there is more there, too, that I will need to continue to explore. I used to be afraid when my shadow came around. I would wonder, "What if it doesn't go away? What if I lose my joy? What if my laughter disappears?" Thanks to my own inner work and the clients I've had the privilege of guiding through this shadowland, I know that even greater joy lies beyond this sadness. It is often when I allow myself to be with my feelings, listen to what they are trying to communicate, and take action on what I'm hearing from them, that the negative state actually begins to resolve. So, I allow myself to be in this state, trust that there is something important that I need to receive and encourage these feelings to come as much as I will allow it to go.

Easier said than done...life often gets in the way. You are busy before the negative emotional crisis, and when it arrives it feels incredibly overwhelming. But here's the thing, there will always be crises that arise in life: terrorists, death, broken arms, bullying. These experiences can be especially challenging for sensitive people. Often those who are the most compassionate have the hardest time with all of these problems that come up, as if they're naturally sensitive to the pain that exists in others' lives. It is often times hard to shut out this pain and their sensitivity can interfere with everyday life. By throwing your perspective off completely, causing you to go into a chronic fight or flight stress situation. This has far-reaching effects on your brain, body, emotions and coping abilities.

So, how do you let go of what's bothering you about the world and focus on what's really necessary? How do you even know what's really necessary? And equally importantly, when you have something in your life that is more than just a negative thought – that feels like a crisis or a major stressor – how do you handle that? How can you keep going, keep your focus and get your priorities straight?

The secret lies in being mindful of what negativity you allow into your space and then intentionally bringing in the positive. During times when you feel anxious, very sad, depressed or angry, you are required to do emotional healing, and can create boundaries to protect your psyche from being overwhelmed with negativity. You may wish to turn off the news, stay away from that person who complains a lot, and put aside anything unnecessary that is unpleasant. For many, a "news fast" can be very helpful for maintaining your focus on the everyday important tasks. The news is overwhelmingly negative, and can make it seem as though the entire world is falling apart at the seams. Change the channel. Discontinue your newspaper subscription. Leave the *Time* magazine at the doctor's office. Likewise, taking a break from social media can bring mental relief: not only will your mind have a break from the comparisons that occur from social media presenting only the most positive side of people's lives, but also the drama of politics, the sad stories, and the obligation of feeling the need to respond to people's comments and posts provides a mental space that you can devote to your inner work.

To bring in positivity, proactively focus on the good things you have around you. Be grateful for what you have, and also for the lessons you've learned through difficulty and challenge. Allow your personal reality to be as positive and fulfilling as possible. Below are some ways you can help make that happen.

To begin with, my favorite way of reshaping the brain to combat negative thinking is to increase positive experiences. You see, if you maintain life as is and don't enjoy yourself, it will be more difficult for your subconscious to understand that you are making a significant positive change. Neurologically and subconsciously, we need data to back up our thoughts, especially the positive ones. Our natural focus tends to be on the negative, which serves a survival response meant to keep us alive. So, when we are changing our thinking, we need positive action to make it believable to ourselves. If you want to worry less but continue to experience the same stresses, it will be more difficult than if you intentionally create habits of enjoyment. Writing down things that you enjoy and then doing them can help shift the focus.

Try listing daily activities that make you feel good. Here are some examples:

- Taking a walk
- Taking a bath
- Eating a favorite food (make sure to list which foods)
- Laughing with a friend (make sure to list which friends)
- Listening to a certain song (make sure to list which songs)
- Admiring the sunset

Now, it's your turn. Write down at least 10 things you enjoy:

1. _____
2. _____
3. _____
4. _____
5. _____
6. _____
7. _____
8. _____
9. _____
10. _____

Of the activities you listed above, circle those that you can do every day. Make sure to do at least one activity that makes you feel good every day. Research on the science of happiness also shows that writing down three things you are grateful for each day has a significant impact in increasing positive emotions.

Let's practice, what are you feeling grateful for right now?

1._____

2._____

3._____

Change Your Thinking By Eliminating Stressors

In order to change unhelpful thinking patterns, you will need to identify and eliminate stressors that cause negative thinking. For example, if you have a tendency to rush out the door in the morning full of the worry about being late, you can get up an hour earlier (and go to bed an hour earlier). If you're like me, you're probably very good at making up excuses such as, "But I can't do such and such because…." Excuses are just another form of avoidance and fear dominating us. We self-sabotage, procrastinate, and stop ourselves from trying because fear is controlling us.

We are still learning so much about the way the conscious and subconscious minds work. In a recent neuroscience study, it was found that the conscious mind is in the passenger seat for most of the time. The majority of the heavy lifting that thinking and decision-making requires stems from the unconscious mind.[41] We know that fear is the root of anxiety, but it is often not based in reality. It is the power of unresolved fear that dominates our unconscious thinking structures which manifests in feelings of anxiety.

Yet, the harder we try not to think about something, the more difficult it becomes not to think about it. So you can stop worrying about *what not to think about* and instead focus your attention on these helpful tools to help you reprogram patterns that are no longer serving you. It starts with looking at your thinking.

---

41 Morsella, E., Godwin, C., Jantz, T., and Krieger, S. (2015) Homing in on consciousness in the nervous system: An action-based synthesis. *Behavioral and Brain Sciences*. Published Online: https://doi.org/10.1017/S0140525X15000643

Step 1: Become Aware of Your Thinking Patterns.

We all have automatic thoughts constantly throughout the day. An incredibly helpful teaching based in meditation and Cognitive Behavioral Therapy is rather than trying to get rid of thoughts and clear your mind, simply allow your thoughts to be without making too much of them. Our Egoic mind likes to think that our thoughts are incredibly important and relevant, but they really are not at all. We have an abundance of thoughts throughout the day and our survival instinct drives us to focus on the fear-based ones in an attempt to keep us safe. If we allow this to go on for too long, however, these neural pathways based in anxiety will become stronger and stronger until, for many people, they grow into a full mood disorder. In other words, unless we change them, unhelpful thinking patterns will only become worse over time. So, let's tackle this head on!

Thinking patterns primarily develop when people are young and are influenced in multiple ways including being raised by a worried parent, a traumatic childhood, regular stress, feeling unable to cope, being told you weren't able to do something, etc. These thinking patterns can result in negative self-talk, such as, "I'm boring, I'm fat, I'm unattractive, I'm no good at math, I'm not the type that _____, It's hard for me to make friends, I get scared easily, Something bad will happen to me," etc. Read through the unhelpful thinking patterns below to see if you tend to think in any of these ways:

All or Nothing Thinking: This is sometimes called "black and white thinking," and is perceiving situations as being only one way or another. Either you are happy or unhappy. Either you are a good parent or a bad parent. Either you do it right or not at all. Either you are eating healthfully or eating poorly. When we think this way, it is discouraging as there is no middle ground. It also prevents us from learning new things for fear of "not doing it perfectly." Write a thought you have or have had in the past that is an example of All or Nothing Thinking:

_____

_____

_____

Minimization and Magnification: We either blow things out of proportion (making a mountain out of a molehill) or inappropriately shrink something to make it seem less important. Some examples of minimizing include making excuses for people – "it wasn't that bad, she was under a lot of stress" – which can be especially troubling when we are in abusive relationships that need to be ended. Magnification can lead to thinking that is overly pessimistic. For example, "If I give in to my child, he'll grow up to be a spoiled brat," or "If I'm late to pick up my kids, I'm a bad father." People also tend to magnify others when they compare themselves: "They're so much better than me." You can see how inaccurate minimization and magnification can be and how it can lead to feeling great worry, hopelessness, worthlessness, or staying in a bad situation.

Write a thought you have had in the past that is an example of Minimization or Magnification:

_____

_____

_____

Should Statements: It's an epidemic how much we "should" all over ourselves and all over our children. Anytime you hear yourself thinking or saying the words "should," "must," or "ought" know that you are creating unhelpful thinking. It's as if we've made up some set of rules, and if we – or other people – don't live within this set of rules, we get angry at ourselves or at others.

While some "shoulds" are hard to argue with, such as "One should not kill others" or even less extreme such as "I should exercise more," "shoulds" limit your ability to find a solution. Using "shoulds" creates a blanket judgement. It can lead to difficulty forgiving ourselves or others and these judgments can interfere with finding a solution. Try replacing the word "should" with "am ready to" and notice how it shifts your energy away from "something is wrong with me" into an empowered state. For example, instead of "I should eat healthier," say to yourself "I am ready to eat healthier." When you eat healthier, you can then change it to "I am a healthy eater" and the affirmation will become locked into a new sense of self as you have the action to back it up.

Write down some things that you "should" about. For example, "I should lose weight."

_____

_____

_____

Now, rewrite those very same sentences but replace the "should" with "am ready to." Notice the difference in your energy. You can rewrite your negative self-talk and programming into that which has possibility. For example, change the "I should lose weight" into "I am ready to lose weight."

_____

_____

_____

Labeling: is another kind of unhelpful thinking style, where we assign labels to ourselves or other people. "She's mean, I'm stupid, I'm ugly, he's a jerk," are all examples of labeling. Children often tend to label as it is a simplified way of understanding someone. "She's mean" can be redirected to "she acted mean." Labeling ourselves and others has us give up on personal improvement and hope for change. It is also oversimplifying and takes people away from the essential emotional intelligence tool of having compassion for others.

Have you ever labeled yourself? What was the label you gave yourself?

_____

_____

How did that label slow down your ability to grow?

_____

_____

Emotional Reasoning: This is when we assume that, because we feel a certain way, what we think must be true. For people with anxiety this is often an issue that comes up again and again. It can often be confused with intuition. For example, Paul would avoid driving on the freeway because, "I don't feel safe so it must not be safe." Another client of mine would feel scared around dogs, so she concluded that dogs are dangerous. As you can see, the problem with emotional reasoning is that we use our emotions as evidence. In other words, our fears prevent us from doing things and we use fear as the reason why we should not.

Have you ever had a feeling that made you think something was true that wasn't necessarily so?

_____

_____

Overgeneralization: This thinking style is developed from seeing a larger pattern based upon a single event, or from being overly broad in the conclusions we draw from our experiences. If you hear yourself say the words "always," "never," "everyone," or "everything," you are probably overgeneralizing. Overgeneralizing is a favorite unhelpful thinking style of siblings. If you are a parent of more than one child you may have heard such statements as "She NEVER has to do the dishes" or "He ALWAYS says bad words and NEVER gets in trouble!" You also hear it a lot in marriages: "She ALWAYS comes home late!" "He NEVER wakes up to care for the baby in the middle of the night!" As you can see, overgeneralizations are NEVER a good thing (just making sure you're paying attention!). Let me rephrase: Overgeneralizations can be unhelpful.

What have you overgeneralized about?

_____

_____

Mental Filter: A mental filter is a perspective that clouds reality. Instead of seeing life through rose colored glasses, most people's mental filter is like seeing through foggy, grey glasses that make reality more negative. For example, when someone gives a compliment, the response may be "Oh, it's nothing." I used to employ this unhelpful thinking style when someone complimented me on my clothes. I would respond "Oh thanks, I got it on sale." In other words, I sent the message to the person giving the compliment and to myself that I wasn't worth the compliment or the clothes. I somehow felt it was necessary to communicate that I didn't spend much money on it. One common example is when you accomplish something and you think to yourself, "That doesn't count."

Write an example of how you may have used a negative mental filter in the past:

_____

_____

_____

Mind Reading is another unhelpful thinking style. It's where we imagine we know what others are thinking. For example, you imagine that someone doesn't call you because they don't like you instead of thinking how busy they must be.

Fortune Telling is predicting the future. For example, "I'll never be like that," or "that kind of stuff won't happen to me," or "I'll probably end up alone." The truth is we never really know what will happen in the future.

Personalization is one of the most common unhelpful thinking styles. It leads to discouragement or anger at others and assumes that everything is your own fault. An example of personalization would be when a child fails at something and their parent thinks, "I must be a bad parent."

Can you think of any times when you've used Mind Reading, Fortune Telling or Personalization?

_____

_____

_____

Step 2: Replace Your Critical Thoughts

Hundreds of thousands of thoughts per day run by your subconscious mind, originally designed to "keep you safe." This running commentary is often negative, as our subconscious tries to maintain the status quo. These automatic thoughts accumulate and create dysfunctional core beliefs, which are developed primarily during childhood. Core beliefs tend to be interpersonal. For example, the belief that you have to be cute/smart/thin/pretty/athletic, etc. to be loved or that you have to accomplish this or that to be "successful." Just because you may feel these core beliefs strongly, doesn't mean they are true. Throughout your life, you've paid more attention to the experiences that support your core beliefs and less attention to those that did not.

Most core beliefs are negative. Our strong emotions surrounding these beliefs make them seem true. Letting go of negative core beliefs involves examining your critical or negative thoughts. Remember, the goal is not to try to control your thoughts, which create your beliefs, but to focus on those that are likely to bring about the greatest change.

Not sure which thoughts to focus on to create change? Here is an exercise to help you. You can do this daily. Take a piece of paper and divide it into three columns. Write down in the far left column automatic thoughts that you are having right now, then in the middle column write down the intensity of the feeling associated with the thought from 1–10 and finally in the last column write from 1–10 how much you believe that thought to be true. This is an exercise used in Cognitive Behavioral Therapy and can be an extremely helpful tool.

Critical thought	Intensity of feeling associated with the thought (rate from 1-10, 1 being not intense and 10 being very intense)	How much you believe the thought is accurate (rate from 1-10, 1 being not accurate and 10 being very accurate)
Example: I'm fat	7	4

Critical thought	Intensity of feeling associated with the thought (rate from 1-10, 1 being not intense and 10 being very intense)	How much you believe the thought is accurate (rate from 1–10, 1 being not accurate and 10 being very accurate)

The thoughts with the highest ratings are the ones that can benefit from modification to bring about the greatest change. Make sure to notice the difference between the intensity of the feeling associated with the thought and how much you believe the thought is actually accurate.

Now, take a moment to write down critical thoughts, state which unhelpful thinking style they fall under, then re-write a critical thought into a realistic thought.

Here are some examples to get you started:

Critical thought	Unhelpful thinking style	Growth-based rational thought
I hate myself	Overgeneralization, negative thinking	I'm feeling upset because I made a mistake, and mistakes are normal.
I'm not smart	Labeling	I need more practice at this skill.
If I try, I will fail	Fortune telling, fixed mindset	If I try, I may fail or not, but I can always try again. "Failing" is learning.
I'm a bad parent for yelling at my child	Labeling	I made a mistake. I will apologize and repair the relationship and work on my personal growth so I hopefully won't yell again.

Now it's your turn. Write down some critical thoughts you have had along with the unhelpful thinking style and a growth-based rational thought you can replace it with.

Critical thought	Unhelpful thinking style	Growth-based rational thought

Critical thought	Unhelpful thinking style	Growth-based rational thought

Step 3: Change the Way You Sleep and Eat

The younger version of myself would have skipped this step, not even bothering to read the section. "I already know that," I would have thought to myself. But actually, even though I had studied neuroscience, I did not fully comprehend the importance of sleep for emotional stability nor was I educated on therapeutic foods. The fact is that we simply cannot properly let go of anger, anxiety or depression if we are sleep deprived or starved of proper nutrition.

What's the big deal about sleep?

Sleep is everything! Although neuroscientists and sleep researchers are still uncovering why sleep is so essential, they articulate that perhaps the most important function of sleep is cell rejuvenation and helping to heal bad memories and stressful emotions. While there are multiple stages of sleep one experiences nightly, emotional processing occurs during a stage called Rapid Eye Movement (REM). Although people are able to live without REM sleep, there can be great cognitive consequences and a lack of sleep makes us significantly more emotionally reactive.[42] Scientists are discovering that our bodies have an innate way of dealing with stressful emotions and working through bad memories

---

42 Tempesta, D., et al. (2018) "Sleep and emotional processing." *Sleep Med Review,* Aug; 40, 183-195.

that is closely tied to sleeping. In the REM stage of sleep, which is when most dreams occur, levels of stress hormones decrease. Although we can dream during other stages of sleep, REM is considered the stage where we process emotions. I've heard people say, "But, I don't dream." Even if you don't remember your dreams, you are still dreaming.

Bear with me as I share with you a very run-on sentence but also one that will likely convince you to sleep more. One of the world's leading sleep researchers, Els van der Helm explains, "Based on the remarkable neurobiology of sleep, and REM sleep in particular, a unique capacity for the overnight modulation of affective networks and previously encountered emotional experiences may be possible, redressing and maintaining the appropriate connectivity and hence next-day reactivity throughout limbic and associated autonomic systems."[43] In other words, when you get enough sleep, you will likely feel less negative emotions, feel calmer, and become less reactive. It's the cure-all, million dollar solution. Over the years, in my psychology practice, I've worked with many people who thought they were depressed or anxious but were actually just sleep deprived. Once they received adequate and regular sleep, the symptoms disappeared!

Some tips for proper sleep include:

- Go to bed at around the same time every night and wake up around the same time every morning
- Avoid looking at screens (phones, television or computers) at least an hour before going to bed
- Don't eat before bed
- Exercise daily
- Incorporate a meditation, stillness or relaxation practice
- Have all the lights off in your room
- Use an alarm clock instead of your phone's alarm so your phone can be out of your bedroom. If that's not possible, turn the wifi off or have your phone on airplane mode.

---

43 Van der Helm, E. and Walker, M. (2009) "Overnight therapy? The role of sleep in emotional brain processing." *Psychological Bulletin,* 135 (5): 731-748.

Therapeutic eating

"Therapeutic eating" is eating with the understanding that what you eat determines your mood as much as what you think. This is not to be mistaken with "comfort food" which is usually full of refined sugar, carbs, dairy and other gut-wrecking ingredients. In the book entitled *Change Your Food, Heal Your Mood*, which I highly recommend, Dr. Kelly Brogan shares how you can reverse depression and other symptoms by changing your eating habits. She recommends that you eliminate processed foods and food toxins from your diet, switch to whole foods, good fats, therapeutic foods and add fermented foods to help support your gut ecology.[44]

Here are some of my favorite therapeutic foods.

- Coconut oil (organic and unrefined), which can help with cognition, antiviral properties and balancing blood sugar. You can consume coconut oil in a smoothie, or take a spoonful and mix it in warm water with a lemon – it's also excellent for cooking and frying.
- Turmeric has an anti-inflammatory, antidepressant efficacy (even compared to prozac) and tastes great with scrambled eggs or as a tea.
- Fermented foods – which are foods with probiotics. Probiotics are so helpful to your healthy functioning that they can even reverse psychiatric symptoms. You can take a probiotic supplement, but there is no better way to get your probiotics than in whole foods that are naturally fermented such as pickles, coconut kefir and sauerkraut. Make sure that you read the ingredient label as many of these foods can be pickled in vinegar and sugar instead of fermented.

Once you've changed your thinking patterns, replaced your critical thoughts, begun eating right and you're sleeping enough you will likely feel significantly better. If you still find the negative emotions coming back, you may need to take it a step further and contact a licensed therapist or counselor who can help uncover the deep-rooted causes.

---

44   Brogan, K. and Habakus, L.K. (2015) *Change Your Food, Heal Your Mood: 3 steps to a happier body and a healthier brain.* Retreived from https://kellybroganmd.com/wp-content/uploads/2016/02/ChangeYourFoodHealYourMoodEBook.pdf

ANXIETY AND STRESS

"Worrying is like a rocking chair: it gives you something to do but never gets you anywhere." – Erma Bombeck

If you sometimes feel anxious, you are not alone. It is estimated that one in every five people will struggle with anxiety in any one-year period.[45] Anxiety is caused by repetitive unhelpful thoughts that have us avoiding certain situations or needing them to be "just" in order to feel comfortable. Some people are unclear as to the difference between fear and anxiety, but they are not the same. Anxiety is long-lasting, whereas fear is often momentary. Although they are different states, fear is involved with anxiety. Having anxiety does not mean that there is something wrong with you. Many people are reported to struggle with anxiety, including actors Johnny Depp, Jennifer Lawrence, Scarlett Johansson, musicians Adele and Justin Timberlake, and athletes David Beckham and Ricky Williams.[46]

You may be wondering what caused your anxiety. The majority of the time there is not a single cause for anxiety but a lifetime of experiences, automatic thoughts and behaviors which have developed into a pattern of thinking. There is a myth running around that in order to cure anxiety, you must know the experience which "caused" your anxiety. However, you don't need to pinpoint the exact "reason" you are anxious; the treatment is the same regardless of the origin. Anxiety can be a vicious cycle as it may manifest as physical sensations (headaches, stomach and digestive problems, shortness of breath, rapid heartbeat, etc.), feelings of low self-worth, fear, powerlessness, and behaviors that create even more anxiety, such as avoidance. For example, I am working with a wonderful teenager right now to help her with anxiety. She often

45   Baxter, A., Scott, K., Vos, T. and Whiteford, H. (2013) Global prevalence of anxiety disorders: A systematic review and meta-regression. *Psychological Medicine*, 43: 362–373. Bromet, E., Andrade, L.H., Hwang, I., Sampson, N.A., Alonzo, J., De Girolamo, G., and Iwata, N. (2011) Cross-national epidemiology of DSM-IV major depressive episode. *BMC Medicine*, 9: 90.

46   Kannis-Dymand, L. and Carter, J. (2015) *How to Deal with Anxiety: A 5-step, CBT-based plan for overcoming generalized anxiety disorder (GAD) and worry*. London: John Murray Learning.

gets stomach aches from her tendency to worry too much, which makes her worry about throwing up, which makes her worry about being embarrassed in front of her friends, which makes her avoid spending time with certain friends, which makes her feel isolated and leaves her feeling even more anxious! You can see how the cycle of anxiety is affecting so many areas of her life.

The good news is that breaking this cycle does not have to be overly complicated. When you work through anxiety, you don't have to "get over it" or learn to be happy all the time. In fact, a core tenet of effective anxiety reduction lies in finding your authentic voice and to learn what bothers you and also what you truly enjoy. You don't have to learn to be happy with every situation, but instead learn to say no to those that you may have avoided in the past if they are not positive. One of the most helpful ways to decrease anxiety is to learn to assess your thoughts.

SADNESS AND DEPRESSION

"Depression is like a woman in black. If she turns up, don't shoo her away. Invite her in, offer her a seat, treat her like a guest and listen to what she wants to say."
– Carl Jung

Sadness and depression are such difficult emotions because they have us feeling disempowered, without energy, and sometimes even numb. It is important to remember that there is a purpose to sadness, though. Sadness has us slow down and be more contemplative so that we can reassess our choices and our path in life. Sadness is our internal navigation system warning, "wrong way, find another route!" Yet, it can be hard to find another route, another path, or another way when we have no energy, when we're feeling worthless, or when we feel like we may as well give up. There are two steps to overcoming sadness and depression; first, pay attention to what your sadness is telling you and second, take action.

If you're feeling sad or depressed, those two steps may sound overwhelming. Let me walk you through them. Also, remember, this is not meant to take the place of a licensed therapist or psychologist. Should you find after reading this chapter that you are stuck, please allow yourself the gift of asking for and receiving help.

Step 1: Pay Attention to What Your Sadness is Telling You

Your sadness can be a gift. It is a gentle calling to listen. Something is not right and you're asked to pay attention. Often, it is much more than what it appears to be, especially when sadness turns into depression.

Step 2: Take Action

I used to wait until I was in the mood to begin a challenging task. Yet, when you're sad or depressed, almost everything feels like a challenging task. For example, have you ever found yourself saying "I'm not in the mood for exercising/writing/cleaning" etc.? The irony is, most of the time, motivation comes after we actually begin a task; "Your error is that you believe that motivation comes first and then leads to activation and success. But it's usually the other way around; action must come first, and then the motivation comes later on."[47] Any meaningful activity has a good chance of brightening your mood. By doing nothing, the negative and critical thoughts can preoccupy you and your attention will go to them, as if you are marinating in a pool of negativity. But when you are engaged in some kind of meaningful task, your mind has something else to focus on besides critical thoughts. Generally, when you hear yourself say "but" in relation to an activity, there is a likelihood that the negative thoughts are in control.

Dr. David Burns, author of *Feeling Good: The new mood therapy*, has an exercise called "How to Get Off Your 'Butt' – The 'But' Rebuttal."[48] It really speaks to me as a psychologist because it helps train our thoughts away from the negative thinking patterns that inhibit so many from living life to their full potential. It's as if the positive part of you is encouraging the negative part of you.

---

47 Burns, D. (1999) *Feeling Good: The new mood therapy*. New York, NY: Harper Collins.
48 Burns, D. (1999) *Feeling Good: The new mood therapy*. New York, NY: Harper Collins.

But	But rebuttal
I really should clean out the refrigerator but I'm not in the mood.	I'll feel better once I do it.
Yes but I'm tired, I'll just do it later.	It will only take a minute, then I won't have to feel bad about myself every time I open the refrigerator.
Ugh! I'm so stupid! Why do I buy all that food that goes to waste?	I'm labeling myself negatively again.
But I'm so tired. Don't I ever get to rest?	I can just do a little now and a little later. It's not so bad.
But…	Doing it will make me feel better.

Go ahead and try this exercise yourself. Start with something you have been avoiding doing on the first left column. It reminds me a bit of the old cartoon images of the person with a devil on one shoulder and an angel on the other arguing with each other, as if the positive and negative sides of yourself are arguing. For many, doing this exercise helps them realize how unhelpful it is to listen to just one side of themselves.

But	But rebuttal

But	But rebuttal

I encourage you to practice this in your thinking as well. When you say something negative to yourself, try the "But Rebuttal" and argue the other side. It will help you become less attached to your thoughts, which is the goal.

The Power of Saying "Thank You" Instead of "Sorry"

When you find yourself showing signs of low self-worth, like over apologizing or not accepting a compliment, change that habit. Release patterns of putting yourself down. Stop saying "Sorry" and say "Thank You" instead. Especially women, we have the tendency to say "Sorry" all the time! When we are late, instead of "Sorry, I'm late," say "thank you for your patience." When we ramble, instead of saying "Sorry, I'm rambling," say, "Thank you for listening." You don't need to apologize simply for existing!

When you're given a compliment, don't return it automatically ("Thanks, you too"), deflect the compliment ("Oh, not really, I guess…") or go on and on (Oh thank you, I had it for years and got it on sale"). Just say "Thank you," already! A simple "Thank you" shows that you deserve the attention and you deserve the compliment. And if you can look directly in the kind person's eyes while you say "Thank you," even better – receive their kindness into your heart. You deserve to be loved, you are lovable just the way you are. So take it in!

The Power of Visualization

The images we create in our mind are so powerful that imagining we are doing something can help us believe we can achieve and lead us closer to our goal, so long as it's done realistically. For example, imagining that you've won the Olympic gold medal will not help you, but visualizing yourself practicing, then visualizing getting tired but continuing practicing, then visualizing yourself in formal training, can help you take the actual steps you need to actually begin training for the Olympics. Effective visualization is critical visualization, where realistic obstacles and efforts are integrated into the visualization. Likewise, optimistic thinking must include realistic challenges in order to help manifest a positive outcome. New York University Professor of Psychology, Gabriele Oettingen's research[49] shows us that dreaming or visualizing about our goal can decrease our energy, as if we are tricking ourselves that we have already succeeded. But, if we include a realistic visualization, it can help us get our minds around the idea that our goal may indeed be realistic. Go ahead and try it yourself:

Do you have something that you've always wanted to achieve? Imagine all five senses: What do you feel, taste, smell, hear and see? How does it make you feel? Now, go ahead and write the steps you will need to take to achieve your achievement. Include possible setbacks and failures, make sure to finish to the end of the exercise to show that you achieved your goal. It's a bit like talking to the positive and negative side of yourself again except this time it's about a goal.

Here's an example:

GOAL: Save money for a family vacation.

Step 1: Budget how much we will need.
Possible Set-Back: It's hard to know how much to budget.

Step 2: Look it up online.
Possible Set-Back: Who has time to look it up?

Step 3: Make the kids do it.
Possible Set-Back: They won't do it.

Step 4: Bring it up in a family meeting.

---

49 Kappes, H.B. and Oettingen, G. (2011) Positive fantasies about idealized futures sap energy. *Journal of Experimental Social Psychology*, 47: 719–729.

Possible Set-Back: None, probably they can do it.

Step 5: Start saving, no more Starbucks or eating out for a while.
Possible Set-Back: That may not be realistic, I need good coffee.

ACHIEVEMENT OF GOAL (You did it! It was not easy, but you did it)!

Now your turn:
GOAL: _____

Step 1: _____
Possible Set-Back: _____

Step 2: _____
Possible Set-Back: _____

Step 3: _____
Possible Set-Back: _____

Step 4: _____
Possible Set-Back: _____

Step 5: _____
Possible Set-Back: _____

ACHIEVEMENT OF GOAL (You did it! It was not easy, but you did it)!

Sometimes we think something will make us happy but it will not, and the visualization process can be a great way to test whether a dream we have will likely bring us happiness or not.

For example, my client Erik chose to visualize selling his company for a large sum. Before he went to bed at night, he would imagine what it would feel like, what he would see, what he would be tasting, hearing and smelling once he got the call from the person who was going to buy his company. His visualization made him feel good, confident and secure, but he was surprised to not feel joy. We processed his response in therapy so he was able to let go of the fantasy that having a lot of money would bring happiness.

Erik did end up selling his company, but he was able to jump past the disappointment that many self-made millionaires feel when they later discover that what they spent decades of their life on would not make them happy. Also, Erik was able to prioritize his family, as he realized his family did bring him joy. By the time he sold his company, he still had positive relationships with his children and wife, unlike many entrepreneurs who lose their family along the way.

ANGER AND FRUSTRATION

"Holding on to anger is like grasping a hot coal with the intent of throwing it at someone else; you are the one who gets burned." — Buddha

Anger isn't bad. When used properly, anger can be a gift. Anger can energize us to make change, can lead us out of a bad situation, can help us change the world. Without anger, there would still be slavery, women would not be able to vote and Hitler would have had his way. Martin Luther King, Jr. used anger to energize the writing of his speeches. He said, "When I am angry I can write, pray, and preach well, for then my whole temperament is quickened, my understanding sharpened, and all mundane vexations and temptations depart."[50] Of course, when anger is left unhealed and turns to hate, indifference or crushes empathy for others, it is the source of destruction and suffering.

Most likely because we are afraid of this destructive aspect of anger, when we feel it, most of us are afraid of it. Afraid of anger taking over, afraid of the consequences it will bring, afraid of being out of control... which is why I believe so much of us focus on how to get rid of it.

---

50 Retrieved from https://gracequotes.org/author-quote/martin-luther/

But why get rid of an emotion that has the potential to energize and empower us? Instead, we can learn to use anger as a tool.

What makes you angry? Chances are, your response will share these traits: 1. The anger will be justified (you are angry for a good reason) and 2. The source of your anger will most likely be another person. To learn how to use anger as a tool, first, you must learn to be fueled by the energy it brings. Often, that simply happens when you stop avoiding anger, pushing it away, or pretending it's not there. If you acknowledge your anger, you can receive the energy that comes along with it. See it as a gift and know it means you need to take action. Next, you can examine what to do when other people make you feel angry.

What to Do When Other People Make You Feel Angry

As much as we think we've got it together, when we get hurt or someone does something that we feel is unfair, rude, or unkind, most humans, most of the time, will allow this to influence them negatively. Chances are, when you unconsciously allow your emotional state to shift into anger, it has to do with how you are perceiving the actions of another person and your idea of what that means to you.

Certainly, a lot of what happens in the world that is done by other people feels like it deserves our anger, sadness, or fear as a response. Just reviewing the news on any given day in any given country, it can be easy to justifiably be angry, upset or scared. From the most extreme examples of war to the daily perceptions of injustice, it is extremely challenging NOT to live as a response to other people's behavior. But good people do bad things. And less than good people do bad things. You can see the dilemma.

When you are feeling angry at the actions of another person and your anger is not helping you create change or is infringing on your ability to enjoy your own life, you can play the "What Must Have Happened to Them to Make Them this Way" game. This is something that they teach us in graduate school except they call it the "empathic hook." Developing this skill gave me the compassion I needed to counsel a man who had murdered his wife and another who had raped someone. I was able to care for and have compassion for them even though I thought I would remain cold and clinical because of the crimes they had perpetrated. Here's how it's done: if you have the opportunity to be able to have a conversation or two with the person you feel anger towards, ask them about their story, their life, ask them about their suffering. The more you learn about their story, the more your compassion will grow and your anger will fade. It can also be helpful to imagine the person as a child.

If you are unable to have a conversation with this person, perhaps they have died or they are a public or political figure that you don't know personally but for whom you have anger towards, do your best to read up about them. Learn about what kinds of experiences people with those character traits likely had. For example, if certain politicians with narcissism and pathology drive you insane, learn that narcissism, at its heart, is based on self-hate. A narcissistic personality develops when a child is seen only as an object or trophy for the parent, not as a real person. The narcissist learns a false idea of love, that love is adoration, and the narcissist cannot be authentic because they never were loved or even seen for who they were, only for how it would make their parent(s) look. Once you can trace the person's behavior to their unhealed wounds, you can have compassion for them.

Once you're able to let go of anger, you can decide how you want to handle the person who triggered your anger. Does this person have to be in your life? What can you do about what is angering you? Remember anger calls for action to be resolved.

But don't be fooled into the fantasy of changing them. When people are wounded so badly that they wound others, change is very slow, and often doesn't happen at all. Unless they are fully engaged with a good licensed therapist or psychologist, meditating and repenting daily, or engaging with another form of personal growth accelerator, waiting for the person that hurts you to change is a recipe for disaster. It's painful when you have a family member or loved one who repeatedly hurts you or others by their unhealed wounds. The easiest way to influence others is to love them and feel compassion for them. Why carry the energy of anger for someone in hopes that they will change? Instead, see them for who they are, a wounded soul, and let them go.

Jealousy Toward Others

Feeling threatened or jealous is a sign that you wonder if you have enough of what's needed to be truly loved. It can also help us to learn what we really want. It may also be a sign that you are underperforming and that the person you are feeling jealous of is taking the steps that you would like to take yourself but fear has been holding you back. If you are jealous of someone, they have something that you would like to have. Yet, once you realize the truth behind your jealousy, you soon realize that your jealousy is simply asking you to let go of your self-doubt and play bigger. How you let go of your self-doubt and how you play bigger and take bolder steps toward your dreams is less important than you taking action and releasing the negative trap of jealousy. Unlock the prison you have trapped yourself in with your jealous feelings and pay attention instead to what you're yearning for. You don't need to feel threatened by how others live or the choices they make. Instead, listen to what you are longing for and feel grateful for the reminder of what you want.

Use Anger as a Tool

Anger is sending you a message that something needs to change. The reason why anger feels energizing is because you are meant to take action with anger. Unlike sadness, which compels us to go inward and contemplate, anger needs a resolution of action. Anger will not be satisfied with talking it away. Listen to your anger. What can you change that will improve your situation?

If your anger is related to a person, in addition to playing the "What Must Have Happened to Them to Make Them this Way" game, you can also feel okay about not being obligated to have a relationship with that person. Even if it's a family member, you can let them go. However, knowing when to let go of the relationship versus when to let go of what you're holding onto in the relationship can be tricky when we are clouded with anger. Often, people want to let go of relationships they are meant to learn from, and hold onto those they are meant to release.

It can be helpful to have a licensed psychologist or therapist to talk to when you are deciding between the two. Being a licensed psychologist myself, one of the rules I consider for my own relationships is, "Is the person open to growth?" If they aren't or are simply too mentally ill, then it can be a good litmus test to understand what you need to do. When people don't heal their wounds and unravel their stories as they age, emotional problems can progress to mental illness. Here's an example: Lynn is a client of mine. She was struggling with the extreme narcissism and self-centeredness of her mother who was almost 70 years old. As her mother had not gotten the help for her untamed emotions, she had grown into an extreme version of all that she hadn't healed. Lynn felt obligated to have a relationship with her mother because she was her mother, but the relationship was so toxic and her mother was not at all open to looking at herself to grow that there was nothing left to do but to release the relationship.

On the other hand, Paul came in wondering what to do about his relationship with his father. Paul's father was also almost 70 and also incredibly self-focused. However, Paul's father was open to looking at himself. When Paul would bring up an issue with his father, his father would actually listen and try to modify his behavior.

It may strike you as strange that adults whose parents are close to 70 years old are still greatly affected by the relationship with their parents, but the truth is that the power of the parent and child relationship never fades. And when parents have unhealed wounds that affect their children while they're still living in their home, this doesn't disappear once the children move out.

Anger Toward Yourself

If your anger is inward, toward yourself, you still need to take action. In one way or another, you have disappointed yourself. You have not been meeting the promise of who you are and you need to get back on the authentic-no-matter-what track. Inner anger is also often a sign of trauma, and of living a lifestyle that felt "safe" but lacks meeting your true potential.

Take Dylan for example. Dylan was angry at himself all the time. He grew up in a poor neighborhood and was bullied, teased and beat up almost weekly. There wasn't anyone to stand up for him to feel safe so he began at a young age to be angry at himself. His anger had turned inward because he was afraid that if he became angry at the bullies that he would be beaten even more. When I saw him in therapy as a young adult in his 20s he was angry and frustrated. His spirit wanted to fight. Even though there were no more bullies beating him up as an adult, the unresolved trauma he had when he was a child had programmed him to believe that he couldn't be angry and he had to remain small to survive. Our work together used his anger to provide him the courage to burst through his old need for safety to explore who he really was. He started speaking up, even disagreeing with people, which he didn't feel safe to do as a child. Not only did his inner anger evaporate, but he was also starting to become confident.

Anger toward yourself can also be habitual. Remember the critical thoughts and unhelpful thinking styles you learned about in the beginning of this chapter? Chances are that if you have anger toward yourself you are practicing unhelpful thinking styles and have some critical thoughts programmed in your hard drive. Incorporating a growth-based mindset can be essential to relieving the pressure of inward anger. Please make sure to read Chapter 9 on the Power of Transformational Communication which will inform you about how to talk to yourself in a way that allows you to be imperfect and still love yourself.

BEING HAPPY, REGARDLESS

We could easily spend our days, our weeks, our months which turn into years that turn into a lifetime, upset by what other people do and don't do. It's hard not to. And then, there are the people we love who are suffering. Unconsciously, we've programmed ourselves away from joy for this fact as well… we allow ourselves to suffer for others, but it does them no good. Our well-intentioned empathy influences our ability to access our potential to help them because we allow fear, anger and sadness to cloud us.

My lesson for distinguishing my happiness from the experiences of others was a gift from my little brother Jeff. He was hilarious, crazy and unusually authentic (with no filter). When we were little, he would chase me around the house making irritating noises while I would scream and hide in locked rooms. We were children of divorce, which meant that we lived with our mother and spent every other weekend and half of the summer with our father. But our mother's house was permissive while our father's house was punitive – one house had almost no rules while the other had many. It was as confusing as could be and Jeff especially got into a lot of trouble. In spite of very different environments, we were always together and were the one constant in life we had for each other. We did almost everything together. I loved my time with him. Years passed and soon we were teenagers. As teens, we had a nightly ritual where we would swim in the ocean at sunset talking about magic and trying to find dolphins. Our relationship was so close that we used to call each other "soul twins."

My brother Jeff and I

We knew we were deeply loved but we had a childhood where drama was a part of daily life. Our mother came from a very neglected childhood and loved us deeply but always struggled with how to raise us as a single parent. On top of it all, I started having seizures at age 5 and was diagnosed with epilepsy and Jeff, having been born three months premature, had extreme learning disabilities and undiagnosed neurological trauma. My heart would break for the difficulties my mother had in raising him and I did my best to make life less stressful for her by being a good student and being as helpful as I could be.

Almost everything she was feeling – anger toward our father, fear of not making rent, resentment toward her parents and siblings, we knew about. We knew every detail of her story and we were caught in the middle of it. I didn't know to interpret her words toward my father and so, as a child, I thought my father must be an awful person because my mother said so.

We soon grew into teens and Jeff, who was shorter than his peers and who had always been vulnerable to needing validation, started using steroids to make himself stronger for his high school wrestling matches. The steroids produced episodes of rage that were taken out on my mother and sister. I was 1000 miles away at college when the rage reached its worst levels. Steroids led to heroin. We're not quite sure how or why he decided to take that next step but when you're used to injecting yourself with needles and you've got anger, sadness and fear inside of you, it's not too great a leap to take.

I was in my late 20s when Jeff was at his worst. He would often show up at my door emaciated, having not eaten for what looked like days. His ribs were showing, pants too big and falling off his body, eyes bulging from his face and a death-like yellowish cast to his skin – it was as though he was trapped in a spiritual concentration camp. I would feed him as much as he would eat and when he went to use the restroom, I would hear him shooting up behind locked doors. I can't possibly express the horror of knowing that the person you love the most in life is behind a lock and may die within minutes, and you really can't do anything about it. The locked door became the drug's portal to separate him from me – it was literal and spiritual. I could no longer reach him. He became lost to me then.

The pain was so great for all of us who loved him, and I know even more for him. The suffering was immense, horrid and shocking. He even ended up in the psychiatric department of the Los Angeles County Jail at one point, which is like something out of a horror movie. His prognosis was bad and we didn't know whether to have hope or to give up. Professionals told us to give up hope. Although my hope was relentless, it felt torturous for us to hold our breath in anticipation of his recovery. It went on for seven years like this. My visits with him eventually forced me to realize that I had to allow some joy to be a part of my life in spite of the suffering my sweet brother was experiencing.

In the end, I got a call that he was in the emergency room and his heart had given way from a drug overdose, and that he might not survive this time. I rushed to see him, and as I walked into the sterile hospital-smell of overly sanitized space there was a shift in energy. I knew this was the last time I would see him. His beautiful greenish-yellow eyes that always had a twinkle in them no matter how far away his spirit was from his body, locked with mine and with tears streaming and heart breaking, I said aloud, "It's ok, Jeff. You can go. We will be ok. I love you." He died minutes later.

What followed was a crashing of hearts and spirits and a mother blaming a father for the death of her child. Anger was transformed to rage, and blame was so present it became tangible. I wasn't sure I would ever truly heal and had even less hope for my mother. In a way, I also lost my hope for my mother that day. Anger ate her from the inside. Although she survived cancer (which she had developed years before), the wounds from her childhood and from losing her son were too much. At this point, I knew that I had to disconnect from the drama so I began the learning process of creating my own reality. I was studying postmodernism in graduate school and the idea that each person manifests their own world based on their thoughts was more than appealing to me; it was my salvation.

Still, my empathy for her led me to try to fix her pain, which as any good therapist will tell you is a recipe for disaster. I gave more than I had to give, I outperformed, I tried to compensate for the loss of my brother and the pain we had experienced, but inside I knew nothing would ever be the same. My mother never asked me for help but her pain was so severe that it was hard not to. Her suffering went on for years, and finally when she fell in love with her last husband we all hoped she would at last find happiness. However, her husband was diagnosed with a severe and rapid-onset form of dementia and died soon after. What a life she had, so much suffering…so I kept on giving, kept on trying to fill her cup. And of course, after more than forty years of this behavior, she came to anticipate and somewhat expect it from me, which led to an important but painful break and a return to authenticity for me as I let go of the obligation of caring for her and "daughtering" the way I had learned it.

It took me 44 years to achieve this clarity and this power of manifesting your own reality. And it is powerful! I'm hoping that with these tools you will get there faster than I was able to and I'm excited for the possibility of you creating the life of your dreams!

So, how will you learn to distinguish your happiness from the emotional state of others? I hope that the story of Jeff will remind you that even when those you love the most suffer, you are still allowed to experience joy.

However, more important than my story is your story.

Your Story

Who are you closest to in life?

_____

_____

_____

_____

_____

Can you think of a time when that person was suffering and you let their suffering become your suffering?

_____

_____

_____

_____

_____

What do you feel obligated about?

_____

_____

_____

_____

Who do you feel obligated to?

_____

_____

_____

_____

_____

Obligations are false relationships based on programming that does not fit our authentic self.

What do you feel guilty about?

_____

_____

_____

_____

_____

_____

_____

_____

_____

Guilt About Being Fortunate

Many people feel guilty about being more fortunate than others, but guilt is a completely wasted emotion – it inhibits us from experiencing connection with others or the joy that is yours to feel. Many live their whole lives out of guilt. Guilt blocks our ability to make authentic choices. Instead of being in a relationship or doing things for others out of a real connection, guilt makes us think that we "should" do something.

Instead of feeling sorry for others less fortunate than you or having guilt about what you have and they don't, be an example of joy for them. The energy of emotion is contagious. Have you ever noticed that when you are with someone who is joyful, your mood elevates? Likewise, when you are with someone who is sad or angry, your mood is depleted? We haven't yet figured this out scientifically, though there has been a small indication of this phenomenon in the study of mirror neurons. So, instead of feeling guilty which at best only neutralizes the mood and at worst depletes others, allow yourself to feel joy.

But, "How can I allow myself to feel joy when the world is so full of suffering?" you may ask. Wars, abuse, atrocities, disease, death, disaster…the amount of suffering cannot and should not be ignored, but you are not meant to suffer for others. Your heart is big and you care about others and want to help but the truth is that your guilt does not help. Guilt inhibits you from being authentic and being in a place of high energy which inhibits you from producing your best work. And your work, when done with joy, does in fact change the world. You may or may not have a career that allows you to help others directly but it's your spirit that really makes a difference.

As a child, I had so much guilt for the suffering of others. Children were starving and I had food! My brother could barely read and I was in the gifted classes. Some of my friends didn't have money for clothes… the inequity of life is so hard to digest and so hard to make sense of. I remember asking my mother, "But how could God allow all of this to happen?" There was no answer but I couldn't help but thinking "How can *I* allow all of this to happen?" and I felt guilty about the difference. I still feel compelled to do what I can to help as much as possible but now I allow myself to not feel guilty.

In college, there was a homeless man who used to sit on the corner of the campus bookstore and give away free jokes. He made everyone laugh. Where I live in California, there is a man who walks up and down a busy highway all day with his hand up waving to each and every car that passes with a sign hanging from his neck that reads "BE POS-ITIVE!" These homeless men see more suffering than you or I likely do, and they have figured out that being in guilt or shame will not help anyone, so they choose to bring joy to the world in their own way.

CHAPTER 6

ACTIVATE YOUR FUTURE

"Your visions will become clear only when you can look into your
own heart. Who looks outside, dreams; who looks inside, awakes."
- C.G. Jung

No parenting book would be complete without mention of the future and our ability to influence it. When we learn parenting tools we are hoping to influence the future of our family. Influencing our own personal future is essential, too. Just as we learned in previous chapters about healing our past and deprogramming our automatic thoughts, a focus on the future is just as crucial to deliver us toward a better life. When we work toward envisioning and achieving our personal goals, we are more often purposeful, confident and joyful, which directly influences our children. When we activate our future, we also model going after our dreams for our children and become happier in the process. In this chapter, we focus on tools to create the life of our dreams.

Most of us pass through life reacting unconsciously to experiences or avoiding bad ones. This is related to staying in our comfort zone and doing things that are often automatically expected of us without questioning them. Some common examples of this include taking whatever job is available instead of envisioning the career of your dreams; following the expected path (college, career, kids) without a vision; wearing what we feel will fit in instead of what truly speaks to our soul, etc. Incrementally, the everyday decisions that we make that we don't give enough thought to end up navigating our life path. Then, 20 years down the line, we end up in a personal crisis wondering: What the heck am I doing with my life? This is a "life happens to me" way of living and it's experienced by most of humanity.

The alternative to "life happens to me" is "I happen to life." You see the "I happen to life" attitude often in entrepreneurs who forge their own careers or in creative people who follow their passion. Although sometimes when it looks like someone is forging their own path in life, behind the scenes they actually are motivated by the Ego and fear-based kind of thinking that going after money creates. You see, every person I've ever worked with that does this deeper work about what truly motivates them is never motivated by wealth alone. Really, none of us are. We want what we believe money may buy us. The author, Simon Sinek, has made a career out of helping people understand their true motivations. He talks about the importance of emotion motivating and inspiring growth of businesses.[51] More importantly, understanding why we are motivated to do what we do manifests into the difference between a full and joyful life and an empty life. How do I know? I've worked with CEOs and Fortune 500 executives in the personal crisis stage of their lives; having everything they ever dreamed of but ending up extremely unhappy. Why? They never examined their true motivations for why they wanted what they wanted. In order to assess our true motivations, we must learn to get past our Ego.

The key to unlocking your dreams and creating the life you want is to move past your Ego. There are many definitions of Ego; I will spare you the psychobabble. Here, we use the term Ego to mean the "I" or the "self" that distinguishes you from others. When we experience feeling better or less than others, that is an indication that our Ego is running the show. When you feel jealous, compare yourself to others, or feel the need to be right or correct others, this is further evidence that our Ego is in control. And our Ego loves to be in control. Ego-based living keeps us from being our authentic selves, has us seeking validation from others, and going after dreams that won't make us happy. The Ego, with its determination to keep you from changing, creates the self-talk of, "I can't do or have this because..." and we often listen and don't bother

---

51 Sinek, S. (2009) *Start with Why: How great leaders inspire everyone to take action.* New York, NY: Portfolio.

trying. Many, unconsciously, feel that they don't deserve such pleasure, or compare themselves to others imagining that those other people have what they want, and think of all the ways they are less than that person. These habits are tricky to break. It's essential to understand why we want something, not just that we want it.

Danielle La Porte (www.daniellelaporte.com) does a beautiful job at helping people find their core desires and has a helpful online program where anyone can discover theirs. Let's go ahead and explore what yours might be now.

Exercise: Core desire

Go ahead and focus on that thing or experience that you've always wanted, but don't let it go or excuse it away, just keep it in your mind's eye. If you can't think of any one thing, just go with the first thing that comes up, no matter how trivial or fantasy-like it may seem. Now, think about how you would feel if you had that. Challenge yourself to be as specific as possible and to think beyond "good and great." Specific feelings such as, "I would feel loved, important, seen, cared for," etc. will be the most helpful to you here.

Take a minute and write down what you want and how you would feel if you had it:

_____

_____

_____

_____

_____

_____

_____

_____

_____

_____

Now take a minute to identify what your core desire is. A core desire is the heart of why you want what you want. For example, if you want wealth, your core desire may be to be free, to feel safe, to feel loved, or all three (or many more). Here is a list of some of the most common core desires. Circle the ones that most resonate with you:

To feel loved	To feel safe	To be free/independent
To be accepted / appreciated / validated	To feel joy	To be free from worry/ taken care of
To feel at peace	To feel authentic/alive	To feel powerful

If you had any trouble with identifying your core desire, don't worry, my friend! The most important desire of all is to seek joy! So, you can just release the need to search and think about what brings you joy. Joy is different from happiness. Joy is a deeper experience, joy is an attitude. Most people aim for happiness. When asked what they want from life, most people say, "I just want to be happy." But happiness is impermanent. One is not meant to be happy all of the time. Happiness is fleeting and circumstantial. But having a joyful spirit can certainly bring more happiness. We lose touch with our innate joy and we try to get it back by quick fixes such as overspending, alcohol, drugs, addictive foods, or even spend our time vegging out on television and movies experiencing the stories of others as if they were our own.

We were born joyful. Every baby has a joyful spirit, it is our birthright, the greatest gift of being human. Think of the joy you experienced as a young child, or the joy you see another child experience, at the simple pleasures in life. Blowing on a dandelion to make a wish, watching butterflies, swinging on a swing....pure joy. Often the simplest experiences bring us back to that state of childhood joy. So, if you aren't sure about what your core desire is, let joy guide you!

Now that you've identified what's behind that something or someone you wish for, take a minute and write down at least 10 other experiences where you feel joy or your core desire. Don't stop at three or four. Keep at it.

When else do you feel this way or imagine that you may feel this way?

1. _____
2. _____
3. _____
4. _____
5. _____
6. _____
7. _____
8. _____
9. _____
10. _____

When people act before understanding what their core desire is, they often end up with results that don't give them what they really want to feel. I've seen it so many times in my practice. The wealthy woman or man who is as unhappy as you can imagine. They thought money would bring them happiness because they never identified their core desire. Most of these people were actually searching for validation, to feel loved and accepted. But because they didn't understand what they were searching for, they never healed to be able to enjoy the wealth they created. They took action before they understood what they really needed. They, along with many of us, had too much action and not enough introspection. Our culture of rushing does not help.

If you can be honest with yourself, really honest, and identify your core desire, your actions will be propelled by healing instead of your Ego distracting you from being honest with yourself about your core desire. And yes, this need to fulfill a core desire probably came from childhood, but that's ok! Everyone has this. Everyone, I promise. I bet even the Dalai Lama is striving.

Now let's work on your subconscious mind to help turn those dreams into reality. In order to effect true positive change, you must disregard how things are, the idea of "the real world." Reality is what we make it and is entirely subjective. We must be honest with ourselves that we are all culturally conditioned for fear. Our primitive mind is often in the driver's seat. We are constantly avoiding pain or numbing ourselves with too much social media, television, sugar. We often enter into a dullness because we think it's safer. Our Ego leads us there and our cultural habits and fear-based programming keep us there. The world can be bright and lively but we make it dull and monochromatic. The "real world" is whatever you believe it to be.

I went with my daughter to see the latest release of DC's *Wonder Woman*. She was confused at the end of the movie and asked, "Mom, don't comic book stories usually have a 'bad guy' – who is it?" We spoke about how Wonder Woman realized that it wasn't about bad or good but it was what you believe. And that's exactly it. It's what you believe. Life is what you believe, what you think about, what you see…. There is an old Indian folk tale about six blind men and an elephant which reminds us of this age-old wisdom:

> There were once six blind men in a village in India. The blind men had heard many stories about elephants but had never come across one. It was arranged for the blind men to experience an elephant. The first blind man was near his trunk, reached up and said "an elephant is like a snake." The second blind man reached up and touched his side, "An elephant is like a wall." The third touched his legs and he thought the elephant was a tree, the fourth touched his tusk and thought the elephant was a spear. The fifth felt the elephant's ear and thought the elephant to be a giant fan. Finally, the last blind man felt his tail and thought elephants were like a rope. The blind men were all arguing about the elephant. It's a "snake!" "wall!" "spear!" "tree!" "fan!" "rope!" They finally realized that if they put all of the parts together that they would be able to see the truth.

As this folktale reminds us, there are many versions of the truth. Truth is an individual interpretation. Of course, we work together to create a collective truth as well. For example, many psychologists, including myself, believe that we create a collective unconscious – which is an unconscious mind shared by humanity. It is a term coined by psychoanalyst Carl Jung, who believed that we inherit knowledge and archetypes (representations of universal figures such as the hero, the wise woman, the mother, etc.). Jung also believed that the images that come to us in our dreams are representations of the unconscious, and many of us psychologists are trained to use archetypes to help people interpret their dreams. It's awesome stuff and a reminder that we create reality together as well as on our own.

In recognizing the importance of perception in creating reality, you can recognize that what is going on in your life is a manifestation of what goes on in your head. If we think the world is bad, it will be. If we think we are lovable, we are…on and on. Ok, so how do you shift your perspective? To change your reality so it's more in your favor?

YOU CAN'T STOP THE FEELING

From the birth of psychotherapy, changing people's thinking to improve their lives has been the goal. Yet the methods have varied according to trends in the field. From using the shape of the head to diagnose emotional disorders through phrenology in the 19th century to Sigmund Freud's "talking cure," humans have been creative with their attempts at changing thinking. We've since learned a thing or two about what works. For many decades now, psychological research has confirmed that what Mahatma Gandhi said is true: "Your beliefs become your thoughts, Your thoughts become your words, Your words become your actions, Your actions become your habits, Your habits become your values, Your values become your destiny."

OK! You say, I'm in! I will change my thoughts and my life will change! Unfortunately the thinking is only the starting point; you will need to take action so you're credible to yourself. If you say to yourself "I eat healthfully" every morning when you wake up but then eat a donut and drink soda during the day you won't believe yourself. No amount of positive affirmations will make up for the fact that your behavior is very different from what you "say" to yourself. Also, as much as we try to "force" positive thinking, we have stuck thought patterns that get in the way and our thinking patterns emerge out of the blue! What can we do?

Instead of scrutinizing every thought and identifying if it's positive or not, I'd actually like to teach you to pay less attention to your thoughts and focus on your feelings. Don't try to monitor your thoughts, that is too complex, just focus on monitoring your feelings. Good and not so good feelings are signs of whether you are on your path or not. The formula is actually very simple: When you are feeling good you are on the right path, when you are feeling bad, you are not.

Let Emotions Guide You

Now, here's the key: when you are having a good feeling, focus your thoughts around it; when you are having a negative feeling, don't. I believe it is impossible to stop negative feelings. So, don't try to stop them, just don't let them linger. One exercise that is helpful is to notice the negative feeling, recognize that it is present and make a note of what could be the origin of that...the real origin. In other words, which of your needs are not being met?

Emotions are our compass – our built in navigation system to tell us when we are going in the wrong direction. When you feel a negative emotion, you are doing or thinking about something that does not match your true essence. When you feel a positive emotion, that is a sign that you are doing things right and headed in the right direction.

AVOIDING PERSONAL GROWTH

Sometimes we know what we need to work on but we avoid it. We know we should eat better, be more patient with our kids, quit smoking, meditate, exercise more, read more books, watch less tv, and on and on. So, why do we avoid doing what we know is best for us?

There are a millions reasons why. Self-sabotaging keeps us "safe." It can be helpful for our rational mind to talk to the frightened part of our mind with a list. For example, if the goal is "eating healthy" your list may look something like this:

1. I'll feel better about myself.
2. I'll have more energy.
3. I'll be healthier.
4. I'll live longer.
5. I'll age better.
6. I'll be a good example for my children.
7. I'll "practice what I preach."
8. I'll reduce my cravings.
9. I'll fit into that dress I love.
10. I'll have better self-esteem.

Go ahead and write your list. Make a list of all of the advantages you will have if you start doing what you need to do. Remember, when writing your list for your goal, avoid using negative words such as "no," "don't" or "can't" as our subconscious mind mostly ignores negative words. So if you say "don't eat junk food," your subconscious hears "eat junk food!"

What I need to do/my goal:

_____

The advantages of doing it:

1._____

2._____

3._____

4._____

5._____

6._____

7._____

8._____

9._____

10. _____

Now, make a list of the positive results that will occur:

1. _____
2. _____
3. _____
4. _____
5. _____
6. _____
7. _____
8. _____
9. _____
10. _____

GOAL SETTING

Making your dreams come true may appear to be complicated, but the process is actually a series of small steps paired with determination. Woody Allen once said "80% of success is showing up." That is, it does not take an extremely intelligent or talented person to realize their dreams; it's about practice and not giving up! In the book *Outliers*, Malcolm Gladwell describes the traits that determine success.[52] He explains whereas once, it was believed that people such as Bill Gates or The Beatles were geniuses and that alone explained their success, he found that Gates and The Beatles, as well as most highly successful people, have simply had the most practice. With determination, doing what you want to be good at, even if you're not at first, and taking small steps to get there...little by little you will succeed.

Yet, the small tasks of daily life often take over. Many of us end up just doing what *needs* to be done instead of steps which allow us to achieve our goals. For many, the daily grind of life has accumulated over so many years that we have even forgotten to dream. For these people, when asked to name personal or professional goals, they cannot think of any. The small daily tasks of life are taking over the practice because the practice is not bringing us joy. You must LOVE the practice and it must bring you joy in order to be repeated often.

How to love the practice? It's rather simple, just pay attention. Slow down. Focus only on that one thing, that one task for a block of time. Turn off your phone, shut down your computer, just give the task the attention it deserves and you will begin to LOVE the practice. It will become a form of meditation for you and you will feel pride when you accomplish just the practice. For me, this process took more than a decade. I have been working on versions of this book ever since my daughter was a baby. But I didn't love the practice. I wasn't paying attention or giving it the focus it required. I would sit to write and feel stressed out by the thousands of other things that needed to be done. I would allow interruptions and not truly invest myself. Of course, there were other factors involved such as fear of judgement, feeling overwhelmed, trying to learn it all to be able to adequately express myself.... But mostly, I didn't allow myself to fall in love with the practice. Writing a book required hours of sitting and listening to the little clicks of the keyboard

---

52   Gladwell, M. (2008) *Outliers: The story of success*. New York, NY: Little, Brown and Co.

and the hum of my mind and nothing else. It wasn't until this year when I began to love the practice of writing that this book had a chance of being born. And although it took me over ten years, it's ok, I did it. And so can you.

Whatever it is. Whether it be to learn the guitar, learn to surf, write a book, start a business, paint a painting, write a song, learn a language, save money, lose weight...we need to love the practice of it. And bring in joy. Joy is the oil that moves the machine, the colors in the sunset, the warm current in the ocean. Joy will be the glue to help you stick to your practice, your goals, and really make your dreams a reality.

How do we cultivate joy? It's rather simple. Just like learning to love the practice: just pay attention. When you desire to feel joy, you will automatically attract that which brings you joy. You will start to enjoy activities that felt like chores. Doing the dishes can be a warm spa for your hands, driving in traffic can be a wonderful opportunity to sing your heart out or listen to your favorite audiobook. Joy will come anywhere you are if you ask for it.

Remember: the most important desire of all is seeking joy! Instead of focusing on what you want, focus on how you want to feel, on your core desire. Most goals are centered around becoming something different or gaining a material object. For example, the most common new year's resolutions typically involve losing weight, making more money, or obtaining some status symbol. However, losing weight, for example, will not in itself make you feel loved and accepted or to feel more joy. Perhaps your goal should be to eat more healthfully and to practice loving your body.

Let's take a minute and give joy the attention it deserves.

Exercise: What brings you joy?

What three activities bring you the most joy?

1._____

_____

_____

_____

2._____

_____

_____

_____

_____

3._____

_____

_____

_____

_____

How can you do these activities more in your life?

_____

_____

_____

_____

_____

What three things make you feel unhappy or take away your energy / joy for life?

_____

_____

_____

_____

_____

What do you need to change in order to eliminate these activities from your life?

_____

_____

_____

_____

If you could do anything, what would it be?

_____

_____

_____

_____

_____

If you could change three things about your life, what would you change?

_____

_____

_____

_____

If you were to die tomorrow, would you have any regrets?

_____

_____

_____

_____

Now, I want you to write three goals that bring you joy or address one of your core desires (to be loved, accepted, safe, authentic, free from worry, powerful, free, etc.)

1._____

_____

_____

2._____

_____

_____

_____

3._____

_____

_____

_____

THE SCIENCE OF LIVING A JOYFUL
AND HAPPY LIFE

Most people aim for happiness. When asked what they want from life, they say "I just want to be happy." But most people don't know what it means to be happy, which is one of the reasons we wonder if we are happy. Happiness is subjective; what it means to be happy is different for every person, and also varies throughout a lifetime. What makes a 3 year old happy is very different than a 13 year old or a 63 year old. With the barrage of mandates about happiness, we're often left to wonder "Am I really happy?" And recent research show us that sometimes, even wondering if we are happy takes us away from being happy.[53] It has been said that "happiness is as a butterfly which, when pursued, is always beyond our grasp, but which if you will sit down quietly, may alight upon you."[54]

So, we want this thing called "happiness" and yet we're not exactly sure what that means. Advertisers know that. Their job is to make us feel unsatisfied with our lives so we can buy the products they are selling. What happens when we don't define happiness for ourselves is that we think happiness means what we watch on movies, commercials, and social media (Facebook, Instagram, etc). Of course, media is designed to entertain us and, due to our mirror neurons, we can't help but to identify with characters on the screen; to feel as if their pain is our pain, their joy is our joy. It's the job of advertisers to make us feel that we are not happy so we will be motivated to buy what they are selling to make us happy. Most would not disagree when we say that most Westerners are obsessed

---

53 Mauss, I.B., Tamir. M., Anderson, C.L., Savino, N.S. (2011) Can seeking happiness make people unhappy? Paradoxical effects of valuing happiness. *Emotion*, 11 (4): 807–815.
54 Retrieved from www.nytimes.com/2013/12/15/opinion/sunday/a-formula-for-happiness.html

with happiness; with the flooding of movies, self-help books, magazine articles, etc. all devoted to the subject of finding happiness. But what exactly are we searching for?

In his book *Happiness: A history,* Dartmouth historian Darrin Mc-Mahon writes that for most Classical philosophers, "Happiness is never simply a function of good feeling – of what puts a smile on our face – but rather of living good lives, lives that will almost certainly include a good deal of pain."[55] What does it mean to be happy? Does it mean that you are always laughing, the life of the party? Does it mean that nothing bothers you and you just float through life? Does it mean that you get everything you wish for? Is it a feeling or a way of life?

The English word for happiness comes from the word "hap" meaning chance or fortune, as in happenstance or haphazard. Likewise, the Chinese character signifying happiness is the same character that indicates luck. So for both West and East, happiness is often seen as something that simply happens to a person or not.

In addition to happiness being different for every person, we also know that happiness is impermanent. One is not meant to be happy all of the time. Happiness is fleeting and circumstantial. Catholic Benedictine monk Brother David Steindl-Rast, known for his interfaith dialogue and his work on the interaction between spirituality and science, speaks of joy being "happiness that lasts."[56] Joy is a lifestyle, happiness is a feeling. But having a joyful spirit can certainly bring more happiness.

Happiness must have meaning. Happiness without meaning is just pleasure.[57] If happiness is just pleasure, we know it's not going to last. How do you seek joy? How do you seek the kind of joy that is connected to growth that provides us long-term meaning? If you keep pursuing pleasure without meaning, it eventually loses its ability to be pleasurable.

For many of us, joy can be found when we are completely immersed in what we are doing. For me, there are only a few things that create this feeling for me. Painting, writing, and public speaking generally take

---

55   McMahon, D.M. (2006) *Happiness: A history.* New York, NY: Atlantic Monthly Press.
56   Steindl-Rast, D. (2016, Jan 21). Anatomy of Gratitude. Retrieved October 21, 2018 from https://onbeing.org/programs/david-steindl-rast-anatomy-of-gratitude/
57   Achor, S. (2013) *Before Happiness: The five hidden keys to achieving success, spreading happiness, and sustaining positive change.* New York, NY: Random House.

me to that state. Mihaly Csikszentmihalyi, the author of *Flow: The psychology of optimal experience*, called this state of consciousness "flow," which he defines as "the way people describe their state of mind when consciousness is harmoniously ordered, and they want to pursue whatever they are doing for its own sake."[58] It simply feels good to be in that state of being completely caught up in what you are doing. I think that's also the reason why movies and television are so popular. It doesn't take much effort to become engrossed in the story and get into a state where we feel like we are experiencing what's on screen. While it's not exactly what Csikszentmihalyi had in mind when he wrote about a state of "flow," I think it explains our obsession with entertainment beyond just the fact that we are exhausted and want to be entertained. When we watch a good movie or show, we become wholly immersed and it takes little effort. Great books also have the ability to put us in this state, but require more effort.

Exercise: Satisfaction with life scale

Below are five statements that you may agree or disagree with. Using the 1–7 scale below,[59] indicate your agreement with each item by placing the appropriate number on the line preceding that item. Please be open and honest in your responses.

- 7 Strongly agree
- 6 Agree
- 5 Slightly agree
- 4 Neither agree nor disagree
- 3 Slightly disagree
- 2 Disagree
- 1 Strongly disagree

____ In most ways, my life is close to my ideal.

____ The conditions of my life are excellent.

---

58   Mihaly Csikszentmihalyi (2008 [1990]) *Flow: The psychology of optimal experience*. New York, NY: Harper Perennial.

59   Diener, E., Emmons, R.A., Larsen, R.J., and Griffin, S. (1985) The Satisfaction with Life Scale. *Journal of Personality Assessment*, 49: 71-75.

_____ I am satisfied with my life.

_____ So far I have gotten the important things I want in life.

_____ If I could live my life over, I would change almost nothing.

- **31–35** Extremely satisfied
- **26–30** Satisfied
- **21–25** Slightly satisfied
- **20** Neutral
- **15–19** Slightly dissatisfied
- **10–14** Dissatisfied
- **5–9** Extremely dissatisfied

Exercise: Defining happiness for yourself

Come up with 30 things that bring you joy without spending too much time thinking about it. Write them down now.

Here are some common examples:

1. Reading a book by the fire.
2. Long walks on the beach.
3. Movie theaters and popcorn.
4. Snuggling with my children.
5. Dancing.
6. The smell of gardenias.
7. Belly laughs.
8. Remarkable sunsets.
9. Freshly squeezed orange juice (food could be a category of its own).
10. Squishy babies.

List of 30 Things that Bring Me Joy:

1. _____

2. _____

3. _____

4. _____

5. _____

6._____

7._____

8._____

9._____

10. _____

11. _____

12. _____

13. _____

14. _____

15. _____

16. _____

17. _____

18. _____

19. _____

20. _____

21. _____

22. _____

23. _____

24. _____

25. _____

26. _____

27. _____

28. _____

29. _____

30. _____

Now, circle or highlight the things on your list that are free, and pick five of these and put them into your calendar. When you prioritize your life around the things that bring you joy, joy becomes a habit.

Now, write down 30 things that you don't like to do but are a part of your life, and what adjustments you could make to bring you joy. Here are some examples:

Things I don't like to do:	How I can adjust:
1. Drive in traffic	Listen to my favorite books on tape
2. Rush in the morning	Get up earlier
3. Get angry	Learn coping skills
4. Have drama with people	Let go of unhealthy relationships
5. Argue with people	Let them be "right" / let it go
6. Take vitamins	Find some that taste good / learn to love them
7. See others in pain	Decide how I will help

Now your turn:

Things I don't like to do:	How I can adjust:
1.	
2.	
3.	
4.	
5.	
6.	
7.	
8.	

9.	
10.	
11.	
12.	
13.	
14.	
15.	
16.	
17.	
18.	
19.	
20.	
21.	
22.	
23.	
24.	
25.	
26.	
27.	
28.	
29.	
30.	

THE EPIDEMIC: JOYLESS PEOPLE

It is the duty of a child's parents, families, society and culture to pre-serve a child's joy. Joy is a birthright – all people are born with joy. Yet somewhere along the line it becomes distorted, usually somewhere in childhood. Then, as adults try to reclaim their birthright of joy, the task can become daunting and certainly requires much more effort.

In Western culture one of the first things people ask each other upon introduction is "what do you do?" and the response is: "I'm a _____." Then comes the judgement. Invariably, most humans will use a person's work to judge their value to the world. Over time, one's profession becomes synonymous with who they are. We tie our careers to our identity. This leaves most people who earn a paycheck from do-ing something that isn't necessarily who they are with a big mess of low self-esteem. And we don't just do this to adults, we start very young. When we ask children "what do you want to be when you grow up?" there is adult judgement awaiting the child's response. We have a cul-tural expectation of ambition of traditional success and we forget about authentic success.

Goldie Hawn shared her story – which is very relevant here – in *Vanity Fair* in the 90s:

> "Happiness was always important to me. Even at the young age of eleven, it was my biggest ambition. People would ask, "Goldie, what do you want to be when you grow up?"
>
> "Happy," I would reply, looking in their eyes.
>
> "No, no," they'd laugh. "That's really sweet, but I mean . . . what do you want to be? A ballerina? An actress maybe?"
>
> "I just want to be happy."[60]

TRADITIONAL SUCCESS VERSUS AUTHENTIC SUCCESS

Traditional success is linked to money, status, and power...authentic suc-cess is linked to joy and happiness. In authentic success, it's not about

---

60 *Vanity Fair* (1992) Solid Goldie (Profile of Goldie Hawn). pp.168–220, March. New York, NY: Conde Nast Publications; p.220, column 3.

"What you do," it's about the feelings you feel when you do it. This is where Daniel Goleman and Martin Seligman come from when they talk about emotional intelligence and the science of happiness. Just because you've got the job you always wanted and a full bank account to make you feel secure doesn't guarantee you will be happy.

In fact, in a study of 792 well-off adults, more than half reported that wealth didn't bring them more happiness, and a third of those with assets greater than $10 million said that money brought more problems than it solved.[61]

We also know that rich people aren't as happy as we'd expect. The richest Americans, those earning more than $10 million annually, report levels of personal happiness only slightly greater than the office staff and blue-collar workers they employ.[62]

So, go after how you want to feel over what you want to have or accomplish. Then, you'll accomplish that which actually brings happiness and end up with what I call Authentic Success, which is a life filled with joy, passion and purpose.

Now, ask yourself these three questions:

1. What do I want?
2. Why do I want it?
3. What am I willing to do to get it?

While most of us can easily answer "what do I want?" the "why do I want it?" may take some digging deeper. Let's take one of the patients I'm working with now, we'll call him Bob to protect his privacy. Bob is a senior executive at a well-regarded company. He makes more money than he really knows what to do with yet he is still pushing harder and harder for more. His "what do I want?" immediate response is "success." Digging deeper, he discovers that "success" really means being considered important. His response to "why do I want it?" initially is "because it gives my family security." Digging deeper, we find a raw need to be seen because he wasn't given much attention or acknowledged as

61 Lyubomirsky, S. (2007) *The How of Happiness: A scientific approach to getting the life you want.* New York, NY: Penguin Press.
62 www.ncbi.nlm.nih.gov/pmc/articles/PMC1201429/ (p. 21)

a child. His response to "what am I willing to do to get it?" initially is "anything." Digging deeper, he realizes the truth is that he would rather not sacrifice time with his children. He would rather give his children the childhood he longed for with a father who is present.

From this simple conversation, Bob's life takes a dramatic shift. After our session he calls his assistant who ends all meetings after 5pm so that he can be home by 6pm to be with his family. He starts to put away his cell phone when with his children and really focuses on being present with them. He finds himself making more eye contact at home and also at the office. He misses some important meetings, but his reassessment of "success" helps him prioritize being with his children over business meetings.

Of course, this shift is difficult. He does take the occasional after 5pm very essential meeting, but he has stopped anything unessential on the evenings and weekends. Ironically, because he has more clarity as to his purpose, he comes off as more confident and emotionally stable, so that by working less, he is actually making more. Since he made the changes and went after the feeling of joy versus what might have fueled his Ego, he comes across as less of a salesperson and more sincere in his communication. His energy is joyful and he is connecting better with clients. Over time, this lead to him getting bigger contracts.

It goes beyond "finding balance." It's about ensuring that the small decisions you make each day add up to something that's aligned with your deeper purpose. Digging deeper isn't something that should wait until you are in therapy. Digging deeper helps us gain clarity as to what motivates us, to ensure we are moving toward something that is right for us.

Now your turn, take a moment to think about what really motivates you...

1. What do I want?

_____

_____

_____

_____

_____

_____

_____

_____

2. Why do I want it?

_____

_____

_____

_____

_____

_____

3. What am I willing to do to get it?

_____

_____

_____

_____

_____

_____

In sum, remember that every micro-decision you make yields a consequence. Just as a ripple in a pond and the flapping of butterfly wings make environmental change, so does every decision.

PART TWO

YOUR CHILD

CHAPTER 7

WHY CHILDREN MISBEHAVE
AND WHAT TO DO ABOUT IT

*"How much more precious is a little humanity
than all the rules in the world."*

– Jean Piaget

Let me ask you something; what would you do if/when:

- Your child screams "I hate you!"
- Your child hits his baby sister?
- Your child is rude to your mother?
- Your child refuses to do her homework?
- Your child starts to scream in front of a group of people at the grocery store when you say "no" to purchasing a candy bar?
- Your child's curfew is 9pm but he doesn't get home until midnight?
- Your child comes home drunk or high?

If you're human, chances are these situations would upset you. Or trigger a fear or cause you to wonder if you have a "bad" child or that you are a "bad parent." Then there's the judgement, and the judgment is real. God forbid your child has a meltdown in a public place. Even if you don't see the glares of judgement, you will probably feel them. I've noticed that our culture is often more tolerant of dogs misbehaving than babies and toddlers crying. Have you noticed the difference between how people react when a child is crying in a restaurant or store versus how people react when a dog is barking or causing a disturbance?

All of this judgement and the shame that goes along with it tells us that we need to "do something" about our child who is disturbing the peace. What is often implied is that we should respond with a punishment. But what this model misses is the recognition that the child is acting out because a basic need is not being met. Remember Maslow's hierarchy of needs?[63] If your child is sleep deprived, is flooded with stress hormones in their brain, or has low blood sugar, the most basic physical needs are not being met. If you threaten them with punishments, you are also taking away the needs of safety and belonging. I know this may sound hard to digest, but bear with me here.

Most parenting books and resources focus specifically on a child's behaviors. If child does A (yells at you), give consequence B (time-out) and A (child yelling) will stop. Behavioral approaches originated from the work of B.F. Skinner, who worked with laboratory animals, not people or children. But unlike dogs, children are much more complex and we are discovering that using a behavioral approach misses much about what is going on with the child. Often, the behavioral approaches actually escalate the behaviors or make them much worse! However, most of us don't know any other way to look at the situations that come up in our parenting. It is what we see all around us. It is what we know. It is a part of who we have been as a society and how we have looked at our children.

Fortunately, we are entering a new era of consciousness in regards to raising children. We now have scientific evidence that through the positive relationship we build with them, our children behave better and actually want to behave better. Psychologists and researchers call it Interpersonal Neurobiology[64] which incorporates studies from psychology, psychiatry, neuroscience, and sociology demonstrating that the mind and brain are shaped by emotional relationships. Relationship-based discipline is revolutionizing the parenting world. Rather than motivating your child to behave through fear or threats, they behave well be-

---

63   Maslow, A.H. (1943) A theory of human motivation. *Psychological Review,* 50 (4): 370–396. Retrieved from http://psychclassics.yorku.ca/Maslow/motivation.htm
64   Siegel, D. J. (1999). *The developing mind: Toward a neurobiology of interpersonal experience.* New York, NY: Guilford Press.

cause it makes them feel good, and they have integrity – and science backs this up.

YOUR PARENTING STYLE

There's more helpful science to be aware of. One of the primary ways scientists have studied the effects of parenting is by understanding a parent's parenting style. As a parent, knowing your parenting style is essential. Perhaps you think of yourself as an authoritative or demo-cratic parent but are actually too punitive or permissive. In the 1970s, a psychologist named Diana Baumrind developed the parenting styles we know today which have been validated over decades.[65] Generally, most parents fall into four parenting styles: Permissive, Controlling (also called Authoritarian), Uninvolved, or Guiding (also called Authorita-tive). Which parenting style most fits you?

Controlling Parenting Style

If you feel your job as a parent is to have your children obey you without having to explain why, if you feel that you need to make your children be afraid of you in order to behave, if you often threaten or use punish-ment to discipline your children, if you send the message that all deci-sions are made by the parent, the Controlling, also called Authoritarian, parenting style is most likely yours. This parenting type has been related to less optimal child outcomes, including lower self efficacy, more ex-ternalizing problems, and rebellion.[66, 67] Over time, when parents be-lieve they "have to" raise their children this way, they often eventually become less empathetic to their children which is associated with the

---

65 Baumrind, D. (1971) Current patterns of parental authority. *Developmental Psychology Monographs*, 4(1, Pt. 2): 1–103.
66 Chan T.W., Koo A. (2011) Parenting style and youth outcomes in the UK. *European Sociological Review*, 27(3): 385–99.
67 Braza P., Carreras R., Muñoz J.M., et al. (2015) Negative maternal and paternal parenting styles as predictors of children's behavioral problems: moderating effects of the child's sex. *Journal of Child and Family Studies*, 24(4): 847–56.

child growing up with increased risk for mental health problems.[68] It is especially related to children with anxiety and depression.[69]

Permissive Parenting Style

Many parents who were raised with a Controlling parenting style sometimes find themselves swinging toward the other end of the spectrum in hopes of not repeating what their parents did to them. Parents with this parenting style often are very nurturing, loving, and feel uncomfortable when their child is upset. Because of this, they tend to be inconsistent with boundary setting and sometimes choose to ignore poor behavior. If you find yourself uncomfortable with setting rules and limits for your child, if you don't demand much of your child, if you find yourself not wanting to upset your child, you likely fall into the Permissive parenting style. This parenting style often includes no specific household and behavioral rules, which can sometimes result in enforcing harsh punishment after becoming frustrated with their lack of control of their children. This parenting type has been related to child outcomes such as lower achievement,[70] lack of impulse control,[71] and lower autonomy.[72]

Uninvolved Parenting Style

If you let your child fend for themselves more often than not, if you minimize rules, if you feel like your child should take care of themselves, you may fall into the Uninvolved parenting style. Further research

68   Psychogiou, L., Daley, D., Thompson, M.J., Sonuga-Barke, E.J. (2008) Parenting empathy: Associations with dimensions of parent and child psychopathology. *British Journal of Developmental Psychology*, 26(2): 221–32.
69   Wolfradt U., Hempel S., Miles J.N. (2003) Perceived parenting styles, depersonalisation, anxiety and coping behaviour in adolescents. *Personality and Individual Differences*, 34(3): 521–32.
70   Baumrind D., 1971. Harmonious parents and their preschool children. *Developmental Psychology*, 4: 99-102.
71   Maccoby, E., and Martin, J. (1983) Socialization in the context of the family: Parent-child interaction. In P. H. Mussen (Series Ed.) & E. M. Hetherington (Ed.), *Handbook of Child Psychology: Socialization, personality, and social development* Vol. 4 (1-101) New York, NY: Wiley.
72   Baumrind, D., Larzelere, R and Owens, E. (2010) Effects of Preschool Parents' Power Assertive Patterns and Practices on Adolescent Development. *Parenting: Science and Practice*, 10: 157-201.

found that the uninvolved parenting style was related to the child's use of coercive practices and a lack of monitoring.[73]

Guiding Parenting Style

If you are warm, encouraging and motivate your children based on your relationship rather than punishing them, your style may be Guiding, also called Authoritative. When your child is misbehaving do you begin a discussion instead of threatening a punishment? Do you explain the reason why you ask your child to do something instead of "because I said so?" Do you set clear rules for your child? Do you have reasonable expectations and also offer support? Do you encourage your child's independence while still providing help when they need it? Do you provide a structure to your child's life, with routines and household rhythms? If so, you're on the right track. This parenting style is considered the ideal, providing balance between having boundaries and expectations, but also being kind, warm and compassionate. Dr. Jane Nelsen, founder and author of Positive Disciple, describes this in an effectively simple way: "kind and firm."[74] This parenting style has been determined to be ideal,[75] and has been related to positive child outcomes such as self-reliance, social responsibility, and adjustment.[76] Again and again, Guiding parenting styles have been shown to be the best approach to raising children. Guiding parenting is related to higher self esteem and

---

73   Baumrind, D. (1989) Rearing competent children. In W. Damon (Ed.), *The Jossey-Bass Social and Behavioral Science Series: Child development today and tomorrow* (pp. 349-378). San Francisco, CA: Jossey-Bass.
74   Nelsen, J. (2006) *Positive Discipline* . New York, NY: Ballantine Books.
75   Baumrind, D. (2013) Authoritative parenting revisited: History and current status. In R.E. Larzelere, A.S. Morris, and A.W. Harris (eds.) *Authoritative Parenting: Synthesizing nurturance and discipline for optimal child development* (pp. 11–34). Washington, DC: American Psychological Association Press. doi:10.1037/13948- 002
Baumrind, D. (1966) Effects of authoritative parental control on child behavior. *Child Development*, 37: 887-907. doi:10.2307/1126611
Maccoby, E.E., and Martin, J.A. (1983) Socialization in the context of the family: Parent–child interaction. In E.M. Hetherington (ed.) *Handbook of Child Psychology: Vol. 4. Socialization, personality, and social development* (4th edn, pp. 1–101). New York, NY: Wiley.
76   Baumrind, D., Larzelere, R. and Owens, E. (2010) Effects of Preschool Parents' Power Assertive Patterns and Practices on Adolescent Development. *Parenting: Science and Practice*, 10: 157-201.

life satisfaction.[77] It has also been found to positively influence social competence and social and emotional skills.[78]

Sounds great on paper, but if you were raised with a too permissive or overly punitive parenting style it can be hard to find the middle ground on your own. Most who know that the way they were raised was not ideal tend to sway too much in the opposite direction: children that were raised with too much fear tend to be permissive parents, parents that were raised too permissively or neglected tend to be either too strict or overly involved. It can be hard to find the middle ground alone, yet raising children isn't something that has to be guessed at. We know what works and what doesn't.

Are you more punitive, permissive or uninvolved? Not to fret. Continue reading and this chapter will set you on track for parenting from a Guiding approach.

Different Parenting Styles Under One Roof

Please know that it's not unusual for parents to have different parenting styles. Almost 90% of all of the parents I know and work with struggle with navigating different parenting styles. Sometimes this can occur as a way of balancing each other out. For example, when her husband is too strict with the children, Juna becomes too lenient with the children. Not only is this confusing for children, it can create anxiety and contribute to a negative home atmosphere. What to do about your partner having a different parenting style? Read *Transformational Parenting* together, attend a Transformational Parenting group together, become a part of our online community *together*. The parents that grow together, stay together. One of the primary reasons for divorce is that one person is doing more personal growth than the other and over time, it becomes hard to relate. The same is true for parenting. Take your partner with you on this journey. It will strengthen your marriage as well as your

---

77   Milevsky, A., Schlechter, M. and Netter, S. (2007) Maternal and paternal parenting styles in adolescence: Associations with self-esteem, depression and life satisfaction. *Journal of Child and Family Studies*, 16(1): 39–47.
78   Ren, L. and Pope Edwards, C. (2015) Pathways of influence: Chinese parents' expectations, parenting styles, and child social competence. *Early Child Development and Care*, 185: 616–632.

child's outcomes. What not to do? Nag, boss, tell what to do, share that you know more...use the Transformational Communication skills you'll learn in the rest of this book to encourage your child's father or mother to grow with you. Even if you're divorced, parenting with the same parenting style is one of the best gifts you can ever give to your child.

Divorced Parents / Co-Parenting

For divorced parents, quite often one of the primary causes of family disharmony in the first place is distinctly different parenting styles. Ironically, once divorced, especially if the child is involved in a shared custody arrangement, it becomes even more essential to practice the same parenting style. Children of divorce can tend to side with one parent or another and different parenting styles further alienates one parent. I'm often asked, "How do I get my ex to get onboard with the Guiding Parenting Style?" Unfortunately, the answer is not simple. Parenting is like religion, it's so personal and so tied to a person's level of personal growth that it can stir up a lot of emotional baggage when questioned. If you have a cordial relationship with your ex, the conversation can be more smooth and can center around the developmental benefits of raising children in a Guiding way.

If you are not on good terms with your child's mother/father, it will be much harder. You can start with a heart to heart talk, sharing this book and others like it (see books in Resources section) about the developmental, neurological and psychological advantages of raising a child this way. You can also hire a professional so you have a neutral third party to explain the benefits. Some of the work I am hired to do has to do with getting divorced parents on the same page. Another way to profoundly benefit your child is to get over your discomfort with being in the same room with your ex and attend a Transformational Parenting or Positive Discipline Class together (see Resources section in the back of the book for where to find those groups). The results can be life-changing. Whatever you can do to get on the same page, do it. It's truly one of the most essential gifts you can give your child. And if you're hoping to avoid your child talking about your relational issues in therapy when they are older, or worse yet, repeating your relationship mistakes, by any means, make it work with your ex to parent in the same parenting style.

Parental Authority Questionnaire

Now that you know more or less your own parenting style, it can be helpful to understand what parenting style you were raised with. Often, we become too punitive, permissive or uninvolved because we are afraid of replicating the hurtful parenting that we experienced. Understanding our own style as well as the style we were raised with can help us gain awareness and be more intentional in our parenting. The following questionnaire will help you determine just that. Because the majority of the time it is mothers who are the primary caregivers, this questionnaire is focused on asking you about your mother, but feel free to substitute the term "mother" for whomever was your primary caregiver. Instructions: For each of the following statements,[79] circle the number of the 5-point scale (1 = strongly disagree, 5 = strongly agree) that best describes how that statement applies to you and your mother. Try to read and think about each statement as it applies to you and your mother during your years of growing up at home. There are no right or wrong answers, so don't spend a lot of time on any one item. We are looking for your overall impression regarding each statement. Be sure not to omit any items.

1 = Strongly disagree

2 = Disagree

3 = Neither agree nor disagree

4 = Agree

5 = Strongly agree

---

79   Buri, J.R. (1991) Parental Authority Questionnaire. *Journal of Personality and Social Assessment*, 57: 110–119.

1. While I was growing up my mother felt that in a well-run home the children should have their way in the family as often as the parents do.

1 2 3 4 5

2. Even if her children didn't agree with her, my mother felt that it was for our own good if we were forced to conform to what she thought was right.

1 2 3 4 5

3. Whenever my mother told me to do something as I was growing up, she expected me to do it immediately without asking any questions.

1 2 3 4 5

4. As I was growing up, once family policy had been established, my mother discussed the reasoning behind the policy with the children in the family.

1 2 3 4 5

5. My mother always encouraged verbal give-and-take whenever I felt that family rules and restrictions were unreasonable.

1 2 3 4 5

6. My mother always felt that what her children need is to be free to make up their own minds and to do what they want to do, even if this does not agree with what their parents might want.

1 2 3 4 5

7. As I was growing up my mother did not allow me to question any decision she had made.

1 2 3 4 5

8. As I was growing up my mother directed the activities and decisions of the children in the family through reasoning and discipline.

1 2 3 4 5

9. My mother always felt that more force should be used by parents in order to get their children to behave the way they are supposed to.

1 2 3 4 5

10. As I was growing up my mother did not feel that I needed to obey rules and regulations of behavior simply because someone in authority had established them.

1 2 3 4 5

11. As I was growing up I knew what my mother expected of me in my family, but I also felt free to discuss those expectations with my mother when I felt that they were unreasonable.

1 2 3 4 5

12. My mother felt that wise parents should teach their children early just who is boss in the family.

1 2 3 4 5

13. As I was growing up, my mother seldom gave me expectations and guidelines for my behavior.

1 2 3 4 5

14. Most of the time as I was growing up my mother did what the children in the family wanted when making family decisions.

1 2 3 4 5

15. As the children in my family were growing up, my mother consistently gave us direction and guidance in rational and objective ways.

1 2 3 4 5

16. As I was growing up my mother would get very upset if I tried to disagree with her.   1 2 3 4 5

17. My mother felt that most problems in society would be solved if parents would not restrict their children's activities, decisions, and desires as they are growing up.   1 2 3 4 5

18. As I was growing up my mother let me know what behavior she expected of me, and if I didn't meet those expectations, she punished me.   1 2 3 4 5

19. As I was growing up my mother allowed me to decide most things for myself without a lot of direction from her.   1 2 3 4 5

20. As I was growing up my mother took the children's opinions into consideration when making family decisions, but she would not decide for something simply because the children wanted it.   1 2 3 4 5

21. My mother did not view herself as responsible for directing and guiding my behavior as I was growing up.   1 2 3 4 5

22. My mother had clear standards of behavior for the children in our home as I was growing up, but she was willing to adjust those standards to the needs of each of the individual children in the family.   1 2 3 4 5

23. My mother gave me direction for my behavior and activities as I was growing up and she expected me to follow her direction, but she was always willing to listen to my concerns and to discuss that direction with me.

1 2 3 4 5

24. As I was growing up my mother allowed me to form my own point of view on family matters and she generally allowed me to decide for myself what I was going to do.

1 2 3 4 5

25. My mother always felt that most problems in society would be solved if we could get parents to strictly and forcibly deal with their children when they don't do what they are supposed to as they are growing up.

1 2 3 4 5

26. As I was growing up my mother often told me exactly what she wanted me to do and how she expected me to do it.

1 2 3 4 5

27. As I was growing up my mother gave me clear direction for my behaviors and activities, but she was also understanding when I disagreed with her.

1 2 3 4 5

28. As I was growing up my mother did not direct the behaviors, activities, and desires of the children in the family.

1 2 3 4 5

29. As I was growing up I knew what my mother expected of me in the family and she insisted that I conform to those expectations simply out of respect for her authority.

1 2 3 4 5

30. As I was growing up, if my mother made a decision in the family that hurt me, she was willing to discuss that decision with me and to admit it if she had made a mistake.	1 2 3 4 5

Scoring:

Add questions 1, 6, 10, 13, 14, 17, 19, 21, 24 and 28 to learn if your childhood had a Permissive parenting style.

Add questions 2, 3, 7, 9, 12, 16, 18, 25, 26 and 29 to learn if your childhood had a Punitive parenting style.

Add questions 4, 5, 8, 11, 15, 20, 22, 23, 27, and 30 to learn if your childhood had a Guiding parenting style.

WHY CHILDREN MISBEHAVE

"Every criticism, judgment, diagnosis, and expression of anger is the tragic expression of an unmet need." – Marshall B. Rosenberg

Children act out because they are in distress, not because they are bad people that need punishment. Acting out is a cry for help, a cry for love. When we respond to poor behavior with anger or punishment, it distances us and invalidates the child's feelings, often sending them deeper into the feeling that caused the poor behavior in the first place. One of the biggest myths is that if we don't punish our children that we will spoil them, but we couldn't be further from the truth. Connecting instead of punishing creates emotional intelligence, allows us to help them process their big feelings, and increases their trust and connection.

Poor behavior is an expression of an unmet need. What is an unmet need? I often refer to Maslow's hierarchy of needs when going through my checklist of what my children may need. I start with the physiological needs: 70–80% of the time a poor behavior has to do with being tired or having low blood sugar (being hungry). The rest of the time, it is often related to a need to feel safe or an emotional need not being met.

You don't want children who are obedient all the time. "Yes I do!" you plead, but just like many traps in life, short-term pleasures are full of long-term consequence. In the short term, perfectly obedient and well-mannered children feel great. In the long term, those children grow up to be people pleasers and even with years of therapy have trouble finding their authentic feelings and happiness. Children should be allowed to disagree, argue, and misbehave; they are trying to figure it out, trying to get their needs met, trying to find their way. Misbehavior shows that they are comfortable enough with us to show us their inner pain. Of course, we want to make sure we help them learn a better way to get their needs met, and we can use parenting tools such as Positive Discipline (in this chapter) and Transformational Communication (Chapter 9) to help them learn without having them be afraid of our retaliation or rejection. If we are too rigid then they will begin to lie and sneak. Rules should instead be simple and few. Offer explanations, "You must be so tired to hit your sister in that way." Look to infer their behavior to help them learn emotional intelligence, "Did you hit your sister because you are jealous that she got a candy?"

The goal is to teach them to articulate their feelings instead of acting them out. When children feel heard and listened to, they have no need to act out. Their feelings are accepted and validated.

What an Opportunity!

When a child acts out with us it is an opportunity for us to help them process their unmet need. Of course, in the moment it will not always feel that way. At times you may feel so angry yourself that you will realize that you also have an unmet need. What to do with all of these unmet needs? It's an opportunity to learn together. Accepting your children then helps you accept yourself. Herein lies a beautiful learning opportunity, to teach your children that life is about learning, and that when they feel a negative emotion it is because something was not aligned with who they really are and how to handle it. As you practice how to handle your own negative thoughts and emotions, you can teach your children and model for them along the way. When we teach them this, we can also remind ourselves that, "Between stimulus and response there is a space. In that space is our power to choose our response. In our response lies our growth and our freedom." This quote is believed to have been stated by Victor Frankl, holocaust survivor and psychiatrist. Regardless, it's essential to remember that we have the power to choose our response. Even in the most challenging times, we can choose to react in a manner that is healthy.

Of course, this requires a change of attitude on our part. Our task becomes less focused on controlling external behavior and more focused on letting go of our need to control behavior. It is a place of acceptance instead of a place of judgement. Have you ever had the experience of being upset, telling a friend about your problem and them telling you what to do instead of comforting you? It doesn't feel great and we do this to children all the time. We are so uncomfortable seeing them upset that we want to fix it right away. When they are sad, we feel responsible and sometimes even resentful. Our thinking may go something like this, "What does he have to be sad about? I took the day off of work. We just spent the day at the park and I just bought him ice cream...now he is crying?"

Big Emotions Are an Opportunity for Growth

Instead of viewing big emotions such as crying, temper tantrums, becoming angry easily, and anger outbursts as something inherently wrong or that needs to be "fixed," the interpretation can shift into a learning opportunity. Through interpersonal neurobiology, we can understand these meltdowns from a neurological perspective. It informs our parenting practices significantly. For example, we know that most young children have not yet learned defense mechanisms to suppress their feelings. The temper tantrums and meltdowns that children express are in fact the way we often feel inside also, but as adults, we have become experts at suppressing or denying emotions.

What happens when emotions are denied? When emotions are denied, there is a consequence. From living in denial or living an inauthentic life, to feeling lack of pleasure or connection to others, denying our emotions is chock full of negative results. Other consequences that result in denying emotions include addictions such as being "busy," overeating, overspending, and generally dissociating from our body. Sometimes we unconsciously create situations to replicate what needs to be healed from our childhood.

Therefore, one of the most powerful gifts we can give our children is to accept them in all of their manifestations: the pleasant and unpleasant. We need to learn to allow them to be in pain. Don't teach them your patterns of minimization or denial, stay present with them, and the emotion will run its course and resolve itself. When we try to thwart the course of emotions and control them, we confuse our biological responses to stress and our yearning for authenticity with mind-games to hide from big feelings.

But it's so hard to see our children in pain! When they experience rejection, or a scraped knee, or a tearful outburst, we yearn to comfort them, as much for them as for ourselves. It hurts us to see them in pain. "Don't cry," "Don't be angry," and "It's ok" are well-meaning communications, but have a disastrous result. We are, in essence, telling them that how they feel is invalid. This unintentionally teaches them that uncomfortable feelings are not allowed. Instead, the best thing we can say is, "I'm here for you."

This avoidance of pain is understandable, it's in the air we breathe. As a society, we have a hard time allowing pain. We medicate fevers, which, within limits, are beneficial and meant to resolve themselves. We over-prescribe painkillers. We are so afraid of pain that we have become addicted to shopping, food, drugs, and being busy in order to distract ourselves from it. But pain does not go away when avoided or masked. The only way to process pain or uncomfortable feelings is to sit with the pain. The only way through pain is to go into it. To allow it to be, to teach us what it is we need to shift, to change – not to ignore it. And pain can increase pleasure. Without pain, we wouldn't recognize happiness. And when you have pain, you can experience a relief from pain and greater appreciation for what you have.

Often, when a child has a tantrum or acts out in anger, it is leftover from a previous time when they did not fully express their emotion. My son has learned this well and explains to me when he's upset, "I'm getting my sadness out." The emotions do not disappear with time.

Emotions stay with us until we release them, either intentionally or unintentionally. When emotions are pent up, they can lead to outbursts in children as well as adults.

The True Meaning of Discipline

When you hear "discipline," do you think "punishment?" Most people do... the meaning has been altered from its original form. The true meaning of discipline is "to learn" or "to teach" which came from the Latin *disciplina*. We know that teaching children *why* behaving positively is important is better than teaching that if they don't behave something negative will occur.

The traditional view of discipline is that our children behave because they learn to be scared of us. This creates not only disruption in the parent-child relationship, but emotional pain. We don't have to teach them to be scared of us in order to behave. One of the major problems with using punishment as discipline is that children learn external motivation (to behave through fear of being punished) instead of internal motivation (to behave because they are motivated to behave). You see, punishment robs children of critical thinking – they comply to our wishes out of fear instead of understanding the reasons why positive behavior is important. In my work with helping adults process their childhood, I've heard "My parents called it discipline, but I now know it was abuse" so many times. Traditional discipline risks our children feeling as though they have been abused. When we are overly tired and our children are afraid of us, our yelling out of exasperation can be interpreted as abusive. In many countries, spanking is illegal and considered abusive. Why risk our children experiencing discipline as abuse when there are better ways of promoting positive behavior?

The trouble is that punishment works (so does bribery) but only in the short-term. When children are raised with punishment, when they come of age to begin to question the behavior of their parents (often just before the teen years), they no longer will tolerate threats and will respond with extra rebellion and defiance. However, when children are raised with internal motivation and critical thinking, the teenage years are much less rocky for everyone and the parent-child relationship endures successfully.

Another issue with punishment is that when we are in a state of anger, we are likely to botch the discipline process, and punish more than we intended. This is often where yelling comes in. I've met with so many parents whose primary parenting goal is to stop yelling, yet when punishment continues to be used, this goal is almost impossible. The truth is that we can only respond to our children (or anyone for that matter) appropriately when we are in a neutral state. As parents, it is our obligation to not become triggered by our children no matter what they did to provoke us.

So, what should I do, you ask? I find that the simplest solutions are the most helpful. When deciding on discipline, ask yourself this: "Will what I say increase or decrease the connection with my child?" If it lessens your connection with your child, don't do it. The first rule of raising children consciously is to prioritize the relationship. Positive behavior is the result of a positive relationship.

Often, there is a misperception that relationship-based parenting means permissive parents who never say "no" to their kids. In fact, the kind of relationship we are going for is a balanced, honest, loving and safe relationship, not an unhealthy relationship. Funny enough, this parent-child relationship that psychologists have found to develop incredible children also happens to look a lot like the relationship that psychologists have found makes the best marriages. Ideally, the relationship we want to have with our children is much like the relationships we want to have in our life in general. These relationships are based on authenticity, feel inherently safe, allow for mistakes and are mostly drama-free. These relationships have love at their core and don't need manipulation. These relationships allow us to be our best selves. The same is true for parent-child relationships.

The Myth of Punishment
When we punish our children, yell at them, spank them, scold them, shame them, or lecture them, it creates fear, not learning. The brain

gets flooded with stress hormones and cannot process our attempts at teaching. In times of intense negative emotion, it can be best to wait at least a few hours after our child misbehaves to teach them how not to. When humans are scared, they cannot learn! "Tough love" creates fear, distance and resentment. In teens, parents often use the idea of "tough love" thinking that they should "know better" by now. But teens need our connection more than ever. It's hard enough to connect with teens, and when we use "tough love" with them it creates isolation from who they need to rely on the most: their parents.

But What About Rewards?

The problem with rewards is they don't help children learn to be responsible, because the parent is the one doing the monitoring. Rewards take away a child's potential for feeling good about their accomplishments and their ability to feel capable. Instead of teaching children how good it feels to behave considerately to others and to achieve on their own, rewards teach children to focus on "What's in it for me?" Rewards rarely produce lasting changes in behavior. When the rewards stop, children often go back to behaving the same way they did before the reward. Research has also shown that children whose parents make frequent use of rewards tend to be less generous than their peers.[80]

Rewards also produce less quality work. People expecting to receive a reward for completing a task (or for doing it successfully) simply do not perform as well as those who expect nothing.[81]

Alfie Kohn has been researching this predicament for decades. His essay, *The Risks of Rewards*[82] explains "There are several plausible expla-

80   Fabes, R.A., Fultz, J., Eisenberg, N., May-Plumlee, T. and Christopher, F.S. (1989) Effects of rewards on children's prosocial motivation: A socialization study. *Developmental Psychology*, 25(4, Jul): 509–515; EJ 396 958.
Grusec, J.E. (1991) Socializing concern for others in the home. *Developmental Psychology*, 27(2, Mar): 338–342; EJ 431 672.
Kohn, A. (1990) *The Brighter Side of Human Nature: Altruism and empathy in everyday life.* New York, NY: Basic Books.
81   Kohn, A. (1993) *Punished by Rewards: The trouble with gold stars, incentive plans, As, praise, and other bribes.* Boston: Houghton Mifflin.
82   Kohn, A. (1994) *The Risks of Rewards.* Urbana, IL :ERIC Clearinghouse on Elementary and Early Childhood Education, University of Illinois.

nations for this puzzling but remarkably consistent finding. The most compelling of these is that *rewards cause people to lose interest in whatever they were rewarded for doing.* This phenomenon, has been demonstrated in scores of studies."[83]

One of the reasons why I feel that even the most connected parents and teachers end up rewarding their children and students is because rewards make us feel good. It's kind of like giving ice cream to a child. It makes you feel good to share it with them, even though you know it's bad for them.

The Myth of Being Permissive

Just as parenting with threats and punishments can be harmful, likewise, parenting with few rules or guidelines can also be scarring. A child is taught that relationships have no boundaries and that love means you can do what you want to do without regard for others. I began my parenting journey on the too permissive side. Just like every parenting cliché, the pendulum was swinging to the opposite of what happened to me. In the beginning, I avoided saying "no" when my daughter was a small child at all costs. When she would ask for more candy, I would offer her a fruit. When she would ask for a toy, I would distract her with a bird outside the toy store. Looking back, I can see this was just a form of fear of conflict that was completely unconscious. I was going for the balanced, kind and firm, Guided, way of discipline but my subconscious fears kept interfering. In my childhood, it was not safe to disagree and so my permissiveness with her was a form of avoiding a feeling I had not yet learned to resolve. What a gift she gave me. I was able to see that my fear of conflict was teaching her to avoid conflict. By the time her brother came around four years later she had taught me to be comfortable saying "no" and I finally was able to update my programming away from what worked for me as a child (to avoid conflict) to a healthier relationship (to be direct in communication). I don't just say "no." I like to give an explanation following my "no" which helps her to develop critical thinking and helps me to communicate my respect

---

83 Kohn, A. (1993) *Punished By Rewards: The trouble with gold stars, incentive plans, As, praise, and other bribes.* Boston: Houghton Mifflin.

(more on that when I share about Positive Discipline). If I hadn't been open to that lesson, my daughter may have grown up in a passive state, accepting what was given to her instead of communicating her needs directly. So you see that being too permissive can create future suffering.

WHAT TO DO ABOUT MISBEHAVIOR

The first resource to handle misbehavior is to prevent it. One of the best ways to prevent misbehavior and to make your children feel special is to spend quality time together. It's so powerful that if I had to pick only one tool for parents to learn I would teach this. If you remember anything about how to handle misbehavior, remember this: the amount of quality time you spend with your child is directly related to their positive behavior. In other words, the less quality time you spend, the worse their behavior. The more quality time you spend, the better they behave.

It's hard being a parent, right? You're busy, exhausted and your child is acting poorly! Poor behavior means you need to spend more quality time with them...but how? When you feel as though you don't even have a moment for yourself and now your children need more of you, it can feel overwhelming. Good news: a little goes a long way. There are so, so many parallels to parenting and marriage that I can't help but compare the two. The more quality time you spend with your spouse, even just for 10 minutes a day, the fewer marital problems you will have.

What children (and most marriages) need is to know what to expect. Plan on spending regular time with each child individually and be sure to communicate when that will happen and then follow through. How much and when is different for every child. As long as it's regular, it will have a positive effect. I usually start with 20 minutes per day. A regular time is essential. It's especially empowering for children if they can choose the activity you will do together. You may want to offer a couple of suggestions and let your child choose from what you suggest or even let them make a list of all of the things they want to do with you. Make sure your phone is off during your time together. As tempting as it is, do not check your phone during your special time with them. My daughter is almost 14, and my son almost 10 and they both still cherish our special time together. I don't think anyone is ever too old to appreciate receiving one to one attention from someone they love.

Many parenting books make the mistake of describing the philosophy but not giving enough tools to actually implement it. So, I want to be sure to share with you one of my favorite set of tools: Jane Nelsen's Positive Discipline,[84] based off of Adlerian psychology which views child misbehavior as a discouraged child. One of my favorite Positive Discipline tools is to remember the simple mantra of being kind and firm, the basis for a Guiding parenting style. But when we are triggered, we often revert to the parenting styles of our childhood or our anger or guilt influences our communication with our children. When we are angry, we tend to overreact and yell or spank. Or the effects of guilt might lead us to be too permissive. We may have guilt about not being around our children more or for not being able to provide them the life we wish we could provide them with. More often than not, parents fall into punitive or permissive parenting patterns when we are trying to not replicate what our parents did to us, and we swing too far in the opposite direction. Positive Discipline provides an easy solution: respond with "I love you and the answer is no." It's a kind but firm response to testing boundaries.

There are a thousand different ways to be kind but firm in your discipline communication. Here are a few examples:

- I know you don't want to clean your room and we can do it together.
- I can see how much you want another cookie but it is bad for you.
- It is bedtime. I do love snuggling and reading to you, but it is now time for sleep.

84   Nelsen, J. (2006) *Positive Discipline: The classic guide to helping children develop self-discipline, responsibility, cooperation, and problem-solving skills.* New York, NY: Random House, Inc.

Many parents ask, why not just say no? Well, in response I ask, if your friend asks you a question to which your answer is no, do you just say no? For example, if a friend asks you to go to a movie with them, do you say "no" or give a reason why? Giving a reason why doesn't mean you have to explain yourself, it gives your children a chance to learn about your decision process so they can grow their own decision making skills, and hopefully when they are away from you, will make healthy decisions. It also shows that you respect them enough to explain. It does not mean that they will always agree or be satisfied with your decision, though. Be prepared for attempts at negotiation, begging and cajoling. Stay firm and stay kind.

Here's a tool I teach parents and also use with my own children when I need some guidance about exactly how to be firm and kind. The acronym is VLEO and stands for Validate, Limit, Explain, Option. If you do it in that order you'll be able to connect with your child, teach them emotional intelligence, be firm and kind and also teach them critical thinking skills. With the exception of infants, a child is never too young to be spoken to this way. In fact, it will also work in all of your other relationships. It's just a good way to communicate with others. I teach the same skill when I work with couples in couples therapy.

Step 1: Validate Feelings

This is one of the first communication tools that we learn as therapists. For children, teens and adults alike, when people come to you with an issue or something they are upset about, there are some rules:

1. Don't try to fix.
2. Don't distract.
3. Don't minimize.
4. Don't make it about you.
5. Don't feel sorry for the person.

But instead of remembering all of the don'ts, just remember to validate and listen. What do I mean by validating? Acknowledge the feeling. Here are some examples:

"That must have been hard."

"I can see you're really upset/sad/angry."

"I can imagine you may feel upset/sad/angry."

It's hard to watch our children suffer and not rescue them from their suffering. However, when we do, we rob them of the opportunity to learn to understand their feelings and create solutions that are empowering to them instead of being reliant on us.

It's also hard to allow our children to have their feelings because we often weren't allowed to have ours. When we were young, we were given the message that our feelings weren't allowed to be felt. When we got hurt, we were told, "You're ok." When we had a problem at school, we were told what to do. When we had tears we were told to "Stop crying." Most people still struggle with identifying even how they feel, let alone the steps they need to take to resolve the problem for the future.

Often you will need to validate and still be firm. "I see that you are upset and you still need to…."

Step 2: Limit

Here is where you set the limit, remind them of the family rule/guideline. For those of us that err on the side of being too permissive, it is also a good opportunity to remind ourselves of the limit. Here are some examples:

"…and we don't hit others."

"…but we only play video games on Saturday."

"…but our family rule is to finish our homework first."

"…and we don't tease people in our family."

Step 3: Explain

The explanation step provides critical thinking skills and helps our children comprehend why we have that limit. For those that swing a bit toward punitive parenting, this step helps release that fear-based motivation and shows our children that understanding why is important so they don't grow up too submissive, or too rebellious when they become tired of being submissive.

Here are some examples:

"…because we are kind."

"...because our bodies need to eat healthy to grow strong."

"...because we respect our teacher."

"...because there are better ways of showing that we are upset."

Step 4: Option

Offering an option is helpful. Just as you would when you're talking to an upset friend. Offering an option shows you care and offers your child a way out of their stuck feeling.

Here are some examples:

"...why don't we go read a book together?"

"...why don't we plan on a day you can stay up late?"

"...would you like to snuggle?"

"...would you like to find a day in the calendar when we can come back?"

"...how about we brainstorm how you can earn money to save up for that toy?"

One of the most helpful ways we can prepare ourselves for not swinging too far towards the permissive or punitive styles is to prepare in advance our responses to common issues. In my parenting workshops, I ask parents to write common issues on index cards, then on the reverse side to come up with kind and firm responses. Take a minute to write in your own in the table provided. Some more examples have been given.

Common issue	Validate, Limit, Explain, Option (VLEO)
Too much tv / phone / video games	Together come up with guidelines around media. Times that media is / is not allowed. Together decide on consequence if media guidelines are not met
Whining for a different outcome (staying up late, more dessert, etc.)	"I hear that you want to stay up late (validate), but it's not good for you to miss sleep (limit and explain). How about you pick a weekend day to stay up late (option)?

Common issue	Validate, Limit, Explain, Option (VLEO)
Hitting sibling	I see that you're upset (validate) but we don't hit others (limit). Would you like for me to come with you to your room and you can tell me what happened (option)?
Not waking up for school	It's hard to wake up in the morning, I understand (validate)! We can't be late for school (limit) as it shows disrespect to your teacher (explain). Would you like for me to help you come up with solutions (option)?

How to Prevent Problems and Handle an Ongoing Issue

An ongoing issue is a sign of a problem in the family system and should be addressed as a family. One simple and even fun way to handle ongoing issues is by implementing regular Family Meetings. Family Meetings are a tool used in Positive Discipline and I've found them to be extraordinarily effective at resolving issues, creating positive feelings and simply sharing in a balanced way. During a Family Meeting, parents let their children help solve problems that come up. As all members of the family help to brainstorm solutions, it becomes less about blame and more about "How can we resolve this?" During a Family Meeting, each person's perspective is relevant so even the youngest and most quiet child feels heard. It incorporates elements of gratitude, respect, relationship, and deep listening, with some fun sprinkled in. Family Meetings are a game-changer for families and extremely effective in improving behavior, relationships and children's confidence.

When you do weekly Family Meetings, you create a tradition of compassion, listening, democratic problem solving and an essential time to express feelings. Kids love Family Meetings because it allows them to be heard and have a voice in the functioning of the family. So much misbehavior is related to kids needing more attention or needing to feel more power – Family Meetings address these spot on. Enjoy! My kids love the Family Meeting time and look forward to it; my 9 year old says "it's cool" and my daughter says, "I feel good knowing we can work things out without getting into trouble." I've guided many families toward this practice and nearly all of the families that use it really love it. It's great for large or small families, even families with only one child. It's an opportunity to be seen as an equal and to participate in the decision-making. What's not to love about appreciating each other, getting buy-in from your kids on good behavior and having a family activity together? The outline format here is derived from Jane Nelsen's "Positive Discipline"[85] and is an incredible tool.

I recommend doing Family Meeting once a week. It can be fun to keep a family album of Family Meetings. The Transformational Parenting online course (www.TransformationalParenting.co) has Family Meeting templates you can print out and complete at your meetings to help you remember the steps and keep track of the progress your family is making.

How to Run a Family Meeting

1. Start with Compliments. Go around in a circle and allow everyone to share what they are thankful for or what they appreciate. You can model this by going first. Often, it's helpful to provide a sentence structure when learning. For example, "Thank you for the _____ (trees, sun, dinner, new jacket, etc.). This sets the mood as positive and gives the opportunity for everyone to connect and be reminded of how they are loved.

2. The next step is Brainstorming for Solutions. Explain to your children that brainstorming is when we think of as many ideas as we can to solve a problem. They can be practical or wild and crazy. After we have had fun brainstorming (with no discussion), we will choose one solution that we all agree on and try it for a week. Choose a problem from the agenda and practice brainstorming. Once your family has made a list, go around and ask your children to cross off anything that won't work. Share the importance of creating a solution everyone can agree

---

85 Nelsen, J. (2006) *Positive discipline*. New York, NY: Ballantine Books.

on. Try it for a week. If it needs revisiting, put it on the agenda again and come back to it.

3. After Brainstorming, you can Plan: share about what's going on in the next week so kids can know what to expect. Another helpful addition in promoting a positive attitude is to ask everyone what they are looking forward to for the upcoming week.

4. Last, but not least is the Fun Family Activity. NEVER skip this, as tempting as it can be with busy schedules. This is the relationship bonding piece that the kids love the most. Let the kids choose an activity you can do for 5–15 minutes together as a family. Some suggestions include charades, family art, card games, guessing games, dominoes, board games, puzzles, Simon says, etc.

Helpful tips:

• Family Meetings are best run during mealtimes because it's one of the rare occasions where everyone is sitting together. Choose a day when all members of your family household are likely to sit for a meal together. Stick to the same day every week and even if you are traveling, home late, or it's a holiday, hold the Family Meeting. The consistency and structure are regulating for children and they feel more secure when they understand what to expect.

• Make sure no one interrupts each other. In indigenous cultures, a talking stick is often used to give a visual aid for whose turn it is to speak and who will listen. You may find it helpful to use an object that gets passed as well. When someone is talking, they hold the meaningful object and no one else talks. It's time for deep listening for the others. When that person is finished, they can pass the object to the next person and they have a turn to share.

• You can print copies of the Family Meeting Template online at www.TransformationalParenting.co. Use one per week. Tape it on the refrigerator, low enough so your kids can reach it. Explain to your kids that when they have a problem or something that's bothering them they can write or draw it on the agenda. Many families like to keep their Family Meeting Agendas as a record of their progress. It can make kids very proud to see, for example, that they used to have frequent sibling squabbles that have been nearly eliminated.

- When it's time for your Family Meeting, take the Agenda and use it to help you remember the steps. If there are no Agenda items (problems / issues to be addressed), you can ask the family during the meeting and write them down in the grey box.

Consequences

It's important not to confuse consequences with punishment. Consequences are decided on jointly and the child has a say in what he or she accepts as a consequence. Consequences are decided on in advance during a Family Meeting or in a conversation. For example, the conversation may go something like this:

The parent, child who hit, and his sister all sit down together.

Parent: "Johnny, this morning you hit your sister Sophia. Let's decide what would be a good consequence to make sure that does not happen again."

Johnny: "I won't hit her again."

Parent: "That would be great, but in case it does happen again, what would be a good consequence?"

Johnny: "To have to clean my room."

Parent: "Well, you have to clean your room anyway. Can you think of something else?"

Sophia: "He should have to give me $5."

Johnny: "That's not fair."

Parent: "What would be fair?"

Johnny: "I guess $3 but it won't happen again."

Parent: "Does that work for you?" (asking the sister)

Sophia: "Yes."

Parent: "Ok, then, we are all deciding that if Johnny hits Sophia again he will give her $3. Sound good?"

Sophia and Johnny: "Yes."

Parent: "OK, great! Let's all high five on it!"

Then, the next time Johnny hits Sophia:

Parent: "You must've been really upset to hit your sister. Do you remember what we discussed as a consequence?"

Johnny: "No."

Parent: "You were to give Sophia $3."

Johnny: "Ok, I guess."

Parent: "Do you want to talk about what upset you and how you can handle it better next time?"

Johnny: "No."

Parent waits a few hours and then asks to talk to Johnny again, gives Johnny alternatives to hitting.

A punishment, on the other hand, is based in the power of the parent and is given on the spot. Here is an example of a punishment:

Johnny hits his sister Sophia

Parent: "Don't hit your sister!"

Johnny: "But she said I was ugly!"

Parent: "Go to your room now or else you won't have dessert tonight."

Johnny: Stomps out of the room angrily "FINE!"

Johnny sits in his room alone and angry for an hour resenting both his sister and his mother. Deciding on a consequence with your child is essential as when the time comes to enforce the consequence, it will not be seen as a scar in your relationship but instead as something you agreed upon together.

When your child has a behavior that you do not want to occur, take a deep breath to make sure your emotions don't get in the way of your communication. It is important that you are not angry or raising your voice otherwise your child will receive fear instead of learning not to repeat the behavior. Calmly explain, "We do not do that. Let's talk about how to make sure that doesn't happen again. Would you like to talk now or later?" The child may be flooded with stress hormones in which case discussing the incident on the spot will not be helpful as she or he will not be able to learn.

You need to make sure that once you decide in advance what will happen that you follow through. This provides children with structure so they know what to expect. My children used to fight in the car all the time. We live in the Los Angeles area and there is often gridlock traffic where we end up in the car for longer than we'd like to. When they were 3 and 7, I made a rule that if they fight I will pull over. Even in the middle of traffic I would calmly pull over (calmly is the key!) and bring out my phone while parked. "Tell me when you're ready," I would tell them. "But MOM!" They would shout. "It's HIS fault! It's HER fault, etc." I just replied, "No worries, guys, just work it out and let me know when you're ready." They figured it out pretty quickly and it gave them great practice at resolving their arguments and letting things go. Once, I was assigned to be a driver on a field trip for my daughter's 3rd grade class. I had five kids in my car and two of them started to argue and yell at each other. I pulled over and stopped the car, while I calmly started to look at my phone. "Why are we stopping?!" asked one of the boys. My daughter explained our rule and told them they had to resolve it before I would drive again. It took about five minutes but they resolved it and the drive back was peaceful.

PARENTING TOOLS FOR COMMON ISSUES

Problem: Siblings fight.

Solution: Tell them to figure it out by themselves and come back with a plan… if they can't do that then you can help them brainstorm.

Problem: Child is addicted to social media, video games or television.

Solution: Set time limits on when screens can be used. Decide together as a family during your Family Meeting what limits are right for your family. For my family, we reserve screen time to Friday afternoons and weekends except for special occasions.

Problem: Your child misbehaves.

Solution: Instead of wondering what punishment to use that will work, instead wonder, "What solution will solve the problem?"

Focus on solutions, stay away from blame, guilt or shaming which only teaches them to disconnect and doesn't help them learn solutions for the future. Instead, ask your child to help brainstorm solutions. Ideally, you'll want your child to be the primary contributor. Once you and your child have come up with a solution, pick one that works for everyone. Give it a week. If it doesn't work after a week, you can brainstorm again and try another solution that you and your child agree to.

THE ROOTS OF VIOLENCE

Imagine for a moment that someone more than twice your size, a giant, yells at you and then hits or spanks you. Not only can you not defend yourself, but you are not allowed to become angry. This giant is your only source of survival, for food, shelter and even love. Sometimes this giant gets angry at you and you are not sure why. You live in fear of being hurt by this giant or losing the love of this giant on whom your survival depends. Because we so badly need the giant to love us, we love the giant no matter how the giant hurts us. When we are hurt physically or emotionally, we learn to blame ourselves instead of the giant. This is what we are to children: we are the giant.

When children live in such a state, their anger turns inward but does not go away. Sometimes the anger gets inflicted on siblings, sometimes on school mates, and often the anger stays in their psyche and becomes a part of them. The brain knows no time. When we are hit, spanked, shamed, yelled at, pinched, tickled too much, touched inappropriately, or made to feel small this feeling of anxiety and can stay with us our entire lives until it is made safe to release. Time alone does not heal these wounds. Left untreated, they turn into inner violence (low self esteem, overeating, undereating, drugs, suicide, etc.) or external violence (teasing others, the need to have power over others, domestic violence, cutting and self-harm, yelling, belittling, suicide, fighting, war, etc.).

Yes, the way we are treated as children has a profound effect on the likelihood of war.

In addition, how much we are held and touched has an effect on violence, especially in the first three years. In order to mitigate stress, children (and adults) need touch and affection throughout their lives in order to tame the neurological tidal wave of stress hormones that arises when we are in fear.

Make no mistake about it: the roots of violence are known. We know that violence is learned; we are not born violent. Many of us were spanked/beaten in our childhood and unless we understand the consequences of continued violence and the reasons why violence continues, we will continue to live in a violent world. "As beaten children are not allowed to defend themselves, they must suppress their anger and rage against their parents who have humiliated them, killed their inborn empathy, and insulted their dignity. They will take out this rage later, as adults, on scapegoats, mostly on their own children. Deprived of empathy, some of them will direct their anger against themselves (in eating disorders, drug addiction, depression etc.), or against other adults (in wars, terrorism, delinquency etc.)" explains Alice Miller, renowned psychologist.[86]

We learn to live in denial of the suffering we experienced as children. Every spanking, put down, manipulation, or shaming appears to have less and less of an effect, but that is because it is internatized and denied. We must survive so we put it away. We cannot live in a vulnerable state so we must tell ourselves that we weren't devastated when we were shamed by our mother at the dinner table, tell ourselves that we don't live in fear of a spanking or whooping by our father or mother…. Just as they tell us, "I do this because I love you" we perpetuate the violence onto our children believing this is the only way. Denial is a dangerous drug and if left unchecked, can perpetuate systems of injustice and inequity as people with power (parents) perpetuate abuse of those without (children). In other words, if we don't look inward to realize the pain of our childhood we will reflect this pain onto our children.

---

86 Shafranske, E.P. (1992) The betrayal of the child: The contributions of Alice Miller. *Psychotherapy Patient*, 8(3-4): 27-40.

Alice Miller calls this denial "emotional blindness." She writes of the possibility of freeing ourselves from this emotional blindness:[87]

> ...by daring to feel our repressed emotions, including our fear and forbidden rage against our parents who had often scared us to death for periods of many years, which should have been the most beautiful years of our lives. We can't retrieve those years. But thanks to facing our truth we can transform ourselves from the children who still live in us full of fear and denial into responsible, well informed adults who regained their empathy, so early stolen from them. By becoming feeling persons we can no longer deny that beating children is a criminal act that should be forbidden on the whole planet.

WHAT ABOUT SPANKING?

It takes a paradigm shift to not do what your parents did to you. I was spanked and no, it didn't make me mentally ill (that I know of) but it did make me afraid of my parents as a little child and I'm sad I felt that way toward them at the tenderest of ages…. When I was in graduate school learning about the emotional and neurological development of the child I learned some about the consequences of spanking. I was working with children at the time so I did some more research and I became aware of how damaging spanking is. It's also much easier NOT to spank and much more fun to enjoy our kids rather than have them be afraid of us.

But it's not always that simple. In some cultures and communities parents feel they must spank their children because disobedient children get shot or put in jail. I worked for almost a decade in South Los Angeles. I was the only Caucasian employee in a 200 person organization. I wrote grants, trained staff and graduate students, taught parenting classes, did counseling with kids and their parents. I loved working there. My heart is still in South LA. What I learned when I was there is enough for another book. One of my biggest lessons came when I was teaching parenting. I had strong relationships with these beautiful parents and

---

87   Miller, A. *The Roots of Violence are NOT Unknown.* Retrieved from https://www.alice-miller.com/en/the-roots-of-violence-are-not-unknown/

their children but when it came to trying to teach them alternatives to spanking, they refused to hear what I had to say. You don't understand, they would plead, "If Jamal acts out when he is a teenager, he may get shot, either by a gang or by the police." I understood as best as I could through my lens of white privilege, but it was, and is so hard to see that cycle perpetuated. Many Caucasian parents I know also spank their kids. It's not an issue of color, it's an issue of fear.

The American Psychological Association published an article stating that "Many studies have shown that physical punishment – including spanking, hitting and other means of causing pain – can lead to increased aggression, antisocial behavior, physical injury and mental health problems for children."[88] Yet spanking remains controversial – perhaps we are in denial about what happened to us. Perhaps people have forgotten how it feels to have pain inflicted upon them by someone they love and trust. Perhaps people are afraid of remembering their own suffering out of feeling ungrateful for their parents' sacrifice. Perhaps parents are afraid that if they don't spank their children that they will grow up to be disrespectful adults. Perhaps families living in unsafe environments feel they need to create a climate of fear for obedience to protect their children from the unsafe environments they are living in. Whatever the reasons, we know there are better ways.

Spanking doesn't work, says Alan Kazdin, PhD, a Yale University psychology professor and director of the Yale Parenting Center and Child Conduct Clinic. "You cannot punish out these behaviors that you do not want," says Kazdin, who served as APA president in 2008. "There is no need for corporal punishment based on the research. We are not giving up an effective technique. We are saying this is a horrible thing that does not work."[89]

In the midst of procrastinating on Facebook I came across a "To spank or not to spank" post. It was on fire with strong opinions and a lot of shaming and judgements.

Here is one of the posts that Elle Lowe from Washington wrote and gave me permission to share:

---

88 Smith, B.L. (2012) The case against spanking. *APA Monitor*, 43, (4): 60.
89 Smith, B.L. (2012) The case against spanking. *APA Monitor*, 43 (4): 60.

A week ago my two elderly Filipino aunts met my baby for the first time and started talking about their grandkids and how they flick the kids hard on the mouth when they're being bad and they were laughing and saying how scared the kids are of them, that even just making the motion makes them run off and / or start acting right. I do not want my kid to be afraid of me. I remember being afraid of my mom. I kept secrets and flinched whenever she got close when she was upset with me. I won't be a perfect parent. And maybe I may break in anger but I hope I don't. I want a different relationship with my kid than my family's relationships with their kids. Time to break the cycle. I want my kid to find other ways of solving conflicts and learn how to deal with his emotions.

Just last month, when I was picking up my son from childcare, I watched a parent ask his son to come with him. The 11 year old was in the middle of a craft project so he pleaded with his father, "just five more minutes?" "No," stated his father, "it's time to go." In defiance, the son didn't budge and kept on with his project. His father then pinched his son's side, "time to go," he said. His father did this in front of me, knowing I'm a parent educator, and also in front of the teacher. I wondered what must be going on with this father and whether he regularly uses this pinching technique. The son was sent the message to respond immediately to his father's requests or else. It made me sad to watch and I could see that the pinch was meant to hurt. It made me sad not only for the boy but also for the father. I could see the unnecessary distancing and distrust that occurred for the son, and some anger too. I could have provided the father with many different options that didn't include hurting his son and hurting the relationship. Often, when parents complain to me about their defiant teens I notice that the teens who are the most defiant have been taught to fear their parents when they are young and the relationship is now broken by the time they are teens. Often, it's very hard and sometimes impossible to repair the years of threatening and hurting. I can't help but wonder how their teen would act if they had been motivated by internal motivation for goodness rather than by fear of punishment.

Now, in 2019, 196 countries around the world have joined the United Nations and have banned spanking. The United Nations Committee on the Rights of the Child issued a directive in 2006 calling physical punishment "legalized violence against children" that should be eliminated in all settings through "legislative, administrative, social and educational measures."[90]

So the next time you are thinking of spanking your child, give yourself a couple of deep breaths and consider the evidence. More importantly, consider your child.

LEAVE THE TIME-OUTS TO ADULTS

"Everything that irritates us about others can lead us to an understanding of ourselves." – Carl Jung

When you are feeling angry, frustrated, overwhelmed, overburdened, or upset in any way when you are with your children, give yourself a time-out instead of giving your child one. Save discipline for when you are calm. We tend to over discipline or under discipline when we are upset. You can use the minutes alone to think about why you are triggered: what emotion are you feeling? When else did you feel that emotion? Or if your mind is not calm enough to think, it can be helpful just to check out for some moments. My favorite time-out place is the bathroom; it has a lock and I can sit and take some breaths.

Dan Siegel states, "So what about time-outs? In most cases, the primary experience a time-out offers a child is isolation. Even when presented in a patient and loving manner, time-outs teach them that when they make a mistake, or when they are having a hard time, they will be forced to be by themselves – a lesson that is often experienced, particularly by young children, as rejection. Further, it communicates to kids, 'I'm only interested in being with you and being there for you when you've got it all together.'[91]

---

90   Retrieved from www.ohchr.org
91   Retrieved from http://time.com/3404701/discipline-time-out-is-not-good/

It's important that you model to your children your full range of emotions, that you are allowed to feel them and, most importantly, that you model not taking your negative emotions out on them. In doing so, it is the most effective way to teach your children to process their own emotions without outpouring them on you.

Instead of time-outs for children, which we know are ineffective long-term and create behavior that's motivated by fear instead of authentic connection, I encourage you to use the model of time-out for yourself when you need it. It is important to remember not to shame your child with communications such as, "Because of your behavior, I need a time-out." Just simply state "Mom/Dad is going to take a moment, I'll be back in a few minutes."

When we find ourselves upset with our children, it's important for us to ask ourselves, why am I really upset? When we become upset by a small misbehavior, it's a sign that we have unresolved emotions. The funny thing about emotions is that they will not go away on their own. Remember: time itself does not heal. Emotions will keep surfacing for years and years until we can process through them and let them go. Unresolved emotions have no timeline, and can be buried from our childhood. Until we can process through our emotions, we will inevitably become upset by someone or something else, regardless of our children.

Although it may feel like our children are intentionally pushing our buttons, the triggering of emotions isn't personal. Our children do not cause or contribute to our negative emotional state. We have a negative emotional state because we have unresolved emotions. However, it is a great opportunity to know that we have not yet resolved something that needs resolving. I think people choose to ignore when emotions rise unexpectedly because they are not sure how to resolve them. Not to worry, just by reading *Transformational Parenting*, you are already raising your consciousness. Just by being aware of the fact that an overreaction is likely due to unresolved emotions, your consciousness will work on the unresolved emotions. In addition the sections near the end of this book "Now What" and "Resources" include further reading and suggestions on how to start or join a Transformational Parenting group in your neighborhood or online.

What to Do When You Yell or React Negatively to Your Child

If you were unable to put yourself in a parent time-out and ended up yelling or scaring your children, it's important to admit you made a mistake. Showing we made a mistake teaches our children that it's okay to make mistakes and also teaches them forgiveness. There are four steps to a perfect apology:

1. Get down to your child's level, make eye contact.
2. Ask for a hug (if you and your child are comforted by hugging).
3. Apologize, admit to your mistakes.
4. Ask your child for help.

Make sure to let them know that you appreciate their help. This teaches them to feel capable, significant, and relevant. Your apology might look something like this: "I made a mistake. I'm so sorry I yelled at you. I should have taken a timeout or taken a deep breath. Would you like to help me remember to take a deep breath if it happens again?"

In order to remain in a calm state when your children are misbehaving, it can help to stop labeling your child's behavior as "good" or "bad." Instead, your goal is to be neutral and to accept the behavior as it is. It is just information. The behavior is not about us. The goal is for children to be allowed to have all kinds of behavior without us getting upset. When we become upset, it is because we have made up some kind of rule such as "kids shouldn't do that," or "how dare she do that to me?" We personalize it or reject it, without allowing it to just be as it is. In doing so, we stifle the need behind the emotion that is being expressed through the behavior. Inevitably, if we continue this pattern, our children learn the same avoidance or ignoring of emotions that we have mastered, which creates not only emotional issues but physical illness as well.

When you think or say phrases such as "he made me feel this way or "you're making me angry!" It's a sign that you're internalizing your child's behavior. Instead, it is our responsibility as parents to control our anger, not our children's responsibility to prevent us from becoming angry. Becoming angry is completely our own responsibility. Our children don't "make us" feel angry, we are often unconsciously reacting to unresolved issues from our our childhood and responding by putting it on them. Unless we are working on personal growth, we are, in essence, choosing anger. No one can make us feel anything – when we feel negatively it is a part of us that has not been resolved.

Likewise, when we have strong emotions about another, it is an indication of that which we most need to resolve in ourselves. We project our feelings of self-hate onto another person because it is safer and because we are unconscious of our feelings. When someone triggers you, you can learn to identify that it is an area that you need to work on. This person that is triggering you is actually giving you a gift to show you what you need to work on. Our wounds are invisible, so those who trigger us provide us with the gift of making our wounds visible. Instead of projecting our anger or hate onto that person, we can receive it as a lesson that we need to learn.

CHAPTER 8

THE CONNECTION CURE

"I define connection as the energy that exists between people when they feel seen, heard, and valued; when they can give and receive without judgment; and when they derive sustenance and strength from the relationship."

— BRENÉ BROWN

Every parent wishes for their child's happiness, but rather than contributing to their happiness, traditional parenting models teach our children to be afraid of us. Just yesterday, I was picking up my son from the aftercare program at his elementary school and as I was signing out, I overheard the father of a kindergarten boy threaten his little son four times in less than a minute. "You'd better come with me now or else." "Hurry up now or else there won't be a treat for you." "You won't get to come here next time if you don't say goodbye nicely." And lastly, when I turned my head in sympathy for the 5 year old boy, the father threatened his son again, "Say hello. Don't be rude or else you'll get it." Yes, this is an extreme example, but you see my point. From the youngest of ages, we cajole our children to "behave" through fear. If it's not fear of us, it's fear of missing out on dessert ("if you don't eat all of your vegetables, there will be no dessert for you"). We try to steer our children like remote controlled beings through fear and when they grow old enough to try to break away from our fear-induced manipulation we call it "teenage rebellion."

Jennifer Senior, bestselling author of *All Joy and No Fun: The paradox of modern parenthood*, gave my favorite TED talk of all time.[92] She talks about parenting as a crisis... how hard it is not to hurt our children, let alone make them happy; how our expectations are unrealistic and skewed. She is right. However, there is a simpler way.

If we parent through fear-based techniques, it becomes very difficult to develop authenticity. After all, how will our children know if they actually love vegetables if they are just thinking about getting the reward of dessert? How will they savor the results of being kind if they are just avoiding being punished? And is it really necessary to punish our children or have them yearn for our approval in order for them to to grow into good humans? The answer is no.

There is another way to motivate them to do good, eat well, and be great people that is much more effective: it's in our relationship with our children. Humans are motivated by relationship over anything else. If we develop a safe, trusting, open and positive relationship with our child instead of one that is dictatorial and based on fear or rewards, their motivations will develop from a desire to connect. When we allow them to have feelings, to disagree, to make mistakes on their own without feeling bad about it, they are able to discover for themselves what motivates them and what brings them joy. When we prioritize the relationship with our children and raise them through connection, happiness becomes a lifestyle rather than a fleeting emotion.

Most parents are just surviving parenthood. Sometimes simply feeding your children or getting them to sleep can feel like a small miracle. When we are worn out, we tend to parent the way our parents did even though we swore we would never do so. We yell, we demean, we stress out, we hit. We were unprepared. Parenting can take us by surprise. To parent consciously prepares us for these moments so we are less apt to create a childhood that our children have to recover from. When we become aware of the impact we have on our children, it allows us to grow into better people and become better parents without trying to follow a prescribed technique or parenting guide.

---

92 www.ted.com/playlists/150/advice_to_help_you_be_a_great

Transformational Parenting is based on the parent-child relationship and the parent's personal growth in a simplified harmony of child psychology, neurology, and child development. It brings in elements of many different styles of parenting. Instead of trying to figure out which parenting camp you fit into (Attachment Parenting, Conscious Parenting, Aware Parenting, Gentle Parenting, Simplicity Parenting, Slow Parenting, Mindful Parenting, etc.), reading ten books and trying to remember what to do and what not to do, we'll go over the best practices of what we know in psychology. Here are the essential practices:

1. Take responsibility for healing your own wounds so you don't pass them onto your children (as you learned in Chapters 4 and 5).
2. Understand that poor behavior is the expression of an unmet need (as you learned in Chapter 7).
3. Prioritize the relationship with your child (more on this in this chapter).
4. Allow your child to be an individual, separate from your own needs and wishes for them (more on this in this chapter).
5. Practice Transformational Communication (you'll learn how to do this thoroughly in the next chapter, Chapter 9).

Memorizing techniques is not necessary with Transformational Parenting. Instead, the ability to have your children do their homework without asking, fight with their siblings less, listen to your requests more, and grow into the best version of themselves while you become the best version of yourself is a practice you will learn and acquire. It will soon become as natural as breathing and you will wonder why you extended so much unnecessary effort in "parenting" before. Although I've listed what is needed to achieve this ability to correct through connection above, your consciousness has most likely already begun to shift as you've been reading this book.

PRIORITIZE THE RELATIONSHIP WITH YOUR CHILD

Imagine being on a yacht in the middle of the ocean, you are sailing to Bora Bora, and you are completely dependent on your captain. You hear a storm and it starts to pour. Suddenly thunder sounds and you feel the ocean lift up the yacht on waves the size of multi-story buildings. The captain of the ship jumps out of the yacht without you onto a lifeboat and motors away quickly leaving you alone. How do you feel?

That's how dependent children are on us. Even when they are teens, we are the captains navigating the treacherous waters of life. Regardless of your situation, age, or background, once you become a parent, it's your responsibility to learn to navigate the ship through those rough waters and to make sure your children feel safe.

Because we are the captain and our children are the passengers, how safe they feel depends more on our emotional response than about how big the waves are – what's going on externally. If we are able to connect, remain centered, and be secure in our path to life, our children will do so as well. I know many children who are going through difficult times but because their "captains" are close and connected to them, you'd never know it. On the other hand, children who are navigating life with less closeness to their parents can feel as though they are at sea without an anchor.

Therefore, our relationship with our children is the most important parenting tool we have. Along with working on our own personal growth, prioritizing the relationship with our children is essential to raising children who feel good about themselves, can achieve authentic success and authentic happiness. No pressure, right?

So how do we prioritize the relationship with our children? What does a parent who prioritizes their children look like? Here are some examples:

- Mike is a busy investor. He is involved in a lot of international deals which require him to be accessible beyond the working hours of his time zone. However, during meal times, he doesn't bring his smartphone to the table. Even if it rings or buzzes, he ignores it, sending a loud message to his family: you are my priority.
- Jo'elle works for herself, which means she has no downtime. However, during the summer months when her children are out of school she takes off Fridays. Her income is reduced, but her kids are so happy to spend the extra time with her.
- Omar has a lot of friends who don't have kids. They invite him regularly to go out with them to events where it's impractical to bring his kids: concerts, sports events, adult dinners, etc. He says no most of the time and his children often overhear his response, "I'm spending time with my kids then. They're growing up so quickly I want all the time I can get with them." His kids have validation that they are, indeed, the most important people to him.

- Juana's daughter Natalia was incredibly miserable at her school. She just couldn't find a group of friends, or even one friend, who she clicked with. She would come home most days in tears. This went on for a couple of years. On top of that, there was some bullying going on, and the school administration wasn't doing anything about it. Natalia felt alone and lonely. Although Natalia's current school was closer to their home, Juana pulled her out and placed her in a new school so she could meet new kids. After a couple of weeks, Natalia found friends and was so grateful for her mother's effort.
- Lisa is not a great soccer player but really wants to be. Her father gets off work early every Tuesday to coach her soccer team (and coach Lisa extra). Lisa's soccer improved and more importantly, so did their relationship!
- Amy's mother was emotionally abusive to her when she was a little girl, often putting her down, calling her fat and telling her to go on diets. This was very hard for Amy and even as an adult, as a result, she still suffers from not being comfortable in her body. When Amy had a daughter of her own she was nervous that her mother would do the same to her daughter. Sure enough, when her daughter was about 2 years old her mother started calling her "chunky" and "cute fattie," even after Amy asked her to stop. Amy told her mother that unless she stopped she would not have her daughter visit any more. Her mother did not stop and so Amy stopped having her mother around her daughter.
- Ben's son Rico didn't like to be kissed by anyone except his parents. Ben's parents would visit regularly and insist that Rico kiss them. At first, Ben felt compelled to please his parents, but after a few times of seeing Rico cringe and being so uncomfortable and looking to his father for support, Ben decided to stand up for Rico and tell his parents that Rico prefers a high five. Rico gave his father a look of relief and Ben knew that he was reinforcing the important lesson of respecting his body.

You'll notice a theme: sacrifice. It's true and cannot be understated. You may have to change your hours, reduce your wages, even change your friends. It's not easy. I have a hundred examples of my own as well. I left a prestigious job at a great hospital because the hours weren't flexible; I monitored or reduced visits from certain family members; I take fewer clients in order to be able to pick my children up from school; I don't answer emails when my children are awake and not in school; on and on. Really, every day is a sacrifice. I used to cherish sleeping in. By nature, I'm a night owl. I'm sure many of you will relate with the torture that is lack of sleep. Talk about boot camp! There's nothing like a newborn to teach you about sacrifice. However, waking up to soothe a crying infant isn't always a strategically planned sacrifice. When you see a need your child has and you develop a plan for what you must sacrifice for your children: that is prioritizing.

Many parents will stop going out at night except for special occasions or special date nights because their children cherish the nighttime routine so much. Or they will move, change careers, become self-employed, leave their husbands, wives, girlfriends, boyfriends, and partners because they aren't good for their children. Sometimes, it will even be as simple as changing what you eat. Your life will be an endless barrage of change all motivated by love for your child.

Yet, with all of the hundreds, maybe thousands of changes you will make in your life to prioritize your child, the single most important way to create a lifelong positive connection that will help your child grow to be an exceptional person is to work on yourself.

ALLOW YOUR CHILD TO BE AN INDIVIDUAL

It's understandable that as parents we can sometimes confuse our children's victories and defeats as our own. When our children fail, it's hard to feel as though we haven't failed too. When they win, we revel in the triumph alongside them. Do you remember in Chapter 4, when you learned about differentiation? Someone who does not have a differentiated self "quickly adjusts what they think, say, and do to please others, or they proclaim what others should be like and pressure them to conform."[93] Does this remind you of traditional parenting at all? We unconsciously coerce or pressure our children to please us.

Another way to tell if we are not differentiated enough is to ask ourselves, honestly, if we personalize our child's behavior. Anytime you hear yourself think or say "he is making me feel..." it's a sign that you are personalizing your child's behavior. As you learned in the previous chapter, when children act out they are simply expressing their pain. It is a way to communicate with us and a cry for help – it's not personal. It is our responsibility to control our anger. Shouting is just as damaging as spanking. Our children don't "make us" feel angry. We are reacting to unresolved issues from our childhood and responding by putting it on them.

As we do our best to allow our children and ourselves to be differentiated from each other, we can use our parenting as a gauge. The relationship with our children is a reflection of how we think of ourselves unconsciously. What irritates you the most about them is what you are irritated the most about yourself. It's important that your relationship not be too punitive (controlling), or too fun all the time (pleasing), which are signs of poor differentiation. Authentic acceptance is the goal.

THE BEST PRESENT IS PRESENCE

Time with your kids matters...every minute...even if it doesn't seem important or pivotal to the relationship, it is. "Time with your kids" means being present, making eye contact and being emotionally available to them. This may sound complicated but it's actually very simple. It doesn't take any special technique to learn, just look at your child, feel how much you love him or her and turn your phone *off*. Kids will tell you what they need..."Play with me mom!" or "Watch this!"

I love my smartphone as much as anyone but it's a silent destroyer of parent-child relationships (perhaps marital relationships, too?). Making eye contact is essential...when we make eye contact with someone we love we experience a decrease in stress hormones and increase in empa-

---

93 https://thebowencenter.org/theory/eight-concepts/

thy (understanding and feeling what someone is feeling). Empathy is a key component to a parent-child relationship. Looking at your phone while your child is playing on the playground doesn't count as spending time with her...neither does vegging out on tv together. I get it, we're all tired, but you've only got one shot at raising a child! Chapter 4, Heal Yourself, will give you strategies to feel less tired and stressed so you can be more present with your child.

Most parents walk blindly into the parent-child relationship, allowing external factors and influences to control the connection. "Work is crazy" they justify, and when they come home and have a bit of time with their kids, they will put on the television and become emotionally distant. Some parents are physically as well as emotionally absent from their children: perhaps they work very long hours and are not present when they are with their children or are simply not around for childhood...in these cases, children typically distance themselves by the time they reach elementary school. Yes, there is love, but not much of a relationship can be built on physical or emotional absence.

PART THREE

ESSENTIALS FOR RAISING REMARKABLE HUMANS

CHAPTER 9

THE POWER OF TRANSFORMATIONAL COMMUNICATION

"The way we talk to our children becomes their inner voice."

– Peggy O'Mara

Communication is programming. What we tell ourselves and what we say to others creates our thoughts, our actions, our motivations and thus, our reality. It is likely that nothing is more powerful in shaping our lives than the way we communicate to others and to ourselves which is why I've devoted an entire chapter to the subject. The way we communicate to ourselves and others is one of the primary interventions used in psychology to help people grow. For example, to eliminate anxiety and depression, Cognitive Behavioral Therapy asks people to change the way they think and speak to themselves. In couples therapy, one of the primary ways to repair and strengthen a relationship is in the way we think and talk to ourselves and our partner. Using Transformational Communication can be life-changing not only in your parenting, but in nearly every aspect of your life. There are five principles for Transformational Communication:

1. Be authentic.
2. Use empathy.
3. Take responsibility.
4. Don't threaten.
5. Encourage instead of praise.

BE AUTHENTIC

Authentic communication means you say what you feel and mean what you say. This sounds simple but it is not simple at all. Communicating authentically can often heal and provide safety for the listener yet it requires the one who is speaking to be vulnerable. Instead of an accusation such as "Why did you do that?" communicating how you feel would include stating the feeling and why the feeling was brought up: "I felt upset that you didn't come when I asked you to. It reminded me of another time I felt upset, I overreacted. I'm sorry."

The opposite of authentic communication is communicating with sarcasm. Sarcasm can be especially confusing for children. When adults reply with the opposite of how they are feeling it doesn't allow the child to have the opportunity to learn empathy and also can make them feel ashamed. When a child asks, "Why are you upset, Mom?" and the mother replies with annoyance, "Why do you think I'm upset, Johnny?" it shuts down the child's attempt at connection. Replying to an innocent question such as "Did you like the movie?" with a sarcastic response and eye roll of "I just loved it" is confusing and makes the child feel as though they were wrong to ask. Sarcasm shuts down authentic communication in its tracks.

I know some kind people who choose to use sarcasm as one of their primary communication styles. I've often wondered why they feel the need to put up walls for others. Sarcasm tells the listener, "Don't go too deep or I'll shame you." Some adults have a sarcastic sense of humor but that is different than a regular sarcastic communication style. Sarcasm means you usually say the opposite of what you mean. Generally, sarcasm has anger behind it. If you find that you use sarcasm in your communication a lot I encourage you to make a *No Sarcasm* rule for yourself. See how you feel differently, see how people open up to you and take a look at why you felt the need to put up walls.

Children need us to model authenticity. Sarcasm is inauthentic, often anger in disguise...it also creates shame. Best not to use sarcasm with children. They tend to take things much more literally than adults do. And when they do understand it, it decreases their respect for your communication. When speaking with children, clear, concise communication will increase your authenticity with them.

USE EMPATHY

One of the best ways to help your child develop positive behavior, emotional intelligence and insight is to use empathy (mirroring) instead of sympathy or diversion.[94] Empathic listening is also called "mirroring" because you are reflecting the emotions of the person you are talking to. It can be communicated by checking in with the person you are talking to. Asking questions such as, "Are you feeling _____?" or statements such as "If that happened to me I might feel _____" helps the person you are speaking to see that you are truly listening and helps you to make sure your interpretations are accurate. There are thousands of ways to check in with someone and to encourage empathic listening. Empathic listening is also incredibly therapeutic and healing and is the basis for therapy. In fact, just practicing empathic listening with someone is enough to heal most wounds and is much more helpful than offering advice or trying to problem solve with the person. This is also true for your child, regardless of his or her age.

Every misbehavior can be an opportunity to practice empathic listening and help your child to learn important social emotional life skills. For example, if your child throws a temper tantrum, once they have calmed down, you can ask "I wonder if you felt (guess feeling) because (guess reason)…I wonder what you can do to (state preferred behavior). This may look like this: "I wonder if you felt upset because your sister was getting more attention…. I wonder what you can do next time to ask for attention in a different way." If you really want to have a powerful positive impact you can use the psychologist Marshall Rosenberg's infamous phrase which is helpful when someone is hurt or a conflict has occurred: "Is it correct that when you (see/hear)…you may

---

94   Paris, E. and Paris, T. (1992) *I'll Never Do to My Kids What My Parents Did to Me! A guide to conscious parenting*. Chicago, IL: Lowell House/Contemporary Books.

feel...because you need...?"[95] Here's an example of that: "Is it correct that when you hear me asking you to turn off your video game you may feel upset because you need more time to relax?"

Empathic listening may sound tricky, but it's a simple way of checking in with the person you're speaking to to see how they are feeling and trying to put yourself in their shoes. For children, it teaches them an important aspect of emotional intelligence, to learn to recognize and name their feelings. It also teaches them that their feelings are valid. For adults, it helps people feel understood and heard. Empathic listening requires eye contact. Again, this sounds simple, but is not always easily done. When you make eye contact with someone, your mirror neurons get lit up and empathy patterns begin to emerge. In other words, it helps you see their perspective and helps them see yours.

TAKE RESPONSIBILITY FOR OUR FEELINGS / ACTIONS

"If your feelings are controlled by how others treat you, then you are in bondage."
– Drew Gullie

Most of us think we are taking responsibility for our feelings but we are not. As adults, no one can make us feel something unless we allow it. It is so common in our culture that we often fail to own our feelings. When we say to our children (or anyone else) statements like "Don't make me mad," or "That made me sad when you _____" we are telling our children that they are responsible for our feelings.

If you were raised this way, you may be thinking "But he *did* make me feel mad / sad / etc." It takes some adjusting to realize that we ourselves were raised to feel like we were responsible for our parent's behavior and that this was incorrect. Expanding your perspective in this area will most certainly also have you realize that your behavior may have changed accordingly, to try to avoid being the cause of your parent's negative emotions.

---

95 Rosenberg, M.B. (2003) *Nonviolent Communication: A language of life*. Encinitas, CA: PuddleDancer Press.

However, one of the core tenets of an authentic relationship and living an empowered life is accepting full responsibility for the circumstances of your life. There are certain words that may very well be a sign that you're not taking responsibility. The words "had to," "can't," "should," "must," and "ought "are not only disempowering, they lead us to believe we don't have control over the negative things that happen to us.

Most people who were physically and emotionally abused will tell you that the emotional abuse hurts more and lasts longer than the physical abuse. Sometimes our communication can unintentionally create emotional abuse. "What's wrong with you?!" said out of anger can lead to depression and feelings of worthlessness as the child grows. Communicating phrases such as, "Now you're really making me angry" can create guilt. "You are so rude" can create shame.

So, what do we do when we are angry? Aren't we allowed to be angry with our children and let them know we are angry at them? Well yes, you could continue to be angry at your children but you will miss a learning opportunity for both you and your child as well as the possibility for increasing the connection with your child.

The key to this is authenticity and emotional regulation. If you are like 90% of humans and have a childhood that you don't want to pass on entirely to your child, you may overdo your attempts at raising your child in trying to "get it right." However, during times of stress when we are triggered by our child, it's hard to remember the "five steps of effective communication." *Transformational Parenting* has you work on yourself so you don't need to remember steps!

When we feel angry or upset, instead of focusing our attention on our children, I would suggest that we look at our own needs rather than our anger toward our children. Rid yourself of thinking that blames others for making you feel a certain way; although our child's behavior may trigger our anger, it is never the cause of our anger.

First, stop and do nothing, just take a breath. If a parent time-out is needed, take one. Second, identify the thoughts that are making you angry. Then, connect to the needs behind your thoughts. To fully express yourself requires expressing what needs you have and communicating your needs directly. When we express our needs instead of our anger or blaming others there is a much higher chance that we will be heard. We may also need to empathize with our children. If we are angry at someone that means that we don't have empathy for them and no matter how nicely we say what we need from them, if we don't have empathy or compassion for them, we will not be heard.

Another powerful technique we can use to let go of anger, as discussed in detail in Chapter 5, is to step back from your thoughts and instead see yourself as the person who experiences the thoughts, rather than as the thoughts themselves.

We use our language to trick ourselves into believing that others are responsible for our feelings. Instead of saying "I'm angry because they _____" you can replace it with "the need I have that is not being met is _____"

Exercise: Identifying needs

Describe the last time you were angry:

_____

_____

_____

_____

What caused you to be angry:

_____

_____

_____

_____

Now take a look at this list of needs and circle those you had that were unmet and which ignited your anger. Words in bold are the basic needs and regular type words are needs that are related to the basic need in bold.

CONNECTION
acceptance
affection
appreciation
belonging
cooperation
communication
closeness
community
companionship
compassion
consideration
consistency
empathy
inclusion
intimacy
love
mutuality
nurturing
respect/self-respect
safety
security
stability
support
to know and be known
to see and be seen
to understand and
be understood
trust
warmth

PHYSICAL WELL-BEING
air
food
movement / exercise
rest / sleep
sexual expression
safety
shelter
touch
water

AUTONOMY
choice
freedom
independence
space
spontaneity

HONESTY
authenticity
integrity
presence

PLAY
joy
humor

PEACE
beauty
communion
ease

equality
harmony
inspiration
order

MEANING
awareness
celebration of life
challenge
clarity
competence
consciousness
contribution
creativity
discovery
efficacy
effectiveness
growth
hope
learning
mourning
participation
purpose
self-expression
stimulation
to matter
understanding

Exercise: Taking responsibility for our feelings and actions

Fill in the blanks with statements you've heard yourself say or think in the past, then rewrite those statements using language of ownership.

I had to _____ vs I did that because _____.

I have to _____ vs I do that because _____.

I can't _____ vs I can _____ instead.

I should _____ vs I will _____.

I must _____ vs I choose to _____.

I ought to _____ vs I want to _____ instead.

"I statements" can help if you're in the habit of diverting responsibility.

ENCOURAGE INSTEAD OF PRAISE

When you praise children for their ability, it makes them focus on looking good – not on learning. Children praised for their intelligence want to keep proving themselves by doing well. This might sound good, but it's actually counter-productive. And if you aren't yet convinced of the unhelpful "programming" that generic praise language creates, check out these studies:

Researchers Claudia Mueller and Carol Dweck conducted a series of experiments on American 5th graders and found that children behaved very differently depending on the kinds of praise they received. When each child was finished with the task he or she was asked to solve, he or she was either: praised for his intelligence ("You must be smart at these problems"), praised for her effort ("You must have worked hard at these problems"), or given no additional feedback (the control condition). Next, these same children were given a second set of more difficult problems to solve and were asked to explain why they performed poorly. The children who had been praised for their intelligence on previous tasks attributed more of their failure to a lack of intelligence. But children praised for their effort responded the same way as controls did – attributing their failure to a lack of effort.[96]

In other words, telling children they are smart can make kids *less* likely to view themselves as intelligent. By praising children for being smart, we teach them that their performance is a definitive test of intelligence. Children might enjoy the initial praise, but when they encounter difficult challenges later – as they must – the praise backfires.

This is even true with preschoolers. In one study, preschoolers were presented with two puzzles to solve and then given one of three types of feedback:

- "Person" praise that emphasized intelligence ("You are a really good problem-solver!")
- "Process" praise that emphasized strategies ("You're finding really good ways to do this!")
- Neutral feedback ("You finished both puzzles.").

Next, the kids were given a much tougher puzzle and they experienced failure. When the preschoolers were offered a similar puzzle weeks later, those kids who had been praised showed more motivation than kids who had received only neutral feedback. But the kids who had received "process" praise showed more motivation than the kids who had gotten "person" praise.[97]

Another experiment yielded similar results.[98] In this study, preschoolers watched a puppet show in which the protagonist drew a picture and was praised by a teacher. Some preschoolers saw the protagonist receive generic praise about his ability ("You are a good drawer"). Other preschoolers saw the protagonist receive praise only for that specific drawing

---

96   Dweck, C.S. (2002) Messages that motivate: How praise molds students' beliefs, motivation, and performance (in surprising ways). In J. Aronson (Ed.), *Improving Academic Achievement.* New York, NY: Academic Press.

97   Lepper, M.R., and Henderlong, J. (2000) Turning "Play" into "Work" and "Work" into "Play": 25 Years of Research on Intrinsic versus Extrinsic Motivation. In C. Sansone and J.M. Harackiewicz (Eds.), *Intrinsic and Extrinsic Motivation: The Search for Optimal Motivation and Performance* (pp. 257-307). San Diego, CA: Academic Press.

98   Cimpian, A., Arce, H., Markman, E. and Dweck, C. (2007) Subtle linguistic cues affect children's motivation. *Psychological Science,* 18(4): 314-316

("You did a good job drawing"). Then the protagonist made a mistake that the teacher commented on. How did the kids feel about the show? The kids who'd watched the protagonist receive generic praise ("You are a good drawer") were more upset about the subsequent mistakes. When asked if they would like to draw themselves, these kids answered no. By contrast, the kids who had been exposed to the specific praise ("You did a good job drawing") were more likely to show an interest in drawing.

So what's the bottom line? Certainly, it appears that telling children they are smart in a generic way such as "You're so smart" can be counterproductive. But this doesn't mean we shouldn't praise our children. As mentioned above, even the "wrong" kind of praise can be more motivating than no praise at all.

What's important is to avoid praise that makes children stop challenging themselves. The problem with telling kids that they are smart or talented is that children become frightened of failure. They've been labeled positively and they don't want to do anything to lose that label. Moreover, children praised for intelligence tend to believe that intelligence is something innate and unchangeable.[99] As a result, these kids are rendered helpless by failure. If you fail, you must not be smart. End of story.

If we keep these principles in mind, it becomes clear what kinds of praise are the most helpful. Instead of telling your child she is smart or talented, try these alternatives:

- Encourage your child for her strategies (e.g., "You found a really good way to do it").
- Encourage your child for specific work (e.g., "You did a great job with those math problems").
- Encourage your child for his persistence or effort (e.g., "I can see you've been practicing" and "Your hard work has really paid off").

Encouraging kids for effort (and not innate ability) may help them develop a better mindset for learning. So:

---

99 Mueller, C.M., and Dweck, C.S. (1998) Praise for intelligence can undermine children's motivation and performance. *Journal of Personality and Social Psychology*, 75(1): 33-52.

DO Encourage the Effort:
- "I love how excited you are about learning something new."
- "You stuck with it and did well! That's great!"
- "I like your effort. Let's work together to help you figure out what you don't understand."
- "That seemed easy for you, let's give you something that challenges you."

AVOID Generic Praise such as:
- "Nice job!"
- "You did great!"
- "You're so smart"
- "What a good boy/girl"

Learning helpful encouragement instead of unhelpful praise takes practice and thinking through the perceived meaning behind your words. Often, some of the most common phrases used with children are sending messages of external motivation and compliance out of fear or of pleasing others. Here's a tough one: what do you think of the phrase "You're such a good boy" or "You're such a good girl"? Is it helpful encouragement or manipulative praise? At first glance, these words may appear to sound beneficial to a child. However, the words are often spoken in response to a child "behaving" to an adult's desires. The message that children quickly learn from such praise is if they do not conform to their parent's wishes, by default, they are a "bad" boy or girl. They also learn the importance of pleasing their parents, and when they grow up, they have a tendency to want to please others. This can lead to not being aware of their true desires and putting themselves last.

Alfie Kohn, an educational scholar and influential author, also saw this fixed mindset years before Dweck published her groundbreaking book from his work in schools.[100] He saw children lacking motivation. Indeed, generic praise has been found to decrease internal motivation. Dweck explains how pervasive this limited thinking has become:

---

100   Kohn, A. (2005) *Unconditional Parenting: Moving from rewards and punishments to love and reason.* New York, NY: Atria Books.

The biggest surprise has been learning the extent of the problem – how fragile and frightened children and young adults are today (while often acting knowing and entitled). Coaches have complained to me that many of their athletes can't take constructive feedback without experiencing it as a blow to their self-esteem. I have read in the news, story after story, how young workers can hardly get through the day without constant praise and perhaps an award. I see in my own students the fear of participating in class and making a mistake or looking foolish. Parents and educators tried to give these kids self-esteem on a silver platter, but instead seem to have created a generation of very vulnerable people. My hope is that my work can help to reverse this trend.[101]

101 Guild, G. (2010, May 28) *Self Esteem on a Silver Platter.* Retrieved from http://geraldguild.com/blog/2010/05/28/self-esteem-on-a-silver-platter

CHAPTER 10

A TEMPLATE FOR AN EXTRAORDINARY LIFE

"Because you are alive, everything is possible."
– THICH NHAT HANH

Templates, blueprints, calendars, and planners are useful guides to help us create and envision our daily life, which adds up to a lifestyle that we create with intention, leading to an extraordinary life. Now that you've begun to deprogram limiting beliefs, realized the importance of healing, begun goal setting, discovered the magic of connection, and learned about the power of Transformational Communication, it's time for you to plan your beautiful, extraordinary life and the beautiful, extraordinary life of your family.

In this chapter, I provide you with daily rituals you can incorporate to improve your life significantly; from when you wake up, to when you are falling asleep. You'll learn a new way to live, to change your brain and to provide your entire family with a daily routine that will add up to a life of possibility. You can and should do these with your children. As with any ritual that you want to become a positive habit, such as brushing your teeth, it is important that it is shared with your household members and not something that has to be done alone. If we had to do these rituals in isolation, they probably would not happen. So, invite your family to do them with you. Learning alongside the ones we love is not only satisfying, but it can also have exponential benefits.

As with any suggestion, please only do what is right for you. However, I will suggest that you do things that make you a little uncomfortable. Your brain needs novelty to grow. By doing things daily that are out of our comfort zone, we allow our brain to develop new branches on its neuron tree (also called dendritic pathways) instead of shriveling up into a sad dried out tree stump. How do you know when you're doing something that's "new enough"? It will feel uncomfortable, awkward, weird, strange, or scare you. It's important to step out of your comfort zone in order to improve yourself day by day. It takes being uncomfortable to grow. Discomfort is the primary ingredient in growth.

Before we get into your daily routine, I wanted to share with you some relevant science: the science of happiness for which most of this chapter and much of this book is based on.

THE SCIENCE OF HAPPINESS

Happiness is our birthright...we are born easily able to access joy. The warmth of the sun, a butterfly, the rain, even a spoonful of peanut butter can be bursting with joy for young children. However, somewhere along the way, our joy gets whittled away and replaced with fear, sadness, denial, dissociation or anger. Of course, these emotions have an important purpose. Anger tells us that we need to take action on something. Sadness tells us to slow down and reflect. Anxiety and fear tell us we don't feel safe and need to make a change. So in no way am I wishing for you to no longer experience these essential emotions. In fact, sadness, fear and anger serve as an important compass to guide us in the right direction when we get off track. What I wish for you is to experience more moments of happiness, more moments of joy and to change your neurochemistry and habits to allow happiness to be a part of your regular operating system.

Altering your life template for happiness is not just meant to help you feel good, although that is certainly nice. There are many other benefits of feeling good. For example, research has shown that people who are happy have better social relationships, have academic and occupational success, good health, and even live longer.[102, 103] And although we

---

102 Lyubomirsky, S. (2007) *The How of Happiness: A scientific approach to getting the life you want*. New York, NY: Penguin Press.

103 Lyubomirsky, S., King, L.A. and Diener, E. (2005) The benefits of frequent positive affect: Does happiness lead to success? *Psychological Bulletin*, 131: 803–855.

know that money doesn't buy happiness, it is interesting to know that happy people even accrue more money. In a study where they followed college freshman 16 years later (when they were in their mid-30s), the happier ones had higher salaries.[104]

So, don't give up on happiness! Even if you can't remember the last time you felt really happy, even if you wonder if it's possible to be really happy again, even if you're not sure trying these routines will be worthwhile, or will work on you, give it a shot! Remember, it takes time to reverse habits and thinking patterns, so give yourself a chance. It always amazes me how willing we are to try a new diet for 30 days, but are so reluctant to try a new way of thinking. Should you wish to challenge yourself, we have a "Happiness Challenge" online: do these rituals every day for 45 days and let us know your results. You can even participate in our pre-test and post-test to be a part of a scientific study to measure happiness – go to www.TransformationalParenting.co to participate.

I will share with you the science of happiness to help you get back to your most natural authentic state, that joyful state that babies and young children often live in. What if you could appreciate a flower, the rain, or the wind with as much joy and reverence as a young child? I believe you can and there's science to back it up.

The science of happiness was the brainchild of Martin Seligman who changed the path of psychology when he suggested as APA president that psychology should stop focusing on what's wrong with humans and instead focus on what's right with them. Over 20 years later, we have amassed a body of research that can inform our daily activities to increase our happiness significantly. What if there were routines and daily rituals you could bring into your life that would make you 40% happier? Would you do it? Studies show that 50% of individual differences in happiness are determined by genes, 10% by life circumstances, and 40% by our intentional activities.[105] So, let's get started!

---

104 Lyubomirsky, S. (2008, July 16) *Happiness Breeds Success…and Money!* Retrieved from www.cnbc.com/id/25709228

105 Lyubomirsky, S. (2007) *The How of Happiness: A scientific approach to getting the life you want.* New York, NY: Penguin Press.

FAMILY RITUALS

Why rituals? The answer is simple: rituals work. They give us confidence, a feeling of certainty and bring hope. Especially when inviting change or charting new waters, rituals are essential. Performance and sports psychology encourages rituals as they increase emotional stability, attention and confidence. Daily rituals are especially powerful as they can create intentional habits.

Personal transformation can be tricky – we all want to do it, but it is hard to break old habits and change old patterns of thinking. Without a ritual, trying to create a positive change or habit often becomes a battle between your primitive and your intellectual brain. The primitive brain is the area that we share with all mammals and reptiles, sometimes called the "reptilian" brain. It's responsible for survival and is motivated by basic pleasures. The intellectual part of your brain, the frontal lobe, located primarily in your forehead, is responsible for our conscience, emotional memory, understanding cause and effect, and making meaning.

Your intellectual brain says "Don't eat that doughnut," but your subconscious brain doesn't pay attention to "don't" and "no" so it just hears "Eat that doughnut," and your primitive brain says "I'm hungry and it looks delicious." In other words, your intellectual brain often battles with your primitive brain – and more often than not, your primitive brain will win.

Fortunately, we can bring in a ritual, which acts as a diplomat or a mediator between our opposing brains. When we have a ritual, something that "just is," and something we do because it's what we do at the same time every day, our primitive brain and intellectual brain relax and stop arguing so we can finally let go of the internal chatter that robs us of our energy, and do what we know we need to do to be healthy.

For example, you've probably brushed your teeth every night without any effort to remember to brush your teeth. This happens because you introduced brushing your teeth into your evening ritual routine when you were a child. You've been doing it for so long that you probably forget that once, when you were a child, your primitive brain argued with your intellectual brain about brushing. If you are a parent, you know what I am talking about. Your primitive brain complained "But I hate to brush my teeth!" while your intellectual brain argued back "You have to or your breath will stink and you will get cavities." And your primitive brain responded "But I'm too tired…" and so on…. But bring in Ms. Ritual and everyone quiets down and the job gets done.

In a recent Scientific American study it was found that rituals performed before stressful tasks increase confidence and lessen anxiety.[106] Worldwide inspiration and basketball superstar Michael Jordan wore his North Carolina shorts under his Chicago Bulls shorts for every game – just one example of many sports rituals that verge on superstition. Also, rituals such as funerals and wakes performed after experiencing loss can help to alleviate grief. Even tearing up the photo of an old boyfriend can help people move on.

Therefore, I propose we channel the power of rituals more intentionally. All you have to do is do them. Start adding one or two at a time. They're all based on neuroscience and psychology and you can integrate them into your life quite easily. Without trying too hard or going to therapy, if you do them daily, you'll see extraordinary changes in your life!

Waking Up Ritual: Rise with the Sun and Body Scan

Because there are many, many studies on the benefits of regulating your circadian rhythm, because we need a full 7–9 hours of sleep for our brains to function properly, because regulating our waking time to the rise of the sun improves mood and energy levels, and because we process trauma primarily when we sleep...start this Waking Up Ritual tomorrow morning!

After a full 7–9 hours of sleep, wake up with the sunrise daily, stretch, think of how lucky you are to be alive. Next, do a body scan to release anything that's holding you back from having an incredible day. Body scans involve paying attention to each part of your body to assess if you're holding tension or any discomfort in your body, and then to focus your breath on that area to release the associated tension. In addition to releasing tension, body scans can help us be aware of any emotional

---

106   Gina, F. and Norton, M.I. (2013) Why rituals work. *Scientific American*. Retrieved from www.scientificamerican.com/article/why-rituals-work/

stress that we are carrying and work intentionally to release it. I find that starting from my head and focusing my attention down to my neck, chest, arms, hands, stomach, legs and feet and the connective parts in between to be an efficient way to become aware of what I am holding.

Breakfast Time Ritual: Receive and Interpret Emotions

If we're conscious enough to even allow ourselves enough time for breakfast, it's rare. Breakfast tends to be one of the more rushed times of the day so why not use that feeling of being in a hurry to our advantage. If you eat breakfast, great, if not, that's ok too...just remember to practice this step when you might normally be having breakfast. When we are rushed, stressed or hungry we are especially vulnerable to old memories interfering with our happiness. So it's an ideal time to Receive and Interpret Emotions. If frustration or anger comes in as you are trying to get to where you need to be, understand the true meaning of anger which is telling you that need to take action on something meaningful to you. We often get frustrated about small things like getting a ticket because we were speeding but the deeper meaning of that isn't "don't speed" (though that's a helpful behavior to modify), the deeper meaning would be to control your emotions so you don't end up speeding. And how do we "control" our emotions? By correctly interpreting them and releasing them.

Fortunately, you don't need to be a psychologist to correctly interpret emotions. Let me show you what we psychologists learn: Anger and all its forms (Agitation, Sarcasm, Annoyance, Rage, Frustration, Hostility, Jealousy, Negative Intensity, Irritation, etc.) mean you need to take action on something meaningful in your life. It fuels us with energy which we can channel to get things done! But if we don't channel that energy toward completing a task we need to complete to feel good again, it can eat away at us.

Sadness and all its forms (Loneliness, Shame, Embarrassment, Guilt, Sensitivity, Depression, Disappointment, Discouragement, Sorrow, Feeling Empty, Grief-Stricken, Hurt, Living with Regret, etc.) means you need to slow down and heal!

And the ever popular Anxiety / Fear and their forms (Busyness, Agitation, Apprehension, Concern, Need for Control, Feeling Edgy, Fidgeting, Hesitation, Feeling Hurried, Jittery or Nervous, Worrying, Being Afraid or Scared, Feeling Tense or Troubled, etc.) mean your mind is trying to tell you that you don't feel safe and need to make a change.

Check in with your emotions throughout the day and listen to the essence of what they are trying to tell you. Understand the true meaning of emotions. When you experience agitation during the day, it is an opportunity to release past experiences. Watch your inner chatter – know that it is not *you*, just your thoughts; let go of the inner voice, instead observe. Don't distract yourself.

Therapeutic Driving

I love practicality! Anytime I can do personal growth while I have to do some kind of mundane task is a huge plus! That's why Thich Nhat Hanh is my favorite monk. He doesn't claim you need to go on a 10-day silent meditation retreat to find contentment, or even sit quietly every day meditating. He teaches conscious multi-tasking. For example, when you are doing the dishes, you can use the warmth of the water on your hands to help you meditate, you can do it while you're walking (even with lots of noise around you in an urban area), and my favorite: the driving meditation. He writes:

> Most people are forgetful; they are not really there a lot of the time. Their mind is caught in their worries, their fears, their anger, and their regrets, and they are not mindful of being there. That state of being is called forgetfulness – you are there but you are not there. You are caught in the past or in the future. You are not there in the present moment, living your life deeply. That is forgetfulness. While you are driving your car, you might notice the tension in your body. You are eager to arrive and you don't enjoy the time you spend driving. When you come to a red light, you are eager for the red light to become a green light so that you can continue. But the red light can be a signal. It can be a reminder that there is tension in you, the stress of wanting to arrive as quickly as possible. If you recognize that, you can make use of the red light. You can sit back and relax – take the ten seconds the light is red to practice mindful breathing and release the tension in the body.[107]

---

107 Retreived from www.lionsroar.com/mindful-living-thich-nhat-hanh-on-the-practice-of-mindfulness-march-2010/

So the next time you're stopped at a red light, you might like to sit back and practice this exercise: Say to yourself while you take a deep breath "Breathing in, I'm aware of my body. Breathing out, I release the tension in my body." The next time you get in the car, let those stop lights, stop signs and traffic that usually irritate you melt away your tension. Along with becoming more aware of your body with the morning Body Scan, Therapeutic Driving will become a regular tool you can use to relieve tension. Traffic never felt so good!

Lunch Ritual: Feed Yourself from Within

The Lunch Ritual is about loving yourself and increasing your self-worth. It is the most primal human need. Inner nourishment is essential to our survival. Yet, nearly every single one of us is starving in this area. It is one of the most neglected forms of self-improvement. Even the field of psychology has been so caught up with lessening negative emotions that it forgets to concentrate on positive ones. Positive psychology, the type of psychology I practice, is different and looks at what someone has that they can build on to improve their lives, but is unusually rare. Most doctors, psychologists and psychiatrists are all about what's wrong with you and forget that we are starving inside and don't love ourselves. Of course, there are multi-billion dollar industries that rely on us not loving ourselves, like most cosmetics, fashion, even food companies, which leave us not only feeling unlovable but broke and fat on top of it.

So, do this for you: every time you sit down to eat lunch, before you put the first bit of food into your mouth, think of something you love about yourself...if that is too hard, imagine yourself as a child, recall an old picture where you were especially cute and think about what you loved about yourself at that age. With each bite, imagine the nourishment of the food filling your heart. You will notice that you eat more slowly and probably much less food as you savor and truly taste each bite. Each bite is a gift you give yourself, a treat. You probably won't need to eat as much sweets to feel like you are having a treat because now the food that you eat will be seen for what it really is, a physical nourishment that can nourish your soul. Look at your hands and cherish all they do for you, how beautiful they are.

And when you use the restroom, which usually comes just after lunch, when you look in the mirror, look at yourself, see how beautiful you are...and if that is hard for you, remember that photo of when you were a child and experience the beauty of yourself at that time. Then look again, see that child reflected in you now. Look deeply into your own eyes and give yourself love. Do this everyday when you eat.

Dinner Ritual: Practice Authenticity and Vulnerability

"Vulnerability is the birthplace of love, belonging, joy, courage, empathy, and creativity. It is the source of hope, empathy, accountability, and authenticity. If we want greater clarity in our purpose or deeper and more meaningful spiritual lives, vulnerability is the path." – Brené Brown

There's a lot of talk about being authentic and vulnerable lately. Brené Brown has practically created a movement with her research on the importance of vulnerability. She has one of the most popular TED talks and is helping people understand the importance of conquering shame in order to heal. Her theory is called Shame Resilience Theory and its goal is to help connect people through empathy, vulnerability and freedom. Her research and others like it recognize that being vulnerable is essential for connection and growth.

By being vulnerable, we are almost certain to connect. Vulnerability is the key to unlocking the door to close relationships. It's an incredible gift that when we have courage enough to practice regularly leads to powerful authenticity. To be vulnerable involves sharing that which we feel ashamed about. We cannot exist healthfully by hiding our secrets or living in shame. Yet the word "shame" is so loaded. We often fail to recognize that each and every day we experience shame because we feel like we will be judged unlovable. It may be the shame of breaking your diet for dessert, shame of yelling at your child, shame of forgetting someone's birthday, or the shame of not feeling good about yourself. The negative voice inside our heads that speaks to us daily when we are anything but perfect magnifies shame.

Ironically, that which we most want to hide has the biggest power to connect us in deeper relationships. One of the fastest and most effective forms of healing involves sharing your darkest parts with others, it's one of the reasons why Alcoholics Anonymous can work. When you share that which you feel ashamed about, people feel connected to you, which has them share more with you, and you share more with them, developing an authentic relationship. But you don't need to be in AA or even therapy to reap the benefits of vulnerability. You can practice sharing things which make you feel vulnerable daily with your family at dinner. It can be something silly like admitting you passed gas or something larger like admitting you lied. My kids love when I share vulnerable stories. The behaviors from my past that still haunt me like when I teased Dean Harwell in 3rd grade or when I cheated on a test. Sharing and regularly admitting to parenting mistakes is also very popular with kids. As parents we make mistakes with our children regularly. When we are aware enough to recognize our mistakes, admit that we messed up and offer a sincere apology it creates a feeling of safety in the relationship, also known as a secure attachment.

Your child doesn't expect you to be perfect, but does expect you to learn from your mistakes. Being authentic with your child often means apologizing to your child for reacting with negative emotion. "I'm sorry I reacted like that" and "I made a mistake" are great responses and should be spoken as often as needed, which for most of us is very often!

Let children know that we don't always have it together. Don't create a false self for your children. By allowing our children to see us making mistakes and trying new things, we help them to learn to be authentic, too. From this they can learn a growth mindset and learn to focus less on how they look to others.

While you are sitting down to eat with your family, share something that makes you feel vulnerable – a mistake you made or something you feel ashamed of…. Vulnerability is the door to connection which heals us. Trust me here, I've been practicing psychology for more than 20 years…we all need to feel validated, we need to feel seen for who we really are. You can start right at the dinner table with your family. Share something that you felt embarrassed about. Share something that you made a mistake about…in fact, if you are a parent, not only will this benefit you, but your kids will learn a growth mindset by you sharing your process which will give them confidence to try new things and not be afraid to make mistakes!

Before Bed: Happiness Journal

It's so easy to focus on what irritates you, what isn't working around you, and how your life just isn't the way you wanted it. If you've written in a journal before, chances are you wrote about difficult experiences more than you did about joyful ones. Our brains function in quite the same way. In order to attempt to protect us from harm, we tend to remember the negative more than the positive. We become experts at remembering and noticing that which feels bad. I'm not knocking this information because it informs you of what to avoid in the future, which is helpful. However, we are missing the other half of the coin: what makes us feel good that we want to seek in the future.

We have the opportunity to train our brain to reconfigure its focus, but we have to focus beyond our primitive brain. The primary reason we tend to remember or focus on the negative rather than positive is that our primitive brain is trying to keep us safe. So, if we just think to ourselves to focus on what makes us feel good, our primitive brain is still most likely in control. Let me show you what I mean. Think of something that makes you feel good. Have something in mind? Good… did you imagine food, sleep or sex? The majority of people will…you can see how limiting our focus can be if we let our primitive brain run the show.

In order to access the more evolutionarily evolved areas of our brain we need to be more intentional in our focus. Writing is one of the most intentional practices one can participate in. It requires our full attention and our creative mind. You'll need a notebook or journal and a pen. It doesn't need to be anything fancy but I would suggest you choose a journal to write in that makes you feel good, something beautiful and of good quality.

- Write down any time you felt joyful, happy, or inspired.
- Write down what lights you up, makes you feel fulfilled, and brings you joy.

- Write down things that you saw that were beautiful, strangers that made you smile, kindnesses you witnessed or experienced.
- Write down what you feel grateful for.
- Keep an ongoing list of joyful circumstances, activities, and relationships.

As mentioned already, writing down things you are grateful for strengthens your immune system and helps you sleep better.[108]

Sleep Ritual: Prime for Happiness

Did you ever notice that what you think about, watch or read before falling asleep will often show up in your dreams? Because we are tired and about to fall asleep, we are slipping into an unconscious state which is a very powerful place for programming your mind. If you don't direct your mind, you may end up inadvertently bringing in anxiety during this time which not only will disturb your sleep but also your ability to release that anxiety. Because we often function from our primitive brain, we tend to give the most attention to negative states, which can be extremely unhelpful at this time of day! Instead, recalibrate your compass to a positive state. How do you do this? Easy: when you fell asleep, recall the nicest feeling you had today, bring up the memory – maybe you felt excited, or grateful, or peaceful, or loved...remember that feeling as if you were reliving it, recreate the way it felt, what you smelled, heard and saw at the time...and if you can't think of anything from your day, think of something from your life. It doesn't matter...your mind has a very non-linear approach to time. Reliving a positive memory right before you fall asleep will prime your unconscious mind for happiness and allow you to process the stress you had during the day more easily. Did you know that we primarily process stress when we sleep? That is why getting enough shut-eye is essential. As someone with epilepsy, I can be the first to explain the importance of sleep for processing stress! If I don't get enough sleep, I have a seizure. Even though you may not have epilepsy, your brain functions in a similar (though less dramatic) way,

---

108 Lyubomirsky, S. (2007) *The How of Happiness: A scientific approach to getting the life you want.* New York, NY: Penguin Press.

in that if you don't get enough sleep stress doesn't get fully processed or resolved. If our brain can't process the negative states we experienced during the day, they just stay with us! Often, this negative energy gets stuck in our body and produces headaches, body aches or worse. So, when you fall asleep at night, Prime Yourself For Happiness – you'll be amazed at the powerful improvement you see!

Practice Quiet (Allow Children to "Be Bored") Ritual

Oh how difficult silence can be. Have you ever been to a home with no music playing, no video games on, no television or movies on in the background, and no need to take up space with words – just quiet? It's almost unheard of. Most homes are filled with noises that distract from creativity, noises that suffocate the imagination and noises that stifle childhood.

Susan cannot be silent for more than 15 seconds. A lifetime of using words to cover up feeling uncomfortable has led her to be uncomfortable with any silence whatsoever. She talks and talks and talks. She fills space with words, often words that are unnecessary. Some people tune her out, others feel agitated. Although her excessive chatter is more extreme than most, it is not uncommon to feel uncomfortable with silence. Have you ever felt uncomfortable with silence? Why? What about when you were with someone else? Did you allow for silence between you or feel the need to begin talking?

This need to talk or to entertain ourselves constantly masks anxiety and distracts us from recognizing our feelings. Yet, quiet invites sharing…ever wonder how to get your child to share about their day? Provide quiet. Quiet creates peace…is your child distracted and having a hard time paying attention to one thing? Provide quiet. Quiet trains the brain to focus. Quiet invites authenticity.

Quiet also invites boredom. When our children complain of "feeling bored" or when we feel bored, it is a sign that we have been distracting ourselves with noise for too long. If you can allow for boredom, boredom will eventually evolve into creativity. Children will find something to do or create something to do. Over time, the idea of "boredom" will fade as they won't have the expectation of distraction and entertainment from something outside of themselves.

It can be challenging to not try to "cure" boredom for our children, to try to help them find something to do. But did you know that the mind needs slowing down in order to be creative? If we keep our children busy and entertain them with activities, movies, video games, sports, parties, and social events, we take away their possibility for discovery of the power of their mind, their creativity, their imagination.

Allow quiet time for the whole family. No phones, tv, movies, video games, music…just some time to be. Warning: children will complain at first; hang in there! I find one of the easiest ways to invite quiet with my children is in the car. When I pick up my children from school, I make sure to have the music off so the car is quiet. I used to initiate the conversation with questions such as "What made you laugh today?" but my son didn't want to answer my chosen topic. Even the creative ways of asking "How was your day" produced the blasé "fine." But I learned from my son. Instead of me initiating the topic, I learned to greet them and just be quiet. Sure enough, he would begin to share about his day, and what he brought up was more interesting than what I would have thought to ask.

Some families invite their quiet time on the weekends when they are making breakfast, others on a family walk, others just sitting on the couch. If we, the parents, can hold back our anxiety enough to allow silence to invite our children's communication, authentic conversations can develop and deeper connections can be made.

What time of day will you invite quiet time? Or will you create this time on the weekends? Write this down now:

_____

_____

Where will you have your family's quiet time (at home, in the car, etc.)?

_____

_____

NOW WHAT?

Now it's time to plan your action steps. In this last part of *Transformational Parenting*, you will develop a life plan to help you grow into the best version of yourself and raise your child to their highest potential. It may be the end of the book, but it's the beginning of a more awakened life for you!

First, take a minute and go through this checklist. If you answer "no" to any of these questions, it needs to be addressed and worked through in a deeper way. If you answer "yes" then you are on track. But don't fret if you answered "no" to any question. This is a process.

1. Do you see parenting as a relationship, rather than something you "do to" your child?
2. Do you recognize that parents go through stages of development just like their children?
3. Do you know that if you get stuck in a developmental stage, probably your child will too?
4. Do you recognize that if you want your child to change, that you must first change yourself?
5. Do you know that you can become your best self regardless of what has happened to you?
6. Do you feel like you deserve good things?
7. Are you able to begin to create your own reality?
8. What is your purpose?

   _____

   _____

   Remember, "purpose" can be as simple as having a deep relationship, a loving connection or creating something you're proud of.
9. Are you more open to making mistakes and being imperfect?
10. Are you ready to let go of "being busy?"
11. Do you understand how sacred the work of parenting is?
12. Do you know what part of your childhood needs healing?
13. Do you know why it's not helpful to avoid pain?
14. Do you have empathy for yourself?

15. How will you prioritize your healing?
16. Do you know that time alone will not heal emotional pain?
17. Do you know how to stop negative thinking patterns?
18. Do you know your relational style?
19. Do you know your thinking patterns?
20. Do you know what to do about anxiety, fear, sadness, anger and depression?
21. How will you follow up to address these emotions in your life (see a therapist, begin a meditation practice, begin a yoga / movement practice, start a therapeutic writing journal, something else, all of the above)? _____
22. Do you recognize some of the stories that have shaped your life?
23. Are you ready to let go of those stories and step into a new you?
24. Are you ready to base your goals on what brings you joy instead of what you think success means?
25. Are you ready to embody a more Guiding parenting style?
26. Can you forgive yourself for parenting mistakes? We can't judge ourselves for what we didn't know before.
27. Do you understand that children misbehave because they have an unmet need?
28. Are you ready to let go of spanking and corporal punishment?
29. Do you know where and when you will take your parent time-out?
30. Are you ready to let your children mess up and fail without taking it personally?
31. Are you ready to let your children have success and achieve without taking it personally?
32. Are you ready to practice Transformational Communication?
33. Are you ready to sit down with your family in a Family Meeting?
34. Are you ready to create (with your family) your family values and traditions?
35. What do you need to deprogram? Are you finding yourself pleasing others? Apologizing for no reason?
36. What will you do to expand your emotional growth this week?

- Gratitude journal?
- Regular meditation?
- Talking to a friend about past trauma?
- EMDR for trauma processing (short-term therapy)?
- Therapy?

DEVELOPING A LIFE PLAN

Life has a way of making its own plan, but that doesn't mean that we shouldn't do our best to plan our limited time. For most goals and dreams, if we don't take the time to plan and schedule time for them, they will not happen. So, if you have goals, dreams and things you hope to accomplish, read on!

The average life span is 27,375 days. Here is a chart to reflect that:

```
x_____x_____x_____x_____x
You're born    6843 days      13,687 days     20,531 days     You die
```

Here is a graph of the average human life in years, cross off the number of triangles according to your age so you can see where you are in your lifespan visually:

```
   △        △        △        △        △
   △        △        △        △        △
   △        △        △        △        △
   △        △        △        △        △
   △        △        △        △        △
   △        △        △        △        △
   △
```

Now write down how many more summers you might have left: _____

How many more summers might you have with your kids until they move out? _____

How many more Halloweens with your kids? _____

You can see how every experience matters!

Most children spend most of their days with their parents until they are 18 and then move out to go to college or to work. It's hard to estimate exactly how much time we will get with our children after they move out. It is likely that if we live in the same city as our children and have healthy relationships with them, we will have more time together. A 34 year-old blogger[109] set about to figure out how much time he has left with his parents. It's just a simple thought experiment and isn't formal science, but I find it helpful to encourage us to be more conscious with our time. He writes,

> I've been thinking about my parents, who are in their mid-60s. During my first 18 years, I spent some time with my parents during at least 90% of my days. But since heading off to college and then later moving out of Boston, I've probably seen them an average of only five times a year each, for an average of maybe two days each time. 10 days a year, about 3% of the days I spent with them each year of my childhood. Being in their mid-60s, let's continue to be super optimistic and say I'm one of the incredibly lucky people to have both parents alive into my 60s. That would give us about 30 more years of coexistence. If the ten days a year thing holds, that's 300 days left to hang with mom and dad. Less time than I spent with them in any one of my 18 childhood years. When you look at that reality, you realize that despite not being at the end of your life, you may very well be nearing the end of your time with some of the most important people in your life. It turns out that when I graduated from high school, I had already used up 93% of my in-person parent time. I'm now enjoying the last 5% of that time. We're in the tail end.

Let's take a minute and soak that in, by the time our children are out of the house, most of our time with them will be gone. As in the example above, we may only have 5% of the time left to spend with our children after they move out even if we live a long life.

Carpe Diem:

Multiply your age by 365, which will give you your current age in days.

---

109   Retrieved from https://waitbutwhy.com/2015/12/the-tail-end.html

Subtract that number from 27,375

How many days, more or less do you probably have left? _____

You will never again have more time than you do right now...

What exactly do you want to do with your precious days left?

How do you want to be remembered?

How do you define success? Take a moment and write down your own definition of success:

_____

_____

_____

_____

_____

YOUR MISSION STATEMENT

Having a mission statement will help you to keep boundaries when life hands you options that may distract you from your mission. You'll want it to be short, concise and reflect what is most authentic to you, not what you think you should do. It doesn't have to be grand or reflect your desire to change the world. It should reflect you, and how you want to be remembered as much as how you want to live your life each and every day. Here are some examples of famous and regular people's mission statements, you'll find they have a lot in common:

Imelda De Los Reis, mother of 3: "My mission is to teach my children how to find authentic happiness by finding it myself."

Sir Richard Branson, Founder of the Virgin Group: "To have fun in [my] journey through life and learn from [my] mistakes."

John Smith, father of 2: "To enjoy each and every second with my family even on the craziest days."

Maya Angelou, bestselling author: "My mission in life is not merely to survive, but to thrive; and to do so with some passion, some compassion, some humour and some style."

Juana Baptista, mother of 2: "To be alive and awake to experience all of the joys life has to offer is my mission."

Oprah Winfrey, media mogul: "To be a teacher. And to be known for inspiring my students to be more than they thought they could be."

Now take a moment to write your personal mission statement. No need to be perfect, you can always modify it later, just get something on this paper that's true for you in this moment:

_____

_____

_____

_____

I'd also like to encourage you to make a family mission statement together with your children and partner (if applicable), which can be done over a few family meetings and updated as your children get older.

Now, based on your mission statement and your priorities, let's make a life plan of the rest of your days. I've followed in Rudolf Steiner's biography tradition outlining life in seven year cycles. Not only is this timing in sync with Erikson and Piaget, it also matches how often most of the body's cells replace themselves, which is every 7 to 10 years.[110] Go ahead and fill in the experiences, lessons and what you learned for ages you already passed, and the experiences, lessons and what you want to learn for the ages that you are not yet. Also, for the ages that you are in or are yet to come, add a goal that feels relevant that you believe will bring you joy. Here is an example from a client of mine to get you started:

---

110   Retrieved from www.nytimes.com/2005/08/02/science/your-body-is-younger-than-you-think.html

Age	Goal for this age	Experiences, lessons and what you learned or Experiences, lessons and what you want to learn
0-7		Birth of my sister, learned how to get attention by being very sweet.
7-14		Birth of my brother. Parents divorce. Had to learn to keep the peace.
14-21		Fell in love. Learned to trust. Traveled to Italy.
21-28		Moved out of place I grew up. I learned that being sweet wasn't really being authentic. Got married, became a mother.
28-35		Mom died. Grieving...learned to be more present.
35-42	Meditate regularly. Start the company.	This is my current age...I hope to learn more patience, and to learn to be lighter in my life.
42-49	Build the company while maintaining freedom with my time. Take my daughter to Israel.	I hope I still remain connected to my kids as they hit their late teen years.
49-56	Go on 15 day cruise to Greek Islands with husband.	I hope to still be married! So I see that I need to plan for more connection time with my husband.
56-63	Live close to my daughter, be an involved grandmother.	I hope to learn to love all of myself, even my aging body--thinking about this age freaks me out. Maybe I need to work on loving myself?
63-70	Retire, move to Mexico.	Grandkids? Hopefully? Maybe I'm a part of a non-profit group? I need to plan more....
70 plus	Open the orphanage.	I hope I'm in great health and as vivacious as I feel some days in my 30s!

As you can see, doing a life plan based on lessons helps you realize what you need to change now to prepare for a meaningful future. Now, your turn:

Age	Goal for this age	Experiences, lessons and what you learned or Experiences, lessons and what you want to learn
0-7		
7-14		
14-21		
21-28		
28-35		
35-42		
42-49		
49-56		
56-63		

63-70		
70 plus		

THE LEARNING HAS JUST BEGUN

Although you're at the end of the book, your learning process has just begun. I've been teaching this work for more than 15 years and I'm still learning, too. I make mistakes regularly and am constantly working on finding a balance. These lessons take time, practice and patience. Let go of judgement, allow yourself to make mistakes, and remember what you learned about growth mindset.

When you are learning these concepts, you may decide to go through these steps alone, go through them alone and then start a Transformational Parenting group afterward, join a Transformational Parenting group online, or get one to one help along the way with Transformational Parenting coaching (at TransformationalParenting.co).

Many of us learn better in a group, especially when it comes to personal growth topics where we could benefit from knowing we are not alone. There are two ways to go about this: you join the online Transformational Parenting group or you can start a *Transformational Parenting* group of your own. Joining a Transformational Parenting group, whether it's with your partner, your ex, your friends, or with some parents from your child's school will accelerate your learning and build community along the way.

If you choose to start a group of your own, as you teach the material, you will hear others' perspectives and it will allow you to have an even deeper experience. Not only will teaching what you have learned help you to become an expert in elevating your consciousness and your own personal growth, but you will benefit the world. When we teach others, we are able to own the material and make it more applicable to ourselves.

How to Start a Transformational Parenting Group

Like a book club with purpose, when you start a *Transformational Par-enting* group, you use the book as your guide. You'll find that your learning, personal growth and friendships accelerate significantly. Also, your children can benefit from a community of parents and friends who raise their children with the same conscientiousness. Here are the steps to starting a Transformational Parenting group:

1. Schedule 10 meetings, once a week at 90 minutes each meeting in a private, quiet setting. If possible, children should not be in the room.

2. Make confidentiality a rule. No one can transform if they worry their friend's children or spouse will hear about their most vul-nerable memories or mistakes. The power of the group to trans-form occurs only when all group members know that what is said in the group stays in the group. Some groups even decide that any sharing, even if it's something benign such as another group member sharing about what movie they saw, is best left in the meeting. That way, there is no questioning what can be shared with others and what cannot: everything stays in the group.

3. Let go of judgments.

4. Avoid interrupting or having side conversations.

5. Turn cell phones off or turn the ringers off. Refrain from looking at your phone during the group.

6. Each week, cover a new chapter, making sure to go in order (i.e., on your first week review Chapter 1, on your second review Chapter 2, etc.)

7. Stay away from the intellectual, instead encourage the personal. You can debate theory all day but it won't help you grow. To re-ally get the most out of your Transformational Parenting group, encourage people to share their own experiences. The more vul-nerable people are, the more they will learn and grow.

8. If you find that someone in your group is having trouble in day to day situations with anxiety, anger, dissociations, or frustra-tion, consider referring to a Transformational Parenting therapist

(www.TransformationalParenting.co) or EMDR therapist who can help you or your friend along the way. Sometimes, emotions and memories that are "stuck" can be processed and healed in just a few sessions.

Let the transformation begin! I'm thrilled to be on this process with you. With this deep inner work, there is no doubt, as we heal ourselves, we heal the world.

ABOUT THE AUTHOR

Jennifer Johnston-Jones, Ph.D. is a licensed clinical psychologist and the founder and executive director of Roots & Wings Institute for Personal Growth and Family Excellence (www.rootsnwings.org). She's helped countless families transform their lives through her therapy practice, work in hospitals and non-profits as well as her speaking engagements for parents, clinicians and educators. Dr. Johnston-Jones lives in the Los Angeles area with her family, whom she absolutely adores.

Want to work directly with Dr. Johnston-Jones?

- Join the Transformational Parenting Group with admission to the annual event at www.TransformationalParenting.co
- Have her keynote your conference, speak at your child's school, your workplace, or your event by emailing: mail@DrJennifer.com
- Limited individual sessions may be available. Go to www.DrJennifer.com to inquire.

You can learn more, and sign up for her newsletter at: www.DrJennifer.com

THANK YOU FOR YOUR PURCHASE

Profits from the sale of this book go to provide free parent education to those who cannot afford it otherwise because there's no better hope for the future than in elevating the way the children of the present are parented.

RESOURCES

MORE FROM DR. JENNIFER JOHNSTON-JONES

www.DrJenniferJones.com
www.TransformationalParenting.co
www.Rootsnwings.org

BOOKS AND WEBSITES WHOSE WISDOM HAS BEEN CITED IN TRANSFORMATIONAL PARENTING; HIGHLY RECOMMENDED READING:

PARENTING WEBSITES

www.TransformationalParenting.co
Positive Discipline Website: www.PositiveDiscipline.com
L.R. Knost: www.littleheartsbooks.com

PARENTING BOOKS

- *The Conscious Parent* (2010) by Shefali Tsabary
- *The Drama of the Gifted Child* (1979) by Alice Miller
- *I'll Never Do to My Kids What My Parents Did to Me! A guide to conscious parenting* (1992) By Eileen and Thomas Paris
- *Parenting for a Peaceful World* (2009) by Robin Grille
- *Parenting from the Inside Out: How a deeper self-understanding can help you raise children who thrive* (2003) by Daniel Siegel and Mary Hartzell
- *Positive Discipline: The classic guide to helping children develop self-discipline, responsibility, cooperation, and problem-solving skills* (2006) by Jane Nelsen
- *Unconditional Parenting: Moving from rewards and punishments to love and reason* (2005) by Alfie Kohn

BABIES
* *The Aware Baby* (1984) by Aletha Solter
* *The Baby Book: Everything you need to know about your baby from birth to age two* (2003) by William Sears

TEENS
* *Reviving Ophelia: Saving the selves of adolescent girls* (1994) by Mary Pipher

TREATING ANXIETY
* *How to Deal With Anxiety* (2015) by Drs. Kannis-Dymand and Carter Great

TREATING DEPRESSION
* *Feeling Good: The new mood therapy* (2008) by David Burns
* *A Mind of Your Own: The truth about depression and how women can heal their bodies to reclaim their lives* (2016) by Kelly Brogan

ACTIVATE YOUR FUTURE
Danielle La Porte: www.daniellelaporte.com
Daily OM: www.DailyOM.com
* *The Law of Attraction* (2006) by Esther and Jerry Hicks
* *Think and Grow Rich* (1937) by Napoleon Hill

TRANSFORMATIONAL COMMUNICATION
* *Mindset: The new psychology of success* (2006) by Carol Dweck
* *Nonviolent Communication* (1999) by Marshall Rosenberg

ACKNOWLEDGMENTS

My first thank you is to you, the reader. With your money and time you voted on this book. Profits from your purchase go to providing free parent education to those who can't afford it. Thank you for being willing to do the work to be your best self for your child(ren) to make the world a better place! It is my honor to be on this journey with you.

This book is a result of the many people who have helped and inspired me along the way. Starting with my parents: my father with his loyal, always-there-for-me-no-matter-what heart. I'd also like to acknowledge my mother for the person I know she really is. I thank you both for all you taught me. I love you.

Fresh out of graduate school, I had the honor to be mentored by the powerful social-justice leader Dr. Jackie Kimbrough who helped me understand the power of psychology paired with advocacy. Around that time, I met Ruth Beaglehole, child advocate and parent educator who lit an inspirational flame in me that still burns. By the time I had children of my own, I was blessed with the mentorship and teachings of Dr. Jane Nelsen, Dr. Leena Banerjee, Dr. Daniel Siegel, and Robin Grille to help me to have the courage and consciousness to raise my children in a peaceful way that often conflicted with the dominant culture.

Thank you to Sarah Ferguson, the Duchess of York, who, like my other mentors, understands and plays a vital role in advocating for child rights. As such, with tremendous grace and generosity, she offered to write the foreword.

Do you know I've been writing this book for more than 13 years? I think I needed that time to develop the unique combination of the nerve to think I deserved to be listened to paired with deep humility I learned being a parent. Thank you to my lifelong friends Dahvia, Cindi, Sasha, Ayesha, Ani, Estela, Gia, Amy, Nate, Connie, Elaine, JP, Alex, Auree, Alison, Laura, Chris, Mickey, Dominique, Rachel, Ben, Giftsy, Laura, Garth, Javier, Janet, Gwen, Kamakshi, Dr. Pam, Melissa, Mila, Christy, Arpie, Kelly, Jessica, Jenn, SLo, Elisa, Annie, and Mia who helped me grow that nerve. They never stopped encouraging the birth of this book and never once rolled their eyes when, for years in a row, for my New Year's Resolution I would declare again and again "This year I'm going to finish the book!" Thanks to your friendship, I always feel your support. I love you so much.

This book is also thanks to my siblings: Lindsay, Jeff and Kristin. I'm the luckiest big sister ever and I'm proud of you all! (My brother died many years ago but he's still present with me so I use the present tense with him). We were lucky enough to have many beautiful souls be a part of nurturing us growing up: stepparents Linda and Barnet; second-moms Eve and Julie; Aunts who live far away but call often just to say they love us: my wonderful Aunt Joan; Aunts who make anything fun: Aunts Debbie and Sherrie; and all of the teachers who took the extra time to care.

Thank you to my Roots & Wings family. Thank you to Marty and Evelin for your childcare support over the years. To my parents-in-law who I adore: Duma and Grandpa Chuck. It takes a village!

Lastly, my deepest acknowledgment goes to my my soul mate Michael who never stops believing in me and to the loves of my life Océane and Orion who remind me everyday of the joys of family. I love you, adore you, and cherish you!

CPSIA information can be obtained
at www.ICGtesting.com
Printed in the USA
LVHW081930170319
610980LV00007B/91/P